Female Studies IX

Teaching About Women In the Foreign Languages

French, Spanish, German, Russian

Editor: Sidonie Cassirer

Prepared for the Commission on the Status of Women of the Modern Language Association

The Feminist Press

The Feminist Press
Box 334
Old Westbury, New York 11568

The Clearinghouse on Women's Studies

The MLA Commission on the Status of Women:

Gloria De Sole, Joan E. Hartman, Leonore Noll Hoffman, Ellen Messer-Davidow, Jean A. Perkins, Kittye Delle Robbins, Deborah Silverton Rosenfelt, Cynthia A. Secor, Barbara Smith

CONTENTS

iii

SPANISH STUDIES

GERMAN STUDIES

RUSSIAN LITERATURE

PREFACE

This volume is part of a long-standing project of the Commission on the Status of Women of the Modern Language Association to promote discussion on women's studies and to identify and advance, on U.S. campuses, courses and programs with a focus on women, particularly courses that relate to language and literature. The earlier volumes in this series dealt with curricular changes and innovations in English and American Studies. The present volume is the result of the first concentrated effort to find out what has been happening in the foreign languages.

The initial impetus for the book came from the Forum "Women Writers, Woman Image in the Foreign Literatures" sponsored by the Commission as part of the Annual Meeting of the Modern Language Association in December 1972. During the months that followed the Commission decided on the project of this survey; contributions were solicited at the Annual Meeting of the Modern Language Association in December 1973. We subsequently sent out some one hundred and fifty additional requests for course outlines and listings to faculty who had indicated an interest in or experience with women's studies courses when listing themselves in the Directory of Women Scholars in the Modern Languages (published by the Commission in 1973), as well as to department chairpersons, and coordinators of women's programs. Although the number of requests had to be limited by the scope of the project, we included in our selection the five most commonly taught foreign languages: French, Spanish, German, Russian, and Italian. The more restricted focus in the present volume on French, Spanish, German and Russian is the result of the contributions we received. Apparently at this time courses with a focus on women are offered primarily by departments of French and, to a lesser degree, Spanish and German.

A main purpose in undertaking this volume was to collect data on who is (or was) offering what courses where. It seemed equally important to include a sampling of the literary research and the pedagogical thinking that feeds into and results from these courses. We would hope that the professional expertise, and the ingenuity reflected in the materials of this volume will have a contagious effect and will contribute to generating more courses with a focus on women, even in the face of the adverse conditions in enrollment and staffing that haunt most foreign language departments today. In putting this volume together we valued the chance to look over the back fence and see what was going on in neighboring territories; we trust that our arrangement in terms of essays, bibliographies, course commentaries, and course groupings will facilitate reference to the various literatures.

We want to express our appreciation to the more than ninety contributors who sent us outlines, syllabi, and articles. Our thanks also go to colleagues in the region who took the time and trouble to assist us with critical comments, suggestions and advice: Sigrid Bauschinger, Associate Professor of German, and Rosalie Soons, Associate Professor of Spanish, both at the University of Massachusetts in Amherst; Page Bancroft, teacher of Spanish at the Stoneleigh-Burnham School; and Carmen Suárez-Galbán, Lecturer in Spanish at Mount Holyoke College. Their help was invaluable to us during this long and complex undertaking. Special thanks go to Thomas Cassirer for his critical comments and his help in editing and proofreading

this book. We are also very indebted to Clover Drinkwater for her editorial
work and to Nonny Burack for the typing of the manuscript. As for the two
of us, Sidonie Cassirer is general editor, and Brigitte Coste assisted in
the selection and editing of the materials.

South Hadley, Massachusetts
October, 1974

Sidonie Cassirer
Department of German
Mount Holyoke College

Brigitte Coste
Department of French
Mount Holyoke College

INTRODUCTION

Some Findings and Observations

The women's movement and women's studies courses are part of a general movement for education reform that is profoundly concerned with American society and the question of social change.[1] It is easy to see why, in
the field of literature, teachers of English departments responded to the
curricular effects of this movement earlier and in greater numbers than
teachers in the foreign languages. The fact that we found even a sprinkling of feminist courses in the foreign language departments for 1971 speaks
for the pioneering spirit of the originators of such offerings and under-
scores the pervasiveness of the movement. The New Guide to Current Female
Studies (Ahlum and Howe 1971) lists 163 courses in departments of English
for that period among the gross statistics of 610 courses with a focus on
women reported for various departments, while we have information of only
a handful of courses in the foreign languages.[2] By 1972, according to our
information, there were some twenty listings of courses in French, German,
and Spanish. In 1973, the last complete year of our sample compilation,
this number increased rapidly, more than two-and-a-half fold, with courses
in French literature tripling and thereby outpacing the other two languages
even further than previously.[3] The limited information we received for 1974
would point to continued growth. These statistics do not indicate, of
course, the cross-currents of thought transcending national boundaries that
are reflected in the offerings themselves whatever their curricular origin.
One has to think only of de Beauvoir's The Second Sex, a standard fixture
on most reading lists of Women's Studies courses. Our sample is also
limited in that we excluded comparative literature offerings in order to
focus on course patterns within the foreign language departments themselves.
    Is it possible to make valid observations about the broad spectrum of
courses of which the collection in this volume can only be considered a
sample? I shall attempt an answer based on the collection itself and on a

---

[1]Florence Howe and Carol Ahlum, "Women's Studies and Social Change"(in
Academic Women on the Move, ed. Alice S. Rossi and Ann Calderwood (New York,
1973), pp. 398, 404.

[2]Female Studies II (Howe and Ahlum 1971), 26, lists an early version
of a course described in the present volume on pp. 213 ff.; Female Studies III
(Howe and Ahlum 1971) lists courses in French on p. 89 and p. 99 (cf. this
volume pp. 69 ff. and pp. 52 ff.). Through correspondence two or three other
courses also have come to our attention.

[3]The breakdown for 1973 shows 39 courses in French, 8 in Spanish, and
8 in German departments. These numbers are bound to be understated since
we did not undertake a systematic over-all survey but worked only with a
selected group (see Preface).

questionnaire that many contributors patiently filled out. This questionnaire touched essentially on three aspects of such a course: First, the
administrative, practical component; we asked for information on class size
and composition by sex, course approval, the place of the course within the
over-all curriculum, and the likelihood of course continuity. A second
component involved the instructor's role as he or she saw it. Student
response was the third. There appeared to be no significant difference
in responses by men and women instructors, and I shall consequently deal
with them as one group.

About 50 questionnaires were returned--nearly 20 percent from men--
three fourths on courses in French literature, almost one fourth in Spanish, with the German returns too small to be statistically significant by
themselves. The responses came about evenly divided from state universities and from private institutions, and more than eighty percent were
from coed institutions. Only a sprinkling of instructors mentioned a tie-in
of their courses with approved or contemplated Women's Studies programs.
By far the largest number of courses seemed to be heavily dependent on the
initiative and continued interest of individual instructors.

Most of the courses encountered no difficulty in approval. While a few
met with administrative "apathy" and "massive skepticism," in other cases
the course was favored and "no effort was spared by the Department chairman . . . to insure its success." The courses frequently fitted into the
departmental offerings as Special Topics courses or, occasionally, as a
special section of the introductory literature course or as a course in
translation to provide an alternative to the foreign language requirement.
In French and German about half the courses were in translation, usually
with a provision for special reading and writing assignments in the target
language for students interested or concentrating in the foreign language.
In Spanish almost all the courses were given in the target language. The
need for language proficiency placed most courses in the upper level offerings. A high degree of language fluency was, regretfully, noted as a
requirement for reading some contemporary women writers such as Christine
Rochefort. As new text editions appear they will make it possible for instructors in the foreign languages to include a greater variety of contemporary readings. In courses in translation the availability of translations seemed to present a problem. The course was "an expensive Xerox
project" for some instructors.

Most of the courses were of necessity conceived to fill a special slot
and to fit within a relatively structured language and literature program.
Yet instructors met the challenge of innovation in a variety of ways. One
approach was to work within the theme course or the survey course and to concentrate on the image of women, sometimes in standard works, sometimes in new
selections. In this way instructors were able to highlight the existence
of constant "myths" and stereotypes of both women and men and, in the words
of some respondents, this produced "a consciousness raising experience."
Other instructors tried to combine a literary approach with an exploration
of the conditions within which women write and authors, both male and female, write about women. Such courses integrated the study of literary
texts with selected background readings whose emphasis varied from the
philosophical to the political and sociological (p. 69, p. 52, for example). Within this general pattern one can discern certain differences

between the various languages. French courses most frequently span the seventeenth to the twentieth century. They stress the treatment of women characters and include works by men and women writers. The less frequently reported survey from the Middle Ages to the twentieth century also follows this pattern. In Spanish there seems to be more emphasis on women writers either as a period course--most frequently of the nineteenth and the twentieth century--or within the general survey course. In German, courses on women writers are infrequent and usually cover the twentieth century. The favored orientation of courses in translation in the various literatures was towards a focus on the female image, mainly in works by well-known male and female writers. Given the problem of obtaining translations, this structure may well have been a matter of practical necessity rather than of choice.

We encountered other approaches that might also have considerable potential. These include a civilization course with an emphasis on the situation of women in the target country, on the institutions and traditions affecting this situation, and, in a wider sense, on the literary image of women. Comparisons with the U.S. in such a course sharpened the self-awareness of the students as well as exposing stereotypical thinking regarding male and female roles in the target country (p. 50). One instructor working with graduate students explored the importance of the woman question in the literary life of the country and its effect on the development of the literature (p. 68). Another type of course combined more than one new field of interest and research. In French, for example, the focus on the francophone world appears to combine well with a study of Canadian women writers since these writers have played a prominent role in the renaissance of French-Canadian literature (p. 73). The focus on women writers also offers a fruitful approach to highlighting the different directions being taken by East and West German literature (p. 210). Obviously, interdepartmental cooperation offers many possibilities, among them a special grouping of paired works in two foreign literatures (p. 118). Almost all the courses seem to have been successful in the classroom. It is too early to tell whether some have more long-range potential than others.

There was, in fact, wide agreement that the courses with a focus on women evoked unusually strong student interest. Many respondents explained the difference in the classroom atmosphere from other courses by the "unusual interest in material and approach," unfortunately without distinguishing between the impact of their own attitude and that of the students. "Students were more eager to participate," classes "more lively, controversial, profitable, enjoyable, upsetting," "a breakthrough," were some of the comments on the questionnaires. In some classes diaries were kept and discussions continued beyond class time. Course evaluations sometimes revealed strong interest and involvement in classes where discussion had seemed lackluster.

Occasionally the special focus helped to minimize the cultural and historical gap: the students "seemed to be a bit surprised that works written centuries ago in France could stimulate so much discussion about the roles and images of women in general . . . the most popular assignment proved to be Laclos' Les Liaisons Dangereuses," runs a comment that expresses the views of several other instructors. In general, however, the students' lack of familiarity with the historical and social background made itself felt as in other courses. Rather uniformly, it was noted that the teacher-student relationship was better and that "students and teachers were more like friends." This benefited the learning process. Students seemed to do more research, write better papers, volunteered for leading class discussions, and were more eager to take part in foreign language discussion.

In the courses we were able to survey there was little, if any, deeply emotional anti-feminist sentiment such as was reported in some early courses with a focus on women in English literature. No doubt the late arrival of these courses in the foreign language curriculum made them beneficiaries of the increasing awareness and acceptance of the feminist point of view.

As to class size: Courses in French literature taught in French and in translation both show a concentration in the ten to twenty-nine student group (12 courses taught in French, 8 in translation). Four courses in French had fewer than ten students, as compared to three in translation. No courses in French had an enrollment of more than thirty students while four in translation were attended by between thirty and fifty-nine students. The limited data we have for Spanish indicate--perhaps inconclusively because of insufficient information--that the courses given in the foreign language attracted more students than the few courses in translation that have come to our attention. Here too the bulk of the courses was in the grouping between ten and twenty-nine students. Three classes had fewer then ten students, one above thirty. Our data do not indicate the role minimum enrollment requirements may have played in class size.

Among the Spanish courses one was reported as proponderantly male, one "half and half" male-female, two all women, and the remainder had a sprinkling of men but were primarily attended by women. It would appear that proportionately more men attended the focus-on-women courses in Spanish than in French. The general pattern of a high female enrollment in French literature courses also holds true for the courses with a focus on women. Only two of sixteen courses in French and six of 16 courses in translation reported an enrollment of 25 percent or more men.

Very rarely were there any participants from outside the academic community in these foreign literature courses. Courses in Spanish, however, at times benefited from another type of "non-academic" enrichment, since some of the students were of Hispanic background and could interpret the literature for the rest of the class through their personal experience as women in a Hispanic culture.

Course data and questionnaires would lead one to believe that about one third of the listings in this volume have by now been repeated or are certain of repetition and that little more than 10 percent can be definitely classed as "one shot" courses. Need for variety in departmental offerings, budget or staff restrictions, lack of room in the existing curriculum are most frequently cited as reasons for not repeating the course, and only rarely are low enrollments cited. However, continuity of some kind may exist even if the course is not repeated. A course first taught in the foreign language may later be given in translation or vice versa. It sometimes is expanded into a comparative literature offering, or a course in a specific literature may later become partially integrated into a broader women's studies course. The course may also reappear in subsequent semesters with a different focus on women writers, or on women in the literature of a specific century or period. The metamorphosis of courses is documented in several instances in this volume. To give just one example: one course started as a winter study project, grew into a large course in translation, and later reappeared as a course in French (pp. 90 ff.).

"What changes would you make if you taught the course again?" was one of the questions we asked. "Sharpen the focus of the course" and "reduce the reading" were the most frequent answers. Others mentioned minor changes in the texts, to maintain the instructor's own "dynamism and growth" and to keep the course fresh; updating of materials; better organization along themes; invitation of outside speakers.

Generally speaking these courses in the foreign literatures highlighted the inadequate and one-sided preparation of students in background knowledge, i.e., the almost total absence of knowledge of the situation of women and of the institutions affecting the lives of women in the target cultures. In courses in translation this lack was sometimes more keenly felt than in those in the target language, where students had some previous exposure to the foreign culture. In courses in translation the combination of students' interest in a foreign literature and the focus on women sometimes proved a demanding task for both the specialist and the feminist in the teacher. "Students had no knowledge at all of France and I spent more time on the frame of reference than I had anticipated" is the comment of an instructor who would have liked to make her course more of a "feminist" course than it turned out to be. Dealing with the foreign culture more than would be the case in the ordinary literature course required special background references and sometimes personal translation projects. The results were rewarding because they established "the universality of female images and myths," runs one fairly typical comment. "Reading The Second Sex before the fiction helped students see things in the French perspective" reports another instructor who ultimately seems also to have been successful in relating the French perspective to the American.

It is clear from the information we have collected--questionnaires and course outlines--that courses with a focus on women in the foreign literatures represent a very ambitious undertaking. Instructors had to move towards three different objectives: the first, to utilize the traditional techniques of literary analysis in teaching an unexplored aspect of the literature; the second, to open up to their students an unfamiliar aspect of the target culture--that is, the situation of women present and past; the third, to help the students relate this knowledge to their own culture and their own situation.

This rapid overview of our project will, I hope, give some indication of the achievements and the potential of courses with a focus on women in the foreign literatures. It also seems evident that further work and initiative is needed in several areas.

Financing is one practical problem which should receive attention. It was astonishing to find that in such a new area of course design only one course, out of nearly fifty reported, received grant support. Yet financial help is essential whether in the form of a research grant, support for the production of new teaching materials, or released time for the faculty member who creates a new type of course. Up to now such support has not been available, nor have faculty in this field made a concerted effort to obtain grant money.

A second area that will need to receive greater attention is that of courses in civilization, as well as composition and conversation. These courses would seem to offer particularly good opportunities for breaking down stereotyped views of women and men, and more generally for presenting students with a more well-rounded picture of the way of life in the target culture. Moreover, these courses, particularly composition and conversation, are frequently taken as a prerequisite by students planning to study abroad. Since at least fifty percent of American students in study-abroad programs are women, it would seem of particular importance to introduce a focus on women into the courses that prepare students for such programs.

The lack of comprehensive cultural information in textbooks remains a problem. Many texts still convey a one-sided, male-oriented view of the foreign culture. Material by women writers could, for example, be introduced for analysis of style, as well as for its cultural content, and this material could serve as a starting point for autobiographical or other essay topics oriented toward women students. More teaching materials should be made available that will incorporate interviews with women of different classes in the target country, as well as literary works dealing with their experiences and concerns.

Courses with a focus on women still are only an occasional venture in the field of foreign language and literature and it is impossible to predict whether, with the present budgetary and enrollment stringencies, these courses will grow at a rapid rate. Yet their statistical significance cannot measure the impact of new thinking that they represent, in approaches, in research, and in broadened outreach into other fields. We hope that the mosaic of individual efforts that is put together in this volume will not only give a better picture of what has been achieved but encourage closer cooperation across fields and disciplines.

FEMALE STUDIES IX

Teaching about Women in the Foreign Language Curriculum:
French, Spanish, German, Russian

Editor: Sidonie Cassirer

Assistant Editor: Brigitte Coste

Prepared for the Commission on the Status of Women
of the Modern Language Association

FRENCH STUDIES

'I Am My Own Heroine':
Some Thoughts About Women And Autobiography In France

by

Elaine Marks

What is an autobiography? What, if anything, distinguishes women autobiographers from their male counterparts? In what way are French women autobiographers different from women autobiographers in other countries? These are the essential questions. Although it would be impossible and presumptuous to hope to answer them satisfactorily we can and should, I think, attempt through them to chart the domain to be explored, to determine what we know or think we know, and what kind of work and thinking still needs to be done.

In his excellent study-presentation L'Autobiographie en France, published in 1971, Philippe Lejeune lists one hundred and six works from Guibert de Nogent's twelfth-century De Vita Sua to François Nourissier's Un Petit Bourgeois (1963) which, according to his definitions, form the corpus of French autobiographical writings. They form a curious group. Eight or more are women of letters: Madame Guyon (1648-1717), George Sand (1804-1876), Marie d'Agoult, known as Daniel Stern (1805-1876), Juliette Adam (1836-1936), Judith Gautier (1846-1917), Clara Malraux (1901-), Violette Leduc (1907-1972), Simone de Beauvoir (1908-). Six at least are in some way connected with the church: Soeur Jeanne des Anges (1602-1665), Madame Guyon, Marcelline Pauper (1663-1708), Mère Sainte-Thérèse de Jésus (1828-1884), Mère Marie de l'Enfant-Jésus (died in 1908), Sainte Thérèse (1873-1897). One is an actress, Mademoiselle Clairon (1723-1803). One is a political figure, Madame Roland (1754-1793). One is a painter, Madame Vigée-Lebrun (1755-1842). It is important to note the increase in women of letters as we move towards the twentieth century. Most autobiographers today, whether men or women, are writers by profession. Writing has been considered by French writers as the great adventure of our age and the writer as the only true hero.

The first woman mentioned in Philippe Lejeune's chronological order is Soeur Jeanne des Anges, the "hysterical" mother superior of the Ursuline convent at Loudon in France. The manuscript which she left was published for the first and only time in 1886, by a medical publishing house, with a preface by the famous Dr. Charcot. I have not read this autobiography, but it is significant that the first French woman autobiographer (further research may change this title) should be classified officially as "hysterical," should have thought herself possessed, and that her work should be considered as having essentially psychological, nay pathological interest. Soeur Jeanne's hysteria casts its real or stereotyped shadow over the genre as it is practised by women even though other less volatile women autobiographers are represented.

There seems to be general agreement among contemporary critics that an autobiography is a first person prose narrative in which the author, the protagonist, and the narrator are identical, that is to say, have the same name, and which covers a sufficient time span to allow for a significant distance between the moment of the narration and the adventure of the protagonist. The autobiography is thus differentiated from the journal or the diary composed of daily entries or fragments and in which the distance between the event and its reporting is considerably reduced. The distinction between autobiography and memoirs is not always clear. In general memoirs focus on the events of a moment in history, what a group of people were doing and saying. Memoirs are closer to an historical account; the first person is the witness, the observer; it is, of course, his story but not necessarily the story of his life.1 Autobiography, then, is perilously close to the first person novel. Were it not for the identity in name between author and protagonist and the presence of other often familiar proper names mentioned in the text, the reader would have no effective way of distinguishing autobiography and novel. The difference between what is fictional and what is real within a given text has become in recent years more and more problematic. What we must note is that writers choose to call certain of their works autobiographies and write them for specific reasons. Writers of autobiographies always state their intentions, and, whatever value we attribute to these intentions, the fact that they exist is important. These stated intentions vary, but the variations do not seem to correspond to differences in the sex of the writer. This is partly due to the phenomenon of the imitation of models. Most autobiographers--men and women--of the nineteenth and twentieth centuries read and assimilated and echoed The Confessions of Jean-Jacques Rousseau. Whenever a paradigmatic work exerts so strong an influence it is difficult to disengage the originality in feeling, tone, or even incident, of some of the writers who come after. Simone de Beauvoir, in the preface to The Prime of Life, the second volume of her autobiography, refers to Rousseau's enterprise as a model for her own.

Philippe Lejeune's separation of autobiographies and journals or diaries into two very different literary forms is certainly valid on aesthetic grounds. But if we are to deal with French women autobiographers we are, I think, at least temporarily obliged to break down the barriers between the two. It would be inaccurate, for example, to speak about French women autobiographers and to exclude, as does Philippe Lejeune, Marie Bashkirtseff. This young Russian aristocrat lived and painted in Paris and kept an extraordinary journal in French from her twelfth year in 1873 until her death in 1884. We know from the several references she makes to it in The Second Sex that Simone de Beauvoir read Marie Bashkirtseff's Journal. Katherine Mansfield also read it; Alice James deliberately avoided it. Marie Bashkirtseff was known to women writers of the twentieth century. It would therefore seem important to consider this late nineteenth-century precursor and not be overwhelmed by Philippe Lejeune's categories. If we want to attempt a study of what characterizes autobiographical works written by women, we must begin by including rather than excluding.

The reader suspects from the preface to Marie Bashkirtseff's Journal that the author died at a very early age. This fact creates a particular atmosphere that surrounds the text and the protagonist--a sadness, a poignancy, a desire to protect. The reader's first encounter is, by contrast, with an apparently hopelessly spoiled and pampered adolescent, a wealthy, talented aristocrat who is alternately generous, intolerant, impulsive, jealous, gay, coquettish, despairing, vain, ambitious, competitive, a compendium of attributes that recreate one of the more prevalent images of the delightful and impossible child-woman. Yet almost from the beginning we are aware, too, of a biting lucidity directed both toward others and herself and increasingly, as the text develops and as illness dominates, a desperate attempt in the face of social pressures and imminent death to study and to become a painter. What is unusual is the manner in which Marie Bashkirtseff sees herself as moving between two mutually exclusive impossible possibilities--marry or paint--and her understanding of the cramped, intolerable situation in which she finds herself. "What I desire is liberty to go walking alone, to come and go, to sit on the benches in the Tuileries Gardens. Without that liberty you cannot become a true artist.[2] . . . It is one of the main reasons why there are no women artists."[2] There are many such cries of despair throughout the Journal, despair at being a woman and despair at being condemned to death while still so young.

On another level, in the domain of feminine narcissism, the Journal of Marie Bashkirtseff is an invaluable document. From the young girl madly in love with a man whom she has never met to the promising painter who wins a prize at the Salon of 1884, Marie Bashkirtseff's greatest pleasure is to be looked at. There is a relationship between the desire, which never diminishes, to be queen, to be famous, to be looked at, and the need to be loved by a superior man, to become a member of the community of intellectuals through their superior man. The search for the superior man as lover is common to all women autobiographers who are not, like Gertrude Stein or Violette Leduc, profoundly lesbian. "To humble oneself before man's superiority must be the superior woman's greatest pride,"[3] writes and reiterates Marie Bashkirtseff. The young Simone de Beauvoir moves from her cousin Jacques to her professor Robert Garric until finally she finds Jean-Paul Sartre. "I would fall in love the day a man appeared whose intelligence, culture and authority would subjugate me."[4] To be seen and also to be the center, to be seen at the center of a salon or an important group, to have admirers and disciples. Such women autobiographers and diarists as Gertrude Stein, Anaïs Nin, Virginia Woolf, Simone de Beauvoir and Clara Malraux share this longing. "I shall be, in the future, the center of the world,"[5] writes Clara Malraux the narrator looking back at Clara Malraux the child protagonist. Towards the end of her life it is clear that Marie Bashkirtseff relies on her Journal to be her passport to immortality which is, after all, another way of reaching the gaze of future generations.

Let us look a bit more closely at the three twentieth-century women autobiographers whom Philippe Lejeune includes. They present interesting contrasts. The family backgrounds of these three women are very different. Clara Malraux (née Goldschmidt) comes from a Franco-German Jewish middle-class family in which money and the value of learning were given equal importance. Simone de Beauvoir was born into an upper-class Catholic family, border-line aristocrats whose ultra-nationalism increased as its money dwindled. Violette Leduc, in contrast to these two Parisians, was born in Arras, an illegitimate child raised in semi-poverty by an unaffectionate mother and a loving grandmother. The images these three women autobiographers create of themselves in their autobiographies are as different one from the other as the initial facts of their lives. The four volumes of Simone de Beauvoir's autobiography develop the image of the exemplary heroine, a model proposed to the reader who, it is assumed, will sympathize both with the desire to free oneself from the family prison and the aspirations towards intellectual freedom and recognition. It is essentially a success story. Clara Malraux and Violette Leduc create images of victims. The reader sees the protagonist Clara Malraux as the victim of her famous husband's misogyny and of her own romantic conception of love. Violette Leduc's protagonist suffers from much deeper wounds. The abandoned child forever cries for her mother, forever loves inaccessible people. She is constantly humiliated, ashamed of the imperfections of her body and the imaginings of her mind.

Both Clara Malraux and Simone de Beauvoir tend to follow a conventional manner of presentation--a chronological narrative that recounts, as in the "realist" novel, the story of a life against the background of specific and well-documented places in time. Although the emphasis is differently distributed, their autobiographies have similar centers of interest: what they tell us about that part of the century and those milieux in which they lived, what they tell us about their attempts to lead their own lives alongside of a very outstanding man whom they loved, what they tell us about these men. If there is more about André Malraux than about Jean-Paul Sartre it is because Simone de Beauvoir achieved a degree of independence that Clara Malraux was never to achieve. Simone de Beauvoir did indeed become a recognized member of the French intellectual and literary world.

The most original writer of the three is Violette Leduc. Simone de Beauvoir and Clara Malraux are simultaneously autobiographers and biographers. They work as much if not more with outer events and the procession of characters than with inner feelings. Violette Leduc never loses touch with the feelings of shame, desire, confusion that drive her to despair and to writing. The events in the three volumes of her autobiography are almost exclusively psychosomatic events translated into a language capable of reproducing in the reader a direct apprehension of the experience it conveys. Violette Leduc is working at a different level from either Clara Malraux or Simone de Beauvoir. She is trying to express something other than a justification of her life in terms of the established notions of success and failure determined by an anxious sense of others' expectations. Violette Leduc does not tell the reader what happened to her and to her entourage in a particular year. Rather she shows a protagonist so embedded in her own universe that there is hardly any separation between microcosm and macrocosm. The obsessions of the protagonist are the only reality. The feelings of shame, desire, and confusion become what the autobiography is all about; and they are pure. They are not put into a conceptual frame that explains them or neutralizes them. Violette Leduc does not pretend to be an intellectual; her organization is solely aesthetic. The absence of any kind of overt moralizing or psychologizing is one of the sources of Violette Leduc's originality.

If we are to look for differences between women and men autobiographers, we should look within the text at the relationship established between author, narrator, and protagonist. What we notice almost immediately if we compare Simone de Beauvoir to André Gide or Violette Leduc to Jean Genet is that the woman narrator tends to see herself as if she were being seen or looked at; her judgement is not sufficient. Someone else must look at her and approve. Narcissus loved himself; Narcissus was alone. The woman autobiographer loves herself being loved. There is perhaps a connection between this reflected vision and the constant references either explicitly or in the imagery to feelings of emptiness and inadequacy and to feelings of envy and rage. Women autobiographers are gluttonous: I want, I want . . . to be famous, or loved, or admired, or immortal. The desire is for something that they lack or think they lack and that others possess or can confer on them. Should they enter into possession of that thing either they no longer want it or it does not satisfy their hunger; emptiness reigns and the cycle of envy, rage, and sadness begins anew. There is certainly a connection between this reflected vision in the autobiographies of Simone de Beauvoir, Clara Malraux, and Violette Leduc and the presence in each case, at a crucial moment in their affective and intellectual lives, of a "superior man": Jean-Paul Sartre, André Malraux, and Maurice Sachs. Jean-Paul Sartre and André Malraux are infinitely more important in the lives of Simone de Beauvoir and Clara Malraux than is Maurice Sachs in the life of Violette Leduc. Many people read Simone de Beauvoir in order to learn about Sartre. Most people read Clara Malraux because of their interest in Malraux. She herself writes, the reader senses, so that she can both set the record straight and talk about her great man. She loves to say his name. Eventually overthrown for another woman, Clara Malraux's pathetic cry is "When I was André's wife."

What is also striking is the relative sparseness of the autobiographies of Gide, Sartre, Genet, and even Malraux when compared to those of the three women. They seem to be haunted, more than the men, by the possibility of total annihilation and oblivion, they are fearful of dissolution and obsessed with mortality. Thus, they attempt to hold on to every detail; nothing will be forgotten. Every feeling that can be recaptured; every incident that can be recollected is recorded as an act of defiance against death. The result of this obsession is great length and often, for the reader, tedium. The men are more selective. They choose, compose, and seem less anxious to include it all than to find a way of communicating a style of life; their preoccupation is more aesthetic than psychological. They move further away from themselves. Why, the question must be put, do women autobiographers consider their feelings to be so precious and so threatened? Why do women autobiographers seem so mysterious to themselves? Is this a weakness, as has always been implied, or a strength? Traditional Aristotelian and Hegelian formal literary criteria have underlined the inadequacies inherent in those works that do not find some abstract means within their structures of objectifying the subjective world. Perhaps these criteria need to be re-examined. Perhaps only women write autobiographies.

Compared to women autobiographers and diarists of the twentieth century in England and the United States--Gertrude Stein, Virginia Woolf, Katherine Mansfield, Mary McCarthy, Lillian Hellman--the French women are distinctive in two apparently contradictory ways. They are more conscious of the degree to which they are determined and manipulated by their families, their milieu, their emotional and intellectual heritage, and at the same time they are more devastatingly lucid, less complacent, in regard to their own sensibility. They are more intellectual and more persistent. This is, of course, a banal distinction. Still, it seems valid. It is one of the reasons why autobiographies from these different traditions are apt to seem so exotic and become so popular when they are translated or transplanted.

The problem is not in defining autobiography or in defining the

French literary tradition, although these definitions could certainly be refined. The problem is with the women autobiographers. What do they do? how? Why is it different from what the men do? And how shall we evaluate her performance and his? What is essential is that we not prejudge differences in terms of better or worse, but that we probe the differences. What do Simone de Beauvoir, Clara Malraux, or Violette Leduc do with language that the men do not do? Can we discover a difference in the way men and women relate to language? The question was raised by Richard Austen Butler in The Difficult Art of Autobiography:

> First I should like to ask why there have not been more women autobiographers. This I think is because they are usually more interested in other people than they are in themselves. One cannot imagine a female Rousseau or a woman like Montaigne. Santa Theresa is perhaps an exception, but there is a reticence which is not found in the true male egotist. Later on I shall be found preferring Leonard to Virginia Woolf in the genre of self-expression, though there is no doubt that Virginia had the greater literary talent. There are many women's names but few candidates for this study.
> There is no female Pepys, much less Boswell. Women are shrewder observers of others rather than of themselves. This observation of the rest of the world is too precious to leave time for introspection. As V. S. Pritchett has put it, they have not by nature the degree of egoism 'which allows a man to split into two and follow one part of himself like a devoted dog.'
> The one possible female Rousseau is the author of The Book of Margery Kempe.[6]

The question is also raised by Anaïs Nin in her Diary:

> I have always believed in a woman's language, a language of sincerity[7] and instinct. This is what I tried to do in my Diary.

We should not dismiss these quotations too hastily even though they both seem to perpetuate unfortunate stereotypes. The purging of the stereotype is more difficult and more ambiguous than has often been acknowledged, since a stereotype is a projection of interiorized attitudes which many of the exorcists harbor themselves. There is also the problem of the rage to destroy that eliminates or forbids the true as well as the false.

Butler's observations, with support from V. S. Pritchett, seem to me partially incorrect. I do not think that women autobiographers are more interested in others than in themselves but rather, as I have already suggested, they are more interested in other people's reactions to themselves. The search for approval and affection is time-consuming and emotionally tiring. The reticence of which Mr. Butler speaks surely does not apply to Violette Leduc, but I doubt that either of these English critics knew her work. Both Violette Leduc and Marie Bashkirtseff contradict V. S. Pritchett's statement about "the degree of egoism" which "by nature" women autobiographers do not possess. The Book of Margery Kempe, the first

English autobiography, dictated in the early fifteenth century, perhaps passes the egoism test because its author was not literate and could not write. An illiterate woman speaking is more acceptable, less threatening, than a talented woman of letters.

Anaïs Nin's statement, often reiterated in the four published volumes of her diary, brings us to the heart of the problem. Is there a woman's language, and if there is, does it specifically involve, as male critics have proclaimed at least since the Romantic Movement, sincerity and instinct? Anaïs Nin, of course, is implying that women have always imitated male models of language and that she, at last, has broken through and is the true woman.

There are two relatively objective ways in which the question of whether or not men and women use language differently can be explored. One involves the kind of testing carried out at the University of California-Berkeley by Jean Walker Macfarlane and Erik Erikson, although as Erikson suggests in "Womanhood and the Inner Space," constructing scenes with blocks and figures is less fraught with variables than are verbal games. Nonetheless it would be worth devising experiments, both by linguists and psychologists, to see if there are two different approaches to language. The other way is more hazardous and involves literary analysis of sentence structure, imagery, vocabulary, etc. I am not quite certain as to how one would evaluate the conclusions. But uncertainty should not deter investigation.

In the absence of an objective methodology I should like to conclude with a quotation from the Journal of Marie Bashkirtseff. "If I had been born a man, I would have conquered Europe. As I was born a woman, I exhausted my energy in excessive language and in eccentricities. Misery!"[8] This lucid cry uttered towards the end of her short life, after a reading of her own Journal, proposes an interesting answer to our dilemma. Men have the possibility of acting in the world; women talk, that is their domain--they put everything into words. Words are their only legitimate outlet. Men use language as a tool among other tools to act upon the world. Women have only language, and thus they tend quite naturally to overindulge. Emptiness, not the intellectual emptiness deduced from the death of God or the absurdity of man's condition, but visceral emptiness, is filled with language. Language is all women possess. It may also be true that women prefer to talk about what goes on inside them, to tell their daily story, and that they use language to reinforce their identity. If this is so, then there would exist a privileged relationship between women and such literary forms as the autobiography, the diary, the journal. It is not, I think, an accident that two of the most important autobiographers in twentieth-century French literature, Simone de Beauvoir and Violette Leduc, are women and that Simone de Beauvoir, one of the central figures in the women's movement, should have written a foreward to La Bâtarde and further that Violette Leduc should talk openly of her passion for Simone de Beauvoir in La Folie en tête. In a sense Simone de Beauvoir and her writings were a model for Violette Leduc as they have been and continue to be for many women in France and elsewhere. One of the lessons we may draw from Simone de Beauvoir as model is that she is most successful as a writer when she writes about herself. This example should not be seen as a sign of inferiority. On the contrary, it should encourage more women to tell their story, to try to tell their story, globally or day by day. "I am my own heroine,"[9] wrote Marie Bashkirtseff in an attempt to justify her narcissism and to denigrate false modesty. We need more women autobiographers of the highest quality, and the road to quality often goes through a valley of abundance. If more women were to repeat Marie Bashkirtseff's phrase we would have fewer Madame Bovarys and more first-rate women writers.

Winston-Salem

Notes

[1] Salon life, in which women played a dominant role, was responsible for a large number of women memorialists in France--secretaries or scribes of their particular group. The narrator in Marcel Proust's Remembrance of Things Past relates how Madame de Villeparisis regains her place in society when it is learned that she is writing her memoirs. Everyone was fearful about what she might tell posterity.

[2] Marie Bashkirtseff, Journal (Paris: Fasquelle, 1955). Vol. II, p. 87.

[3] Ibid., p. 80.

[4] Simone de Beauvoir, Mémoires d'une jeune fille rangée (Paris: Gallimard, 1958), p. 145.

[5] Clara Malraux, Apprendre à vivre (Paris: Grasset, 1963), p. 80.

[6] Richard Austen Butler, The Difficult Art of Autobiography (Oxford: At the Clarendon Press, 1968), p. 22.

[7] "Entretien de Pierre Lhoste avec Anaïs Nin," Les Nouvelles Littéraires, Jan. 7, 1971, p. 6.

[8] Marie Bashkirtseff, p. 443.

[9] Ibid., Vol. I, p. 48.

I.   On Autobiography

Lejeune, Philippe. L'Autobiographie en France. Paris: Armand
    Colin, 1971.

Starobinski, Jean. "The Style of Autobiography," Literary Style:
    A Symposium. Edited by Seymour Chatman. New York: Oxford
    University Press, 1972.

II. Major French Women Autobiographers of the Twentieth Century

Beauvoir, Simone de. Mémoires d'une jeune fille rangée. Paris:
    Gallimard, 1958.

_____. Memoirs of a Dutiful Daughter. Translated by James
    Kirkup. Cleveland and New York: World Publishing Company,
    1959

_____. La Force des choses. Paris: Gallimard, 1963.

_____. Force of Circumstance. Translated by Richard Howard.
    New York: G. P. Putnam's Sons, 1964.

_____. Tout compte fait. Paris: Gallimard, 1972.

_____. All Said and Done. Translated by André Deutsch. New
    York: G. P. Putnam's Sons, 1974.

Malraux, Clara. Le Bruit de nos pas. I. Apprendre à vivre, 1963;
    II. Nos Vingt ans, 1966; III. Les Combats et les jeux, 1969;
    IV. Voici que vient l'été, 1973. Paris: Grasset.

_____. Memoirs. Translated by Patrick O'Brian. New York:
    Farrar, Straus and Giroux, 1971.

Leduc, Violette. La Bâtarde. Paris: Gallimard, 1964.

_____. La Bâtarde. Translated by Derek Coltman. New York:
    Farrar, Straus and Giroux, 1965.

_____. La Folie en tête. Paris: Gallimard, 1970.

_____. Mad in Pursuit. Translated by Derek Coltman. New York:
    Farrar, Straus and Giroux, 1971.

_____. La Chasse à l'amour. Paris: Gallimard, 1973.

III. An Essential Precursor

    Bashkirtseff, Marie. _Journal de Marie Bashkirtseff_. 2 vols.
        Paris: Fasquelle, 1955.

    _____. _The Journal of a Young Artist_. Translated and abridged
        by Mary J. Serrano. New York: Cassell and Company Limited,
        1889.

IV. A Point of View

    Erikson, Erik H. "Womanhood and the Inner Space," _Identity:
        Youth and Crisis_. New York: W. W. Norton and Company, Inc.,
        1968, pp. 261-294.

Women Writers in France: The "Initiators"

by

Germaine Brée*

A list of names of women writers would mean as little as a historical
survey. But I think a quick look at a cluster of early French women writ-
ers--significant figures in the realm of letters, whom I call the "inia-
tors"--may prove fruitful in spite of the distant social and cultural
milieu and the intervention of from four to two hundred years. Of these
women, Christine de Pisan (1364-1430?) is the first. Born in the fourteenth century, she preceded the other three of whom I shall speak by a
hundred and twenty to two hundred years. But she is, in every respect,
their precursor; and in some respects she is the first modern French woman
we know. She moved to France from Italy when she was three years old, for
her father, Thomas, who was a doctor and an astrologer, was sent as an en-
voy from the Doge of Venice to the court of Charles V, whose councilor he
subsequently became. A man of learning as well as wealth, Thomas saw to
it that the daughter, of whom he was very fond, would read and write, besides French, Latin and her native Italian. At fifteen, he chose for her
among her suitors "the one who had the most knowledge with bonnes moeurs,"
good character. The marriage was a most happy one, as witnesses one of
her ballads, "Douce chose est, que mariage (A Sweet Thing Is Marriage),"
and as she tells us in yet another poem:

> His company was
> So pleasing to me when he was
> Close by! There was never a woman alive
> More contented with her lot.[1]

But in 1380, the fortune of the family began to change: her father's pa-
tron and protector, King Charles V, died; the Dauphin was a sickly boy who,
when he became King, was given to spells of insanity. In a France where,
during those waning years of the century, the feudal system was fast disintegrating, the rivalries between such powerful and ambitious figures as
the King's uncles--the Duke of Orléans and the Duke of Burgundy, who eventually made an alliance with the English--plunged France into a new phase
of the Hundred Years' War; and anarchy reigned until such time as a young
girl, Joan, took it upon herself to lead the French armies to victory and
the Dauphin of France to his coronation at Rheims.

The death of Charles V spelled ruin for Christine's father, who
soon followed his king to the grave. Ten years after her marriage, when
she was twenty-five, Christine's husband died of the plague, leaving her
with three small children to care for. It was then that she began to
write, in the deep distress of that loss.

Today, a month ago,

---

*From: Women Writers in France: Variations on a Theme by Germaine
Brée. New Brunswick, N.J.: Rutgers University Press, 1973, pp. 16-31.
Reprinted by permission of the Rutgers University Press.

                    My dear one left me
                    My heart is sad and numb
                    Today, a month ago.
                              (P. 33)

She later recalled her plight: "When he was in the flower of his age,
competent and ready, as much in knowledge as in wise and prudent ascend-
ancy and control, about to rise to high positions, Fortune took him from
me in the flower of his age, when he was thirty-three years old and I was
twenty-five. And I remained alone with the charge of three small children
and a large household" (p. 35). Alone and facing ruin, with no protectors,
cheated and harassed by unscrupulous dealers, "desiring more to die than
live," she nonetheless took up the fight. "And you may understand that
for me, a woman weak in body and naturally fearful, it was hard work to
make of necessity a virtue" (p. 37). It was then that she started to earn
her living by the pen, acquiring a modest economic independence that guaranteed her a personal freedom rare for a woman in those days.
        Against the backdrop of war, court life at the time revolved around
Queen Isabeau. It was turning in upon itself and reviving the courtly
modes of the past, the themes and decor of l'amour courtois. Writers in
those years sought patronage at court. Literature was a highly conventional affair and the task of writers was ritually to celebrate their patrons and the events of court life in the intricately patterned verse forms
of the day. It was a fellow poet, Eustache Deschamps, who taught Christine
the rules of the game: "I started to forge pretty things," she writes.
And so that her son would have a proper education, she also started to
study:

                    Son, I have no treasure
                    To enrich you!
                    For treasure, I now
                    Shall note for you
                    Some teachings. (P. 49)

Christine took to learning with passion:

                    . . . for I am fated
                    To occupy my life with learning
                    And I'll never wish
                    To leave that path.
                              (P. 57)

And so began her extraordinary career as a "scholar among women." She
produced fifteen volumes of work contained in seventy large notebooks.
Her writings became increasingly broad in scope, as she undertook the vast,
objective treatises on politics, on the art of government, on peace, that
won her a comparison with Boethius. Rambling and overdocumented with erudite quotations and allusions though they may seem to us, to her contemporaries they seemed modern and learned.
        Her first success came when she launched the controversy concerning
women. Her target was the famous Roman de la rose, a long poem in two
parts: the first is a compendium of the rules of courtly love; the second, by an antifeminist cleric, Jean de Meung, is an exposition of the

                                  12

traditional medieval attacks on the misdeeds of Eve. It was one of the most widely read books of the time, a typical literary exercise showing two traditional, contradictory and equally mythical male images of woman, the courtly and the clerical. As scholars have suggested, it is probably because Christine had a direct experience of what the nature of the relations between men and women really was outside the closed circle of courtly ritual--that is, brutal and demeaning for women--that she undertook to challenge those relations in a long poem, Epistle to the God of Love. She attacked male attitudes to women in no uncertain terms and from the point of view of her own experience. What did a woman encounter in her dealings with men? Lack of respect, extortion, defamation, betrayal. As far as she was concerned, the Roman de la rose and Ovid too (another favorite book of the time, and in her eyes a manual on how to deceive women) were fit only for burning. She thought, of course, within the conceptual framework of her time concerning the hierarchy of the sexes, drawn from the familiar story of the Creation and the Fall.[2] So she based her arguments upon the wide gap between the image of man in his role as representative of God's reason and order and the realities of his conduct; and between Jean de Meung's antifeminist description of women and the women she observed, herself among them. In other words, she held up to men a far more realistic image of themselves and their failure to live up to their role and blamed them for misrepresenting women in their books. She suggested too that, had women written those books, a different light would have been thrown on the subject.

It would be tedious to recapitulate the arguments aligned, but Christine's was a passionate and yet sensible defense that won for her the protection of the Queen, and, more significantly, the friendship of a powerful and enlightened ecclesiastic, John Gerson, the Chancellor of the University of Paris. Gerson was aware that the times were changing and that the old codes of behavior were disintegrating; and he seems to have appreciated the basic rationality of Christine's approach. Daniel Poirion, a medieval scholar, sees in the conjunction of the two figures, Christine and Gerson, the first signs of a totally new social configuration, announcing the humanistic and rational Renaissance.

"For the first time in France," writes Poirion of Christine, "the story of a literary work cannot be separated from the study of a personality. Here is . . . our first author, and that author is a woman. And because she is a woman, [as a writer] she avoids many shortcomings of the period."[3] One of these being, of course, the gratuitous pedantry of the age. In her case, he notes, one feels that the expression and the feeling coincide exactly; speaking for herself, she spoke for all women. "I took as example myself and my way of living, as a natural [normal] woman, and in the same way also the other women I frequented, princesses, noble ladies, ladies of middle or low condition, who, most kindly, told me their private and secret thoughts." Christine was committed to the defense of "toute l'université des femmes," present and to come.

It is pleasing to note that after some years of silence in a retirement caused by the violence of the civil wars, Christine took up her pen again, alone among the writers of her time, to celebrate Joan of Arc, when the rumors of the Maid's exploits reached her in 1429, as "the honor of the feminine sex":

> A sixteen year old girl . . .
> For whom arms are not too heavy
> It seems in fact that she thrives
> On them, so strong and hardy is she
> And before her, her enemies are in flight[4]

It did not surprise her at all that God had chosen a woman to save the country; to those who pointed out that the Church had condemned Joan, she answered: "What Dame Joan has done was well done, and by the commandment of God."

I shall recall, more briefly, three women writers of the Renaissance. The first is Marguerite d'Angoulême (1492-1549), later Queen of Navarre. She was the sister of Francis I, to whose career she devoted her energies. A woman active in politics who shared the Renaissance passion for knowledge, she started out better equipped than Christine, for she was thoroughly well-grounded in the major classical and medieval texts that formed the corpus of knowledge at that period, and she was familiar besides with Dante and Petrarch. She gathered in her entourage some of the best minds of the time. During the Renaissance, learning enjoyed an unrivaled prestige in court circles, and Marguerite was one of the many women of the high no-bility who mastered that learning. Like Christine, she wrote prolifically, in a great variety of forms in both verse and prose; dialogues, oraisons, spiritual meditations, plays, a spiritual autobiography, and finally, the famous unfinished collection of sometimes ribald short stories in the tra-dition of Boccaccio, the Heptameron. In her handling of the traditional conte, she modified its intent and structures, giving it a new depth and significance. She was a studious and deeply meditative woman with a broad and often trying experience of life in a society where highborn women were pawns in a political power game. In the humanistic learning of the time she sought a personal understanding of life and of the Christian religion. Underlying her work is her personal spiritual odyssey. She was drawn to the new philosophical trends, the Neoplatonism which was to bring about a reassessment of the doctrines of the Church. Like Christine, she too ap-pears as an innovator: "Beyond the fact that philosophical and religious poetry in France goes back to Marguerite, that she is the first mystical poet in our literature, we owe her something more precious and greater still: a scrupulous attention, honest and unswerving, to the movements of consciousness, the appearance of the 'moi' [the self], in literature."[5]

The contrast could hardly be greater than with Louise Labé (1524?-1565?), a generation younger, and certainly no Neoplatonist. Celebrated in her time as the "French Sappho"--a term we shall encounter again in one form or another--she produced only one small volume of purely lyrical love poetry and a Debate of Love and Folly, a dialogue in five parts, highly original in form, which today's critics are looking at with renewed in-terest. She lived in the city of Lyons, then in its heyday as the second capital of France, called the "French Florence." It was at the time the city of printers, close in spirit to the free and brilliant way of life of Renaissance Italy. Louise Labé was the daughter and later the wife of wealthy merchants, ropemakers--thence her name, la Belle Cordière. Her father idolized his daughter and saw to it that she got a first-rate edu-cation: in Greek, Latin, Spanish, Italian. She knew Dante, Boccaccio, and Petrarch, and learned the art of music; she later had a fine collec-

tion of books in her library. She rode horseback in male attire and
jousted like her brothers. She married late for the time, at twenty-five,
a man thirty years her senior, who seems to have left her the greatest
freedom

This was a time of small circles or clubs of men and women enamored
of the new culture. In Louise's circle there were many celebrated poets,
both male and female, precursors of the better-known Pléiade group: Ron-
sord, Du Bellay, Rémy Belleau, etc. Her house and garden became the gathering place of a brilliant and talented circle of friends, who practiced the
Renaissance art of civilized living, cultivating poetry, music, friendship,
and love until the Wars of Religion plunged the city into disaster and
ruin. Clément Marot, the protégé of Marguerite de Navarre, was one of
her circle, as was Amadis Jamyn. The inner circle of the "Lyonnais" poets
comprised such figures as Maurice Scève and another gifted woman poet,
Pernette du Guillet. Louise sought no protectors and needed none, for she
was an independent woman. It was to a friend, Mademoiselle Clemence de
Bourges, that she dedicated her slim volume of love poems, justifying
their publication:

> Since the time has come, Mademoiselle, that the severe laws
> of men no longer prevent women from applying themselves to
> sciences and disciplines, it seems to me that those who have
> that facility should employ that worthy freedom which our sex
> desired so greatly in the past to study these and to show men
> the wrong they did us by .depriving us of the good and the
> honor which these [studies] could bring us; and if one of us
> should reach such a level as to be able to put down her con-
> ceptions in writing, she should do it carefully and not dis-
> dain fame and make of it an adornment rather than [adorn her-
> self] with chains, rings, and sumptuous clothes, which we
> can only really count as ours through the use we make of them.[6]

Though not made to command, women, she felt, should be the companions as
much in "domestic as in public affairs, of those who govern and are
obeyed" (p. 12). She points to the good that comes from writing as one
who has experienced it. Pleasures and feelings pass instantly, she notes,
"but when it happens that we have put our conceptions into writing, even
though our brain afterwards pursues an infinity of affairs and moves incessantly, taking up what we wrote a long time later, we come back to the
same point and the same disposition in which we then were" (p. 15). And
this, she adds, gives "a singular pleasure." Clearly the experience is a
personal one, and it is expressed in the limpid, musical language that
characterizes her poems. The feeling seems strangely modern that makes of
writing the vehicle of "time regained"! For a long time it was the woman
Louise and her love-life that fascinated critics, moved by the passion and
sensuousness of her poems; what astounds us today is rather her originality,
her unique mastery of the poetic idiom she developed, almost untouched by
the current mannerisms of the day.

For the last of these exemplary women, I admit I have a personal
sympathy: Marie de Gournay, the "French Minerva," who was to become Montaigne's spiritual daughter, a relationship that was recognized in their
day. Born in 1566, at a time when the Wars of Religion were about to

plunge France once again into chaos (there were eight wars between 1552 and 1598), she was the eldest of six children and seems to have been a particular favorite of her father, who died when she was eleven. In order to survive, the family retired to the provinces, where this extraordinary young woman taught herself how to read and learned Latin "without the help of any Grammar," together with some Greek, while stubbornly refusing to get married. In 1584, when she was eighteen, she fell upon a book that had just come out, the Essays of Montaigne. It came as an illumination. Happily for her, since her family had begun to think she was mad, Justus Lipsius, "the most erudite man in Europe," proclaimed the then-obscure Essays to be a great book. On the strength of this corroboration, Marie de Bournay persuaded her mother to take her to Paris, where she wrote to Montaigne, asking to see him. He called on her, fascinated, he said, by the judgment she had made of his essays: "She a woman and living in these times and so young and alone in her province . . . a circumstance worthy of high consideration."[7] He was to entrust to her the editing of his work after his death. In the meantime, like Christine, she had become head of the family, a family in debt; like Christine, she decided to live by her pen, and concurrently fulfilled her task as head of the family nobly. For herself, she adopted a way of life that was truly new. She resolved to "have no other husband than her honor enriched by the reading of good books." She took a house in Paris; then, when money became scarce, she moved into a small apartment with a companion and a cat, and, besides devoting much time to the defense and promotion of Montaigne, wrote mightily and fought mightily too in the battles of the day, some of which concerned the intellectual capacity of women. She produced a novel, treatises on education, language and poetry, and a defense of her own way of life; she was a deeply committed woman of great integrity. She was also a perspicacious critic and a magnificent satirist. And she won out. Attacked and lampooned by some, she became nonetheless a highly respected figure in Parisian society; her salon was frequented by the most active and interesting men of letters of the time; indeed, it was from that salon, it has been suggested, that the idea of the French Academy was launched. She lived, active and honored, to the age of eighty.

I have sketched these portraits briefly; they should suffice to kill once and for all any stereotyped image of the feminist writer, so diverse are they: scholar, philosopher, poet, critic. Yet all these women do have certain things in common: the fight they put up in favor of the emancipation of women, of "honneste liberté"; and the manner in which they themselves lived their own freedom. All four could have signed Marie de Gournay's treatise on the Egalité des hommes et des femmes (Equality of Men and Women) and her Grief des dames (Complaint of Ladies). (Some of these "griefs" are taken up again in Parturier's Open Letter to Men, more particularly the exasperating complacency of rather stupid men who refuse to listen to women who are more intelligent and better informed than they are.) All four claimed for women the right to an education and refused to accept current opinions on the natural inferiority of a woman's mind. One could quote endlessly from what they wrote on the topic. Even the apparently most uncommitted of them, the poet Louise Labé, exhorted women to raise their minds above distaff and spindle; to learn for "their own contentment and to show they could surpass men in that realm."

One can detect certain similarities in the social situation of these women that may explain their careers: three of them belonged to an aristocracy that in itself freed them from certain forms of social constraint; it was the flowering of a liberal spirit in the bourgeois society to which she belonged, coupled with her wealth, which gave the fourth, Louise Labé, her independence. The women benefited from the great prestige of learning in the circles in which they moved; all four were passionately drawn to books and because of special circumstances had access to them. Because they were women, they had not been shaped in the scholastic mold. It was perhaps because of their very position as "outsiders," not admitted to institutions of learning, that, in a time of rapid social change they were able to some extent to detect more clearly than most of their male contemporaries some of the essential trends and social myths of the moment.

They lived at a time when a form of culture and with it a way of life were drawing to an end, and by their own independence and integrity, in their sphere, they broke away in small measure from obsolete constraints. They flourished within small, select circles of men and women where a certain decorum prevailed between the sexes that counteracted or masked the injustice of the condition against which they rebelled. They all seemed to have felt the need for the sustenance of feminine friends and found comfort in feminine examples of achievement. It would seem, at least for three of them, that an initiation into learning through the interest of an indulgent father was an important factor in their development.

There was, however, no dominant male figure in their adult lives to impose upon them a certain way of living. All four moved freely beyond the narrow limit their society ascribed to feminine life; and all four enjoyed the friendship and respect of eminent men, who were in touch with the new concerns, knowledge, and ideological trends of the time. They seem to have had one great advantage as writers: for them, writing was never a game, a pastime, or an erudite display, gratuitous, of knowledge. It was rather a means to self-knowledge and perhaps self-affirmation; thence their originality. That originality too perhaps explains why their quality as writers eluded not so much their contemporaries but later scholars intent on generalizing and cataloguing. They astonished their contemporaries, not because of their "feminine" qualities, but because they thought and wrote as well as the best of men.

17

Notes

[1] Françoise du Castel, Damoiselle Christine de Pizan: veuve de Me Etienne de Castel, 1364-1431 (Paris: Editions A. et J. Picard, 1972), p. 29. Subsequent quotations from Christine de Pisan are all drawn from this work and will therefore merely be referenced in the text. For the sake of convenience, I shall follow this practice with other authors.

[2] It has become customary today to refer to an older version of the Creation presented in Genesis 1:26-28, according to which men and women were created together: "So God created man in his own image, in the image of God he created him; male and female he created them," as opposed to the other, more familiar version in Genesis 2:18-24.

[3] Daniel Poirion, Le Moyen Age II, 1300-1480, Collection Littérature française, 2 (Paris: Arthaud, 1971), p. 206.

[4] Françoise du Castel, Damoiselle Christine, p. 90.

[5] Yves Girard and Marc-René Jung, La Renaissance I, 1480-1548, Collection Littérature française, 3 (Paris: Arthaud, 1972), p. 242.

[6] Louise Labbé, Oeuvres poétiques de Louise Labbé (Paris: Le Club Français du Meilleur Livre, 1967), pp. 9-17.

[7] I have drawn my information from Marjorie Ilseley's authoritative book, A Daughter of the Renaissance: Marie le Jars de Gournay (The Hague: Mouton and Company, 1963). All quotations of Marie de Gournay's are from Ilseley, and the translations are hers.

The Status of the Frenchwoman Today

by

Anna Raitière

"Yesterday morning, all Paris enthusiastically acclaimed the Star of the Fourteenth of July." So wrote the popular newspaper Le Journal du Dimanche the next day. This "Star" of Bastille Day 1973, fêted everywhere and congratulated by M. Pompidou, was a young woman of twenty, Anne Chopinet, first in the class lists at the Ecole Polytechnique. For the first time since the School was founded, a woman carried the banner and led the procession of marching troops. This unprecedented event, reported in every newspaper, brought home to the French that in one of the toughest university competitions, from which until quite recently women were barred, a woman had headed the lists, beating all the male entrants.[1] And as the journalist Thierry Maulnier of Le Figaro pointed out, the crowd which acclaimed Anne Chopinet was certainly not made up overwhelmingly of feminists.

The enthusiastic reception given to this young woman is symbolic of the progress made by women, slowly but irresistibly, toward emancipation and the recognition by the general public of what women are capable of achieving, given the opportunity.

I

The background of the Frenchwoman's struggle

The work that brought the status of women into focus after the Second World War was Simone de Beauvoir's The Second Sex (1949). The author's approach to the problem was so unorthodox that the book was on the whole little understood at the time of publication. But one young woman of twenty-seven, Geneviève Bécane, a legislative assistant in the French Senate, has this to say, "As a teenager I was brought up with Simone de Beauvoir's book at my bedside. At school it was banned; we passed it around under the desk. For us it was an extraordinary experience."

In The Second Sex Simone de Beauvoir expounded two somewhat disconcerting basic theories. First, that "femininity" is much more a cultural than a natural trait. "One is not born a woman, but rather becomes a woman."[2] Second, a woman is regarded as existing in relation to the central figure--man. But while The Second Sex made little impression on the public at large, it was one source of inspiration for a study on American womanhood in the fifties--Betty Friedan's The Feminine Mystique. By the time this book appeared in translation in 1964, the French public was in a better frame of mind to accept the demise of certain myths, and the book had a great success in France. In the meantime, Simone de Beauvoir's arguments have gained a measure of acceptance. Today we actually find a Churchman writing, "Woman as such does not exist. The 'Eternal Feminine' is a myth."[3] Studies on women have mushroomed. Since 1963, an entire collection entitled "Femme," published by Denoël-Gonthier, has been devoted exclusively to women of all countries.[4] In most good bookshops in France today there is a special section for "Women" which as likely as not will stand next to studies on other minority groups--"Indians" or "Blacks."

The feminist movement in France

If we try to find which of the women's groups in France most resemble the feminist movements in the United States, the two that at once come to mind are the "MDF" (<u>Mouvement démocratique féminin</u>) and the "MLF" (<u>Mouvement de libération des femmes</u>). The MDF is a discussion group established in 1963, and comprises some 3,000 members, the more influential among them being non-communist left-wing intellectuals and the rest mostly middle-class women with no political affiliations. The main theme of the MDF is democracy within the family, in employment, in matters of morals, and in life generally; and at these four levels, the MDF finds alarming disparities between the sexes and urges appropriate political action by women. In fact, in its studies, it has invariably managed to find the political roots of the problem--a fact which particularly impressed Betty Friedan during a visit she paid to France in 1967. But by encouraging its members to take political action, the MDF has lost many of its supporters to political groups--some to the Socialist Party, some to the MLF.

The MLF is a loosely knit group (it does not even have a chairman at its meetings) set up in 1968. The number of adherents is estimated at about 4,000, although there is no formal membership. The Movement has no specific program--in fact, various tendencies are represented in it--but its fight is mainly against anti-abortion legislation and in favor of total freedom in regard to contraceptive methods. So far, it has published five numbers of a periodical, <u>Le Torchon brûle</u>. Not long ago, Simone de Beauvoir expressed the view that the status of women had shown little improvement over the past twenty-three years and abandoned her allegiance to the non-activist groups, deciding instead to militate with the MLF. In December 1971 she joined a street demonstration in favor of the right to undergo abortion freely and without charge.[5]

In spite of their small numbers, the MDF and MLF do have an educational influence on the general public. The MDF has helped to make known in France the work of American sociologists such as Betty Friedan, Kate Millett and Elizabeth Janeway. The MLF acts as a goad to the public, making people stop and think by putting forward "far-out" iconoclastic ideas and helps to create an awareness of the situation. On the other hand, the <u>Union des femmes françaises</u>, which is attached to the Communist Party, has a traditional rather than a feminist outlook. The journal it publishes, <u>Heures claires</u>, follows the familiar pattern of "fashion, beauty, health, home."

The views of feminist groups in France on their counterparts in the United States are interesting. Yvette Roudy, a writer and English-language specialist, finds their work very helpful. "Do not forget," she says, "that the emergence of the MLF was crystallized by two factors: the events of May 1968 in France and the influence of American feminism. American women gave a fresh spurt to the feminist movement when it was in the doldrums" and thus helped feminism in France. But, she adds, "As far as women's participation in governmental decisions is concerned, they are no more successful than we are."[6]

II

Women and public law

The pessimism expressed by Yvette Roudy and Simone de Beauvoir is not shared by Geneviève Bécane.[7] According to her, progress has unquestionably been made in the matter of social awareness, as reflected in the fact that today women enjoy far more rights than, say, fifty years ago and in the whole trend of recent public and social legislation. Since 1944 Frenchwomen have the vote--they were among the last in Europe to acquire it--and they have the right to be elected to public office and to enter the government service.[8] In addition, nearly all the competitive entrance examinations for these posts are now open to women, though this situation is only recent, as we saw in connection with Anne Chopinet. Women are still excluded from certain technical professions such as those of mining or civil engineering, and generally speaking from posts of responsibility such as Prefect and the higher echelons of the police force. The competitive examination known as the agrégation is still segregated, with a numerus clausus for women, which means that, for example, in the sciences the Administration offers 201 places to women as against 294 to men.[9]

Laws relating to the family

Under private law, over the past ten years or so various legal instruments have been enacted by Parliament granting a wife a measure of equality with her husband. She has now, for example, rights with respect to her child, the term "paternal authority" having been replaced in the texts of laws enacted since January 3, 1971, by "parental authority." (But the habit is so ingrained that when a young teacher tried in June 1973 to deposit part of her salary in the Caisse d'Epargne, the nation's official savings bank, in the name of her child, she was told that she must produce an authorization from her husband.) The words of the marriage contract read by the mayor to young couples today reflect this new spirit of equality. "Marriage partners owe each other mutual fidelity, help, and support . . . . They are jointly responsible for the moral and material upbringing of the family." The cost of maintaining the family is to be met by "contributions proportionate to their respective abilities." This means that since 1965 the husband can no longer insist that his wife may not have a separate occupation, although he does have the right to insist on a contribution to the household. But the husband is still the "head" of the family. He has the right to choose the first place of domicile, though he must have the wife's consent in choosing any subsequent one. In the event of conflict concerning the children, the woman does not yet have complete equality. Nor has she in the handling of property, where she is merely "associated" in the management of the family's assets, the husband being still the "head." (This is hardly surprising, considering how poorly women are represented in the French Parliament.) For example, the husband can gamble on the stock market, and the wife can do nothing to stop him, even if she is likely to be ruined as a result. And it is perhaps not generally known that as far as the tax authorities are concerned, a woman cannot act in her own right even if she is financially independent. She must give her husband particulars concerning her earnings, whereas he is not obliged to divulge his, since it is the husband who completes and signs the statutory joint statement even if the couple were married under the system of separate maintenance.[10] Thus the woman does not yet have complete equality with her husband.

But social patterns evolve, and gradually, under the weight of economic and social pressure, force the law to evolve with them. Reform of the paternity laws dates from July 20, 1972. Today, a child born out of wedlock has in general the same rights as a legitimate child, and a child born of an adulterous union can be recognized by its father and in certain cases can claim legitimacy status. In addition, a wife now enjoys a privilege from which she was debarred hitherto, namely the right to contest the paternity of her husband so as to be able to give her child the name of its real father, if for example she divorces and marries him.[11] The law endeavors in this way to protect all children.

In cases of adultery, the Penal Code still treats the spouses differently. The man can only be punished--and by no more than a fine--if he keeps a mistress in the home of the couple, whereas the penalty for infidelity on the part of the woman, wherever it is committed, is imprisonment. If a husband catches his wife in the act and kills her, he can plead "extenuating circumstances." The converse does not hold.

The divorce laws are criticized in every quarter for their ponderous procedure. Divorce by mutual consent does not yet exist in France. It is one of the planks in the platform of some of the opposition parties, but Parliament and Government are reluctant to make any move. Divorce is less common than in the United States (about one marriage in ten), but the level of child support payments is much lower--far below the one-third of the father's salary frequently awarded in the United States. Worse still, child support is often paid late (65 per cent of cases) or not at all (25 per cent). But since November 1972, if payment is not made promptly, the law gives the divorcee or the "bachelor mother" the right to have recourse to the law to obtain what is due to her--if necessary by a lien on the father's salary.[12] In the United States there is of course a drive by women's groups against alimony and child support payments. But in France no formal distinction is made between alimony and child support, and the latter is the more usual practice, the amount depending on the mother's earnings.

But the burning issue, about which a great deal has been written, is that of abortion. The right to undergo abortion is debated, not in a few radical groups as might be supposed, but throughout French society.

In the electoral campaign which preceded the last general election in France, all parties, left and right, and the Government itself, raised the problem of abortion, all the more readily in that a recent court case had made the headlines in the press and on television and had stirred public opinion profoundly.[13] When the new Assembly convened, a dozen parliamentary bills, ranging from unrestricted freedom to conditional freedom, were put before Parliament. The National Medical Council entered the lists--for and against--and many jurists did the same. At the time of writing, the bill which has the best chance of survival would authorize abortion in three specific cases only: pregnancy due to rape or incest, grave risk of congenital malformation, and danger to the physical or moral health of the mother. The more progressive elements find it too timid because, as presently drafted, it takes no account of economic and social considerations and does not permit the woman to decide if and when she wants maternity. Others regard it as a real electoral bogey. Hence further demonstrations are to be expected, next fall and thereafter.

As for contraception, M. Neuwirth, a Democratic Republican Union Deputy, who was responsible for the "Neuwirth Law" of 1967 legalizing the use of contraceptive methods, recently denounced angrily what he described as the "deliberate sabotage" of the law.[14] In the first place, two years elapsed before the implementing legislation on the pill was enacted--in the main complicating its use. Then the newspapers carried articles alleging that the pill causes women to put on weight, grow hair, or lose their hair, and that it sometimes causes cancer; the result is that only 6 percent of women in France use it. What is more, these 6 percent are mostly intellectually or socially privileged women, whereas the women in the lower income brackets, who stand to benefit most by the pill, are the ones who make least use of it, especially as the cost of the pill is not refunded by the State health services. In the meantime, thousands of Frenchwomen disregard the law and the controversy and have abortions, either in France or abroad. Whether or not it is right, legally or morally, for them to do so, it is a fact that they are having them. "What they are demanding is not the right to have abortions but facilities for having them safely." On this note Le Monde suggests that the debate be closed "at any rate until the fall."[15]

The obstacle to the liberalization of the abortion and contraception laws is not so much Catholic tradition as fear on the part of a Government that advocates a high birthrate for a declining population. France still remembers the years between the wars when the French economy was weakened because there were too few births. (This fear, incidentally, explains the family allowances paid to all families, rich or poor, after the birth of the second child.) Hence, the political parties in favor of liberalized abortion laws try to drive home the argument that contraception and freedom to have abortions do not reduce the sum total of children that will be born but rather enable families to decide when they will have children.[16]

Adopting a different approach to the problem, M. Neuwirth induced the National Assembly to set up, under a law enacted on July 12, 1973, a "Board of Sex Information, Birth Control, and National Education." From now on, any establishment where a certain minimum number of women are employed must provide an information service on all problems relating to family matters and family planning. The achievement already made in the publishing sphere is noteworthy--five illustrated volumes, intended for the family, form an Encyclopedia of Sex. The same information is presented in each volume, but it is adapted from the first to the final volume to appeal to different age groups.[17] Since September 1973, "sex information" has been required to be provided as part of the natural science classes for children in the French equivalent of the American sixth and seventh grades. "Sex information" dealing with the emotional and moral aspects of sex is made available outside school hours, if the pupils want it and the parents give their consent.

Thus, after sitting on the fence for a long time, France, curiously behind the times in a field in which other countries would expect it to be in the vanguard, is rapidly catching up.

III

Women and employment

"Equal pay for equal work" says the 1946 Constitution. In practice, the most serious problem for women is the gap between men's and women's salaries—in professional grade, and in many instances where seniority, qualifications, and job descriptions are the same.

The female labor force constitutes an important sector of the economy: 7,850,000 working women or 37.5 percent of the active population. Between the ages of 20 and 55, there are more working women than housewives. Between 25 and 34, mothers tend more and more to go back to work after the birth of their first child, and the main interruption, which takes place after the second child is born, is less and less common. Let us also explode one or two myths. "Women work to supplement the family income." Not always, since the employment figures include 3,200,000 widows, divorcees, and unmarried women. "Woman's place is in the home." Yet the majority of the 150,000 newcomers to the ranks of working women each year are married. "Women are not fitted for responsibility at professional level." There are 250,000 women at executive level and 28,000 at managerial level.[18] Upwards of one salaried employee in three today is a woman. This is one of Europe's highest rates of employment for women, and it is also higher than the rate in the United States.

Unequal pay for equal work

For doing the same work, five million women earn 7.5 percent less than men. At technician level the difference is 15 percent, and at executive level it is over 20 percent.[19] And if we leave aside the notion of equal work, the gulf between the average amount of net annual salaries paid to men and women in 1970 was 32.6 percent, as compared with 35.2 percent in 1967.[20]

In spite of legislation ratified by the Government in 1954 which formally recognizes the principle of equal pay, the law on equal pay for men and women was only promulgated on December 22, 1972, a historic date for the history of labor legislation in France. As of that date, an employer can be prosecuted for discrimination on grounds of sex. Unfortunately, it is a law with no teeth, since the penalty is a paltry fine. If the penalties and the means of enforcing the law are inadequate, the only remedy for women is to make representations at trade union level to have their rights respected. As a matter of fact, the principle of equal rights for men and women is not observed anywhere in Europe, and the Commission of the European Communities is worried about it. It has reminded its member states that women should have the same opportunities as men to reach higher income levels, and it has decided to bring actions against States which do not observe the law.

Without going into details that would be out of place here, two factors in particular have proved a drawback to women in the field of employment—the fact that their professional training is often not up to the level of that of men and the tendency for women's careers to be broken off for family reasons.

Vocational guidance and professional training

Although in theory there is equality today in professional training, women have tended for a long time, by tradition and because of the way they see themselves, to gravitate toward the so-called "female" occupations i.e., "white collar" jobs (saleswomen, shop assistants, etc.) and secretarial work (the modern counterpart of the convent, as Françoise Parturier calls it) which account for three-quarters of the daughters of middle-class families. Apart from these categories there are what might be called the "do-gooders" (social workers, family helps) and the "look-gooders" (models, beauticians, hairdressers). Most of the jobs in these categories are badly paid; openings are in low-level jobs, chances of promotion are poor, and unemployment is rife. Few women turn toward industry, toward the hundreds of jobs available in technology today, or in general toward the more highly paid occupations. In fact, on the employment market, female labor plays a supernumerary role, since if staff has to be laid off, it is the women who are let go first. Labor experts suggest that a good way of increasing the numbers of women in economic life would be to give vocational guidance without reference to sex and to foster greater professional stability. Gradually the female labor market would lose its specifically female character and would finally merge into the national labor market.

In 1947, a girl wishing to enroll in the technical program at a lycée had to apply to the Ministry of Education for permission. Twenty years later the Ministry on two occasions (in 1966 and again in 1967) issued circulars reminding students that the technical programs were now open to candidates of both sexes. It was wasting its time. Some lycées still have no female applicants. (At the advanced technical educational level, where students are trained to be engineers, there are virtually no women--under 1 percent). Here as elsewhere, the opportunity is not enough; the will must also be there, and parents, especially working-class parents, are very narrow in their outlook: 45 percent of   ents do not consider it essential for their daughters to be taught a real skill; 33 percent consider it quite useless to think in terms of any occupation for them except those of housewife and mother of a family.[21] Girls brought up in a strictly traditional home atmosphere assimilate this image of what they should do in life, and by the age of 16 they are thinking of marriage and children as the be-all and end-all of their existence. They forget--or they do not know--that French women have a life-expectancy of nearly 76 years. They marry earlier; they are mothers earlier; and they survive for an average of 35 years without family responsibilities, including 9 years as widows.[22] Thus there is a need to make parents and daughters aware of the value of education.

Consequently, the Comité du Travail Féminin, an information and documentation agency established in 1971 under the auspices of the Ministry for Social Affairs, has now recommended an increase in career information to families, and above all, priority consideration to job placement for female graduates of technical and industrial institutions. The attitude here is the same as that of the Affirmative Action committees in the Unites States toward minorities. A change in motivation to work is already taking place. In a 1972 survey of 1,000 women aged 18 to 25, 95 percent said they could not conceive of a life without earning a living; of these, 27 percent said they wanted economic independence. This represents an increase over a survey carried out in 1968. Expectations of obstacles and discrimination may itself be a factor responsible for girls shying away from industrial and technical studies. This is suggested in a recent survey.[23]

Extended professional training

Women can now learn the latest techniques in their profession, improve their knowledge where it is inadequate, or even acquire new knowledge. The law on extended professional training and continued education dates from July 16, 1971. All business concerns employing more than 10 persons are required to spend 0.8 percent of the wage total (2 percent by 1976) on the training of a proportion of the staff (2 percent of the total manpower strength). The complex scheme allows for training on the job or permits the employee to take time off for improving job skills. Even nonworking women can apply to the national education authorities and be admitted to the program. Such an ongoing experiment is reported from the Dijon region where about 30 housewives of between 25 and 50 years of age with an average of 3 children each have arranged, with the help of advisers, for a two-year course, culminating for most of them in opportunities for skilled occupations and for all of them in a sense of personal achievement.[24]

There is also plenty of room, however, for tilting the scale against women. In one undertaking with 3,000 employees, half of them women, only the higher technical grades, all males, enjoy the advantages of the extended education plan. Secretaries in the firm have asked to be allowed to take courses in English, but since this would qualify them for better jobs elsewhere, the management turns a deaf ear. Of the persons trained in 1970 by the Association for Adult Professional Training (AFPA), only 7 percent were women. Yet it was a record year in this respect. On the other hand, the secretary-in-charge at a private psychiatric service for children took part during the year in 4 group therapy sessions lasting 3 to 5 days each, merely for the asking. To quote her on the subject, she found that the experience had "opened up new horizons" and had been "most enriching."

Even though extended education does not necessarily mean that promotion will follow, and tends at the moment to favor the male, the opportunities it offers the individual to catch up, to learn new skills, or to develop, is welcome. But here as elsewhere, Frenchwomen will still have to fight to fortify their position and to take advantage of all the options open to them.

Women executives

But even though there is no obstacle in the way, given the same qualifications on both sides, the doors to posts in the higher echelons do not open readily to women. A very small minority of women rise to posts of responsibility in the government service or in private enterprise. The number of women increases as we descend the hierarchical ladder: 1 per cent at the upper executive level, 3 percent of engineers, 6 percent of supervisors, 11 percent of technicians, and 60 percent of employees generally. Even in the government service, where women are unusually privileged, since they occupy the majority of posts (51 percent), they fill only 11 percent of the senior posts. In the teaching profession, where

26

women are in a majority from the nursery school (95 percent) to the secondary school (65 percent), they become a minority at the higher education level. The senior posts in the universities--rectorships and deanships--are virtually all held by men. Charleville has the only woman Inspector of Studies.[25] France has recently appointed its Ambassadress, Marcelle Campana, en poste in Panama, and at the Quai d'Orsay one woman, Simonne Servais, among 180 men holds the title of Minister Plenipotentiary.

The situation is so bad that it has finally begun to worry the authorities themselves. On November 29, 1972, the President of the Republic called for a study of all existing regulations concerning admission to the 900 major State bodies "to verify whether or not they include provisions amounting to a numerus clausus for women" and "for measures designed to remove all legal obstacles to equality of the sexes in regard to access to civil service posts."[26] But the struggle will be hard. The practice goes back to Genesis, where Eve was fashioned from one of Adam's ribs, coming after him and formed out of him.

Thierry Maulnier worried about the success of Annè Chopinet at the Polytechnique. What would happen if there were not enough professional openings for the two sexes? Women have not overcome every obstacle by proving that they are intellectually the equals of men. It is after they have graduated from the Grandes Ecoles, when those who have headed the the lists are no longer willing to accept respectable but obscure research assignments, and stake their claims to posts as President of Renault or of an oil company, that the competition may become bitter--unless their placement too is given priority status, as recommended by the Comité du Travail Féminin.

Child care

In France, children can be put in a crèche or day care center from birth (or from the time they are two months old) until the age of three, when they can be sent to a nursery school. The quality of these institutions is excellent. Under the strict supervision and the ample and competent staff provided, the children develop as well in every respect as in their mother's care. The present trend is to open up the crèche to more parental participation, for the good of the parents and that of the children.

But the number of crèches is pathetically small--700, with a total of 37,488 beds, and half of them in the Paris region. (According to the World Health Organization there should be twice that number for that region alone.) And these have to cater for 400,000 children under three years of age whose mothers go out to work. The Comité du Travail Féminin estimates that by 1975 the number of mothers in this category will be 800,000. Only four mothers out of every hundred have so far managed to have their children enrolled in a crèche. The rest fall back on grandmothers or mothers' helpers or baby-sitters, with no special qualifications.[27] According to statistics from INSEE some 48 percent of nonworking young married women attribute the fact that they are not working to the impossibility of finding someone to look after the children.

The need is so great that the question of setting up crèches was part of the platform of all the political parties during the last electoral campaign. The Government itself has promised to install 2,000 crèches within five years. But there seems little likelihood that this figure will be attained. The cost to the State of installation and operation is very high. The day-to-day running costs are divided between the parents, who pay up to one third (1 to 14 francs, or approximately 25 cents to $5, a day) according to their means, and between the municipality and the State. Since January 1972 the neediest families are entitled to a child-supervision allowance.

To cope with the present shortage, crèches operating from 6:15 a.m. to 7:15 p.m. have been started in the nursery schools of the Paris region. At Bordeaux, thirty schools accept babies in this way. There are also about fifty crèches in France attached to industrial firms. This is an excellent arrangement, so long as the employee lives quite close to her place of work and does not have to cope with the problems of carrying her child back and forth over long distances during rush hours.

There is a major project on foot for "Baby Centers" which would combine three institutions ordinarily run separately--the crèche, the day nursery, and the nursery school--which would cater for children between three months and six years of age. These Centers would be open day and night to cover all possible working hours, and would be run by a team of specialists and parents, under the supervision of a pediatrician and a social worker.

There is no ideal solution for mothers who go out to work. Some will always be reluctant to have someone else look after their child. (Yet oddly enough, it is the mothers with more than one child who are most eager to work and not childless women.) But more and more crèches are the answer. The Comité du Travail Féminin recommends that they should be compulsorily set up wherever large-scale reconstruction or urban building schemes are undertaken and that such child-care facilities should be regarded as a public service in the same way as the public school system.[28]

IV

Under-representation of women in the French Government

At the most recent INSEE census (1968), the French population comprised 51.3 percent women and 48.7 percent men, and the population eligible to vote included 53 percent women and 47 percent men. Yet only 2 percent of deputies, 1.7 percent of regional councillors and 4.4 percent of municipal councillors are women.[29] There are 8 women out of 499 deputies in the National Assembly, 5 women out of 283 members of the Senate, and no women in either the Court of Justice or the Constitutional Council. (In Sweden 48 out of 360 members of parliament are women, and there are 2 female ministers.)[30] It is surely astonishing to find so few in government. The disproportion between the female electorate and the number of women representing it is so great that the very structure of society is in jeopardy.

Strangely enough, after Liberation Day, the number of women in the French Parliament was greater than it is today: there were 32 in 1946 as compared with 8 in 1968. The explanation of this decline is the change in the voting procedure. When the list system was in force, the political parties themselves put up women candidates, who had a chance of being elected even if they were at the bottom of the list. But since 1958, when the single nomination form of voting was introduced, each party presents only one candidate, and a woman is seldom chosen, because the party thinks that a man has a better chance of being elected. Hence women are no longer even put forward as candidates--except in constituencies which are counted as lost anyway, as was the case with a female socialist candidate in the XVIth arrondissement in Paris, the rightist sector par excellence. For this reason, a return to the list system with proportional representation is being urged by the legalistic and reformist groups on the grounds that it is more democratic than the present majority vote system with a single candidate, and it is part of the platform of the leftist parties. (The way in which women are presented is very important. In Norway recently, women suddenly found themselves in a majority in the Oslo Municipal Council--48 out of 85--because their names had not been automatically placed at the end of the list.)[31]

The number of women who fail to use their votes is twice that of men. Women are far less eager than men to become involved and militant in a political party--maybe because they usually find themselves given secretarial tasks or put down to organize discussion-dinner sessions. As of January, 1973, there were only 5 women on the Executive Committee of the Democratic Center Party, 5 out of 81 on the Committee of the Socialist Party, 2 on the Executive Board of the Republican Democratic Union (UDR)-- the party of the Government--and a mere 7 out of 107 on the Central Committee of the Communist Party, even though the female membership amounts to the respectable figure of 27 percent.[32] In other words, within the very parties that favor equal rights as a matter of course, the men shy away from facing the problem of minority status, since otherwise they would have to take positive action and agree, or refuse, to share their powers-- an unpalatable choice either way.

Women assert themselves more easily in trade unions where they can exert direct pressure for resolving the problems that affect them. The proportion of women at the top is relatively good, though less than in the rank and file, where it constitutes 25 percent of the members of the CGT, 40 percent of those of the CFDT, and two-thirds in the National Education Federation.[33]

But the problem is a socio-cultural one. Women also have to overcome a learned and internalized sense of dependence and inferiority. In a survey of 1,000 women between 18 and 25 years of age, 47 percent said they would not let a woman doctor operate on them, 57 percent would not ride in an airplane piloted by a member of their sex, and 39 percent would not willingly ride in a bus with a woman driver. (Admittedly there are few women holding these occupations in France, and people fight shy of the unfamiliar.) But in a group of 60 women of all ages, every single one said she would prefer to be under the command of a man. "I prefer a man so that I can work my charm on him," says one. Another says "As far as I am concerned, men are superior."[34] This sense of inferiority is also expressed indirectly. One working woman says proudly, "I earn such-and-such a salary. Not bad for a woman."[35]

In short, the Frenchwoman has won her independence, but she is still hamstrung. She has come of age but still feels herself a minor. Geneviève Bécane, the young woman not yet thirty years of age working at the Luxembourg Palace, addressed herself in a recent interview to the situation which French women of her generation experience today. "Is your life very different from that of your mother?" I asked her. "Oh, certainly. I don't

live the way my mother did. She stayed home all day looking after the
household and the children. She was by definition economically dependent,
and emotionally dependent too. Her personality was nourished exclusively
from outside: she lived through her husband and her children, always on
the receiving end. It must have been very difficult for her to keep her
balance psychologically. Nevertheless I am convinced that in my generation (the under 30's), the few remaining difficulties we have are trace-
able to the education we have received, where women were essentially
brought up to be wives and mothers. We are now confronted with life as it
really is, a life very different from the idyllic picture shown to us from
childhood. The result is that we are pulled in both directions. I think
our generation still feels a sense of guilt because we are not the kind of
women our mothers were. We feel psychologically torn inside between several female models, and we do not yet have the courage to accept ourselves
wholeheartedly. We are not altogether sure what we are. We can no longer
live for family and children alone, as devoted wives and mothers. On the
other hand, life entirely on the masculine plane is not satisfactory either; the difficult and often very painful problem is that of striking a
balance between these two models. We are the generation caught between
two opposing concepts of women. It is not easy."

I put another question to her. "What about emotional independence?
It is relatively easy to become economically independent. But emotional
independence is much more difficult." "That is absolutely true, and I
have no answer to give. Is there such a thing as a feminine temperament,
or is it all a matter of education? At any rate I do think it is harder
for us to achieve emotional independence. I know it from my own experience, and I see it in my friends. Economic independence is necessary; but
it is not enough." Whatever the burden of the emotional stresses experienced by the "link-generation," Geneviève Bécane does not lose sight of
basic social issues and goals. "Women will not be free until society is
free. There can be no freedom for women without social change; and this
must take place in conjunction with men, not without them or in opposition
to them. Young couples have made a start by refusing to accept all the
stereotyped roles in which they are cast beforehand. In the more privileged sectors of the young generation, distinct progress has been made."

The persistent economic, legal, and social inequities that exist in
spite of the progress made, as well as problems of coming to terms with
the changes which have already taken place, outline the continuing tasks
and challenges for the Frenchwoman today, and for Françoise Giroud, holder
since July 16, 1974 of the new Cabinet-level post of secretary for the
condition of women (secrétariat d'Etat à la condition féminine) created
by President Valéry Giscard d'Estaing.*

York College
of the City University
of New York

*English version of an article "La Française devient majeure," pub-
lished by <u>The French Review</u>, Vol. 48 (October 1974).

[1]Of the 300 who passed, 7 others were women, including a Vietnamese, 19 years of age, who took first place in the competitive examination for women.

[2]Simone de Beauvoir, Le Deuxième Sexe (Gallimard, 1949), V. 2, p. 13.

[3]Abel Jeannière, Anthropologie sexuelle (Aubier-Montaigne, 1969), p. 138.

[4]Some recent studies are: Claude Alzon, La Femme potiche et la femme bonniche (Maspero, 1973). Colette Cotti, La Femme au seuil de l'an 2000 (Castermann, 1968). Francine Dumas, L'Autre semblable (Delachaux et Niestlé, 1967). Charles Ford, Femmes cinéastes (Denoël, 1972). Suzanne Lilar, Le Malentendu du deuxième sexe (Presses Universitaires de France, 1969). Françoise Parturier, Lettre ouverte aux hommes (Albin Michel, 1968). Yvonne Pellé-Douël, Etre femme (Editions du Seuil, 1967). Also the writings of Evelyne Sullerot, not to mention the large number of studies on women without partners, abortion, and sexuality.

[5]Alice Schwartzer, "La Femme révoltée," La Nouvel Observateur, Feb. 14, 1972, pp. 47-54.

[6]Yvette Roudy is co-author with Lydie Péchadre of La Réussite de la femme (Denoël, 1970). She directed a monthly magazine, La Femme au vingtième siècle, the organ of the MDF. Inside the movement she organized courses in oral expression on selected topics to give women the self-assurance they lack so as to express themselves easily in mixed groups. She teaches at the Université de Paris-VII.

[7]Author of "Le Statut de la femme mariée," Après-demain, January 1972, pp. 14-16. I take this opportunity to thank Geneviève Bécane and Yvette Roudy for the interviews they very kindly gave me.

[8]De Gaulle felt that he had to give a reason, and he cited women's activity in the Resistance against the Nazis (Jeanière, p. 30).

[9]Elisabeth Caporal, Denise Mourad, Lucien Rioux, "Sept millions de femmes hors-la-loi," La Nouvel Observateur, Jan 22., 1973,

[10]Claude Servan-Schreiber, "La Décolonisation des Françaises," Le Monde, July 22, 1973, p. 15.

[11]"Les Femmes en 1972," L'Express, January 1, 1973, p. 23. Before that, if a woman separated from her husband wished to make it possible for the real father of her child to recognize his child later on, she had to declare him to be of "mother unknown." The most extraordinary situations ensued as a result.

[12]Ibid.

[13]On October 9, 1972, a girl of 15 1/2 years, Marie-Claude Chevalier, came before the Children's Court, accused of having undergone abortion. An eminent Catholic doctor, Professor Milliez, gave evidence on her behalf, as did also two Nobel Prize winners, Professors Monod and Jacob, and a large number of well-known literary and artistic figures. As a result, within two weeks the 1920 Act forbidding abortion and laying down heavy prison sentences for persons convicted of undergoing abortion or aiding and abetting the crime had, in effect, become unenforceable. In May 1973, the sentencing of a woman doctor at Grenoble unleashed a demonstration by 6,000 to 8,000 persons. The abortion law as it now stands is without any doubt a dead letter.

[14]The abortion figures vary between 300,000 and 1 million a year. According to Dr. Marie Prigent, over 2,000 Frenchwomen undergo the operation every day, in dangerous conditions ("Sur la liberté de l'avortement," A-D, January 1972, p. 8). Two charter flights a week take off for England and Holland.

[15]Le Monde, July 1, 1973, p. 16

[16]Especially since the fertility rate for Frenchwomen (an average of 2.47 children) is higher than that of any other group of women in Europe, except Norwegians. Comité du Travail Féminin, Bulletin, No. 1 (Dec. 1972), p. 1.

[17]Published by Hachette. Vol. I for the age group 7-9 years; Vol. II for 10-13; Vol. III for 14-16; Vol. IV for 17-18; Vol V. (by far the bulkiest) for adults.

[18]Statistics from INSEE employment surveys 1968-1972. Quoted in Comité du Travail Féminin, Bulletin, No. 4 (June 1973), p. 1, and No. 1 (Dec. 1972), p. 1.

[19]France-Soir, May 28, 1972, p. 1. In the United States, for equal work, this discrimination would be 10 to 20 per cent (New York Herald Tribune, Paris, July 14, 1973, p. 3). Other examples: on the basis of equal qualifications a woman in the "white collar" grades earns 23 percent less than a man, in the "workers" grades 32 percent less, and in the executive grades 34 percent less (L'Express, January 1, 1973, p. 23).

[20]Gisèle Charzat, Les Françaises sont-elles des citoyennes? (Denoël, 1972), p. 148. The survey carried out in 1970 by INSEE indicates that on the average, women receive only 68 percent of the monthly salaries paid to men. The differential applies at all levels from manual to executive. Please note that Gisèle Charzat's study was used throughout this article for basic information concerning women in politics in France.

[21]Péchadre and Roudy, p. 92.

[22]The French Review, V. 46 (1973), p. 908.

[23] L'Express, May 8, 1972, p. 1972; La Femme du vingtième siècle (March–April 1968), p. 13; Comité du Travail Féminin, La Formation professionnelle continue, p. 17.

[24] Christiane Coeurdevey, "La Formation professionnelle continue, Après-demain (March–April 1973), p. 39.

[25] Le Monde, July 22, 1973, p. 15; Le Nouvel Observateur, July 22, 1973, p. 73.

[26] Le Nouvel Observateur, July 22, 1973, p. 73.

[27] Comité du Travail Féminin, Bulletin, No. 2 (Jan. 1973), p. 2; Evelyne Sullerot, Les Françaises au travail (Hachette, 1973), p. 211.

[28] Comité du Travail Feminin, Bulletin, No. 2 (Jan. 1973), p. 3, Sullerot, pp. 236–237.

[29] Charzat, pp. 16–17; Le Monde, July 22, 1973, p. 15.

[30] There is a woman President of the Conseil de Paris, Nicole de Hautecloque, and a Secretary of State for Social Action and Readaptation, Marie-Madeleine Diénesch. An exception to the general rule is that there are more and more women mayors, 539 in 1970. A large sector of public opinion seems to be less opposed to women in local government than in the Assembly. The more conservative tend to think that administering a township is somewhat like running a household; and in actual fact, almost half of these women mayors are "ladies"--local landowners for whom running their commune is the equivalent of the charitable work they did in the past (Charzat, pp. 102–103).

[31] L'Express, May 8, 1972, p. 114.

[32] L'Express, Jan. 1, 1973, p. 116. It may be recalled that the main political parties at present are, from left to right: the Communist Party, the United Socialist Party, the Socialist Party, the Left Radical Party, the Radical Party, the Democratic Center, the Republican Democratic Union (UDR, the Government Party) and the Independent Republicans, plus a number of minor leftist and rightist groups that are formed and in due course fade out.

[33] The CGT (Confédération Générale du Travail) and the CFDT (Confédération française démocratique du travail) are two important labor unions. The CGT is the larger and older of the two, and is constituted mostly of skilled and semiskilled workers and professional blue-collar workers. It follows rather traditionally rigid communist views, whereas the CFDT, which may rank second after the CGT among labor unions, is more progressive in its outlook and inclines towards a dialogue between the classes.

[34] L'Express, May 8, 1972, p. 111. But why is it that the group

that expressed the greatest degree of confidence in women surgeons (72 percent) were girls of the "peasant" class? It would seem that the women accustomed to hard manual labor were the ones with most confidence in
female skill.

[35]_Le Nouvel Observateur_, January 22, 1973, p. 73.

A Letter to Marguerite Durand from Paul and Victor Margueritte

by

Fernande Gontier

The work of Paul (1860-1918) and Victor (1866-1942) Margueritte revolves essentially round two interrelated ideas for which they fought all their life: woman's liberation and mankind's freedom. Throughout their writings, one can see their constant concern for woman's liberation; more than half of their novels deal specifically with this subject. In 1899, they started a vigorous campaign for the right to divorce not only by mutual consent, but by the consent of any one of the two parties as well. This campaign was so successful that a number of writers, journalists, and politicians soon joined in. Polls published in December 1900, January and February 1901 by two major political and literary magazines, La Presse and La Revue, show writers such as Pierre Louÿs, Jules Renard, Henri de Régnier, and Marcel Prévost agreeing with Paul and Victor Margueritte on the issue of equal rights for women and for their children born out of wedlock.

In 1922, the publication of Victor Margueritte's novel, La Garçonne, met with an unprecedented success and gave rise to passionate and widespread controversies. The novel's title, La Garçonne--a word used by the author to mean the "emancipated woman"--became at once an integral part of the vocabulary of the twenties. The result was that woman's liberation grew into a popular issue and was no longer considered a uniquely legal and literary one. Feminine emancipation became identified with women's attempts to free themselves from sexual taboos and double standards and attain equality as individuals. The first novel of its kind to speak openly of sexual taboos, La Garçonne prompted such extreme reactions in the public that Victor Margueritte was accused of "immorality" and crossed off the Order of the Legion of Honor.

Paul and Victor Margueritte focused their attacks on the Napoleonic Code, introduced in 1804, which gives very limited rights to women. The letter below, addressed to Marguerite Durand, a well-known feminist and founder of the newspaper La Fronde, was written in 1904 for the centennial of the Napoleonic Code. It strongly denounces the Code and gives full support to the women's struggle.

University of Rochester

7 Boulevard Beauséjour XVI
2 Villa Beauséjour

Samedi

Madame,

Nous joignons de coeur notre pensée aux vôtres, au sentiment de stricte équité qui dicte votre protestation.

Il est juste que, le jour même où tant d'hommes célèbrent à

grand orchestre le Centenaire du Code Civil, la voix de
vaillantes femmes s'élève pour dénoncer quelques-unes de
ses lois d'oppression. Elles ont été faites en dehors, au
dessus de la femme. Epouse, mère, citoyenne, la femme n'était
alors qu'une mineure. Elle a grandi, depuis cent ans.

Ce Code qui, lui, a vieilli d'autant, --ce lourd édifice
suranné, ce ne sont point les guirlandes, l'écho des discours
officiels, --c'est la pioche qu'il lui faut.

Paul et Victor Margueritte

7 Boulevard Beauséjour XVIe
2 Vila Beauséjour

Saturday

Madam,

We join our heartfelt thoughts to yours in the feeling of
strict justice that dictates your protest.

It is only right that, on the very day when so many men celebrate with such fanfare the centennial of the Civil Code,
the voices of courageous women rise up to denounce some of
its oppressive laws. Those laws were made regardless of and
over the heads of women. Spouse, mother, citizen, nevertheless, the woman was then only a minor. She has grown up in
a hundred years.

This code itself has grown that much older; this heavy, an-
tiquated edifice deserves neither garlands nor the echoes of
official speeches--what it needs is the pickaxe.

Paul and Victor Margueritte

Published with the authorization of the Bibliothèque Marguerite Durand,
Mairie du Vième arrondissement, Paris.

Women in Contemporary French Society: A Brief Annotated Bibliography of Materials Suitable for a Civilization Course

by

Jeannette Bragger

HISTORICAL PERSPECTIVE

Abensour, Léon. La Femme et le féminisme avant la Révolution. Paris: E. Leroux, 1923, xxii + 477 pp.

Still the most complete study of the role of women and the importance of feminism in eighteenth-century France. Written by one of the few male French scholars of the early twentieth century who was an out-spoken advocate of women's rights. Suitable for outside reading, especially for graduate students and undergraduates with some knowledge of eighteenth-century French history. The book is divided into two parts: I. "La Femme en France au 18e siècle." Chapters on education, legal and political rights, women in the Church, the position of women in the various classes. II. "Le Féminisme au 18e siècle." Draws primarily on the writings of the philosophes. This part should be supplemented by the chapter on "Féminisme et roman" in: Georges May.   Le Dilemme du roman au 18e siècle. New Haven and Paris: Yale University Press and Presses Universitaires de France, 1963.

Other books by Abensour:

Le Féminisme sous le règne de Louis-Philippe et en 1848. Paris: Plon, 1913. xvi + 337 p.

Histoire générale du féminisme. Paris: Delagrave, 1921. 326 p.

Le Problème féministe. Un cas d'aspiration collective vers l'égalité. Paris: Radot, 1927. 185 pp. (TC)*

Bardèche, Maurice. Histoire des femmes. 2 vols. Paris: Stock, 1968. Vol. I, 384 pp.; Vol. II, 460 pp.

Descriptive with numerous illustrations. Statistical data included in the chapters dealing with the twentieth century. As he explores the myths surrounding women from ancient times to the present, the author emphasizes the continuous evolution toward the twentieth-century struggle for liberation. Volume II of this study deals with the Middle Ages to the present and would perhaps be of greatest interest in a culture course. No attempt is made to divide the book by countries. The author proceeds by centuries, using French social institutions as the basis of his analysis. From this "point de départ" he

---

*Items marked (TC) were added by Thomas Cassirer (University of Massachusetts, Amherst).

discusses the role of women in all the major countries of the world. Although somewhat lengthy and densely packed with information, this work can provide students with the names, places, and historical events that have shaped modern society.

Eaubonne, Françoise D'. <u>Histoire et actualité du féminisme</u>. Paris: Editions Alain Moreau, 1972. 398 pp.

A comprehensive study of the history of the feminist movement. Evolution and modification of women's role from ancient civilization to the present day. Most recent information: Chapter II, Part 3: "Le Radical-Féminisme et nous." A look at several countries, including the United States, to determine their influence on the feminist movement in France. Discussion of the Mouvement de libération des femmes (MLF), its founding in 1968, its activities and affiliations. Description of the meetings of "Les Etats Généraux de la Femme." Suggested as a basic text for a civilization course.

<u>La Femme</u>. Recueils de la Société Jean Bodin pour l'histoire comparative des institutions. 2 vols. Bruxelles: Editions de la Librairie Encyclopédique, 1959. 347 pp.

A collection of articles dealing with the status of women in different parts of the world. For France see especially Vol. II, Chapter XXII: Pierre Petot, "Le Statut de la femme dans les pays coutumiers français du XIIIe siècle au XVIIe siècle"; Chapter XXX: Jean Portemer, "Le Statut de la femme en France, depuis la réformation des coutumes jusqu'à la rédaction du Code civil"; Chapter XXXII: Jean Hemard, "Le Statut de la femme en Europe occidentale au XXe siècle." Deals with women in public, private, economic, and social life. Excellent notes with detailed bibliographical references. Emphasis on changes in legal status.

WOMEN IN THE TWENTIETH CENTURY

Chombart de Lauwe, Marie-José et Paul Henry. <u>La Femme dans la société</u>. Travaux du groupe d'ethnologie sociale. Paris: Centre National de la Recherche Scientifique, 1963. 439 pp.

A study of the image and self-image of woman in various social groups. Based on questionnaires given to families of different social status and to students. The first part of the book deals with the theoretical and methodological aspects of such a study (i.e., what are the variables, what questions must be asked, etc.). Very useful in the organization of a course. The book deals with such topics as "equality and the couple," "equality and the family," "evolution of social structures to meet the changing image of women," "evolution of the family structure," etc. Includes a detailed bibliography on women in the working world.

Confédération Générale du Travail (C.G.T.). <u>Les Femmes Salariées</u>. Paris: Editions Sociales, 1973. 247 pp.

Proceedings of the 1973 Congress of the C.G.T. (i.e., the Communist trade unions). Chapters on: <u>les salaires</u>, <u>la promotion</u>, <u>les condi-</u> <u>tions du travail</u>, <u>la maternité et les problèmes familiaux</u>, etc. (TC)

<u>La Femme à la recherche d'elle-même</u>. A series of articles by leading fem-
    inists. Paris-Genève: La Palatine, 1966. 288 pp

Proceedings of the "Semaine de la pensée marxiste." Contains a good
deal of information on the economic situation of women in France, on
problems of maternity and freedom, the use of leisure time, etc. Interesting because it presents points of view of Communist intellectuals. Concludes with debate on the meaning of "liberation" between
Ménie Grégoire, one of the leading non-Marxist feminists, and Claude
Vaillant-Couturier, member of the Central Committee of the Communist
Party and spokeswoman for the Communist conception of women's
liberation.

Grégoire, Ménie. <u>Le Métier de femme</u>. Paris: Librairie Plon, 1965.
    317 pp.

The author, a noted journalist, is well known for her investigation
of the status of women in society. Her book is based on interviews
with one thousand women of all ages and professions. The eight questions asked deal primarily with the "image" of women. Stereotyped
views are seen as the major stumbling block to the liberation of
women. The author suggests solutions favoring women in such areas as
education, part-time work, professional training, social and political involvement. Well-documented.

Guélaud-Léridon, Françoise. <u>Recherches sur la condition féminine dans</u>
    <u>la société d'aujourd'hui</u>. "Travaux et Documents," Cahier No. 48.
    Paris: Presses Universitaires de France, 1967. 123 pp.

The author, a researcher for the National Institute of Demographic
Studies, provides a statistical analysis of some of the principal con-
cerns of women. Women and education, professional activity, etc.
Should be used as a reference text. Basic bibliography.

Parturier, Françoise. <u>Lettre ouverte aux hommes</u>. Paris: Editions Albin
    Michel, 1968. 148 pp.

A journalist and writer, Françoise Parturier is an active feminist and
a leader in the movement to gain equality for women. <u>Lettre ouverte</u>
<u>aux hommes</u> is her response to Francis Jeanson's <u>Lettre ouverte aux</u>
<u>femmes</u> (Paris: Editions du Seuil, 1965). Her book is a cleverly pre-
sented dialogue between herself and anti-feminist, traditional men.
Through the use of irony and the "light touch that stings," she ex-
poses the principal stereotyped ideas men have of women.

Sullerot, Evelyne. <u>La Femme dans le monde moderne</u>. Paris: Librairie
    Hachette, 1970. 248 pp.

A prominent sociologist, Evelyne Sullerot has dedicated a major por-
tion of her work to the study of women. Critical of the traditional
patriarchal society, she recognizes the changes that are occurring,

putting women slowly but surely in their rightful place. Her book is divided into topics such as "Révolution de la démographie féminine," "Les Femmes et l'éducation," "Des Lois et des réalités," "La Femme dans la vie publique." Her choice of topics could be used as the basis for course organization. Many graphs, statistics, and illustrations. Good basic bibliography. The index makes it an easily usable reference text. Very up-to-date.

MOUVEMENT DE LA LIBÉRATION DES FEMMES

Andrade, Béatrix. "Celles qui crient," L'Express, May 8-14, 1972, p. 45.

A very short but informative article on the Mouvement de libération des femmes and its members.

Muchnik, Nicole. "Le M. L. F., c'est toi, c'est moi . . . ," Le Nouvel Observateur, No. 459, Aug. 27-Sept. 2, 1973, pp. 54-64.

Origins of the French MLF. Divisions within the group created by two principal factions: 1) "les féministes," 2) "celles de Psychanalyse et Politique." Includes a chart of the most important dates of the movement beginning with 1791 and Olympe de Gouges to 1968 (founding of the MLF).

ETATS GENERAUX DE LA FEMME

Mauduit, Jean et **Anne-Marie Raimond.** Ce que les femmes réclament. Paris: Fayard, 1971. 458 p.

A report of the essential documents formulated at the three-day conference, Etats Généraux de la Femme, held in Versailles in 1970.

Mauduit, Jean. La Révolte des femmes. Paris: Fayard, 1971. 254 p.

As "Secrétaire Général" of Elle and organizer of the conference, Etats Généraux de la femme, the author presents his assessment of the meeting in Versailles. In discussing the condition of women in France he also touches on topics such as urbanization, public health, education, pollution, leisure time, politics, etc. A good exposition of French life in the 1970's. States both the feminist and antifeminist positions.

GENERAL ISSUES

I. ABORTION

Although the following five articles deal specifically with the problem of abortion, each brings out the question of women's rights, women's place in society, and the social attitudes and prejudices which prevent women from exercising their rights as free individuals. The pros and cons of marriage, maternity, and child-rearing are examined.

Accoce, Pierre. "Médecine: Les Françaises sont mal loties," L'Express,

May 7-10, 1973, pp. 42-43.

An account of Professor Robert Debré's fight to change the abortion
law of 1920, which prohibits abortion for any reason. A very useful
article for the statistics it presents on birth rates and physical
and mental handicaps. Reports the result of the "Entretiens de
Monaco" of April 28, 1973.

Aymon, Jean-Paul (Enquête de Renée Manevy). "Françaises, vous qui savez
. . . ," L'Express, May 21-27, 1973, pp. 77-80.

An enumeration of the main participants in the struggle for the re-
vision of the 1920 abortion law. Discussion of the events and people
which have put pressure on the government to change the law. Numerous statistics. Well-documented.

Bessières, Annie. "L'Avortement comme un défi," Paris-Match, No. 1254,
May 19, pp. 96-97.

The problem of abortion has led to the formation of a group called
"Choisir" in Grenoble. The author discusses the role played by such
prominent women as Annie Fessey-Martin and Gisèle Halimi.

Chabalier, Hervé. "Avortement: Fin de la clandestinité?" Le Nouvel Observateur, No. 445, May 21-27, 1973, pp. 50-52.

A discussion of the origins of the abortion law of 1920. How and why
did it come into being? Proposals by the Socialist and Communist
parties to change the law.

Halimi, Gisèle. "Le Combat de Bobigny," Le Nouvel Observateur, No. 470,
Nov. 12, 1973, pp. 74-75 ff.

Account of a "cause célèbre," this article presents the trial of six-
teen-year-old Marie-Claire Chevalier charged with breaking the abortion
law of 1920. As the defense attorney in the case Gisèle Halimi points
out that there is more involved than the trial of one person. The ultimate goal is "faire le procès d'une loi, d'un système, d'une politique." Well documented, supported with statistics.

II. EMPLOYMENT

Aumont, Michèle. Femmes en usine: Les Ouvrières de la métallurgie
parisienne. Paris: Editions Spes, 1953. 156 pp.

A study of 80,000 women working in factories. Working conditions,
salaries, union activities, etc. Although somewhat outdated due to
increased mechanization and more recent legislation, this study reveals the inequities that existed as late as the 1950's.

Callet, Christine and Claude de Renty du Granrut. Place aux femmes.
Collection "Les Français qui changent la France." Paris: Stock,
March 1973. 284 pp.

Eight million women are professionally employed in France. A discussion of the jobs they hold, the wages they receive, the conditions under which they work.

Employment of Women. Regional Trade Union Seminar, Paris, 26th-29th November 1968. Final Report. Paris: Organization for Economic Co-operation and Development, 1970. 385 pp.

The question of women in employment touches on the wider problem of women as members of the community. The report begins with a statement by Madame F. Guéland-Léridon regarding the place of women in contemporary society, masculine and feminine roles, demographic changes, education for women. Accurate statistics. Proposed measures to correct inequities. For France see especially the reports by Evelyne Sullerot, Alain Girard, Simone Troisgros, Marcelle Dehareng, and Jeannette Laot.

Guilbert, Madeleine. Les Femmes et l'organisation syndicale avant 1914. Paris: Editions du Centre National de la Recherche Scientifique, 1966. 500 pp.

A very detailed examination of the working conditions of women and the role of trade unions between 1881 and 1914. List of articles (annotated) that appeared in the press at the time. An essential text for anyone interested in employment or the impact of the press on public opinion.

Heymann, Danièle. "Jusqu'où vont-elles aller, les femmes?" L'Express, May 8-14, 1972, pp. 30-46.

Article based on a survey of 1000 women between the ages of 18 and 25. Touches on various aspects of the place of women in society, but deals specifically with the conflicts between the desire for a professional life and the responsibilities of the home. Good background article for a general picture of the situation.

Sullerot, Evelyne. Histoire et sociologie du travail féminin. Paris: Gonthier, 1968. 397 pp.

The author traces the working conditions of women from the Middle Ages to the present. Historically, women were employed not for their talents and abilities, but according to the economic needs of a nation (i.e., jobs with no prestige). Sociological point of view: in a society where work is highly valued and regarded as a source of satisfaction and pleasure, women should have the same rights as men to share these satisfactions. Well-documented.

_____. "Le Travail et les femmes." Interview of Evelyne Sullerot by Sophie Lannes, L'Express, May 21-27, 1973, pp. 169-211.

Evelyne Sullerot discusses the results of a survey taken of 1300 women of all ages and professions. One hundred and twenty-six questions were asked of each woman. Many important statistics. Among the questions discussed are: education and training, why women want to work, discrimination in salaries and working conditions, role of trade unions, the guilt complex working women have toward their husbands and children. Ms. Sullerot emphasizes that these problems are not simply feminine problems but concern all members of society.

III. WOMEN AND THE PRESS

Braude, Beatrice. "Marguerite Durand: Journalistic Mother-of-us-All,"
  Ms., March 1973, pp. 33-35.

   A very informative article discussing the role of Marguerite Durand
   in journalism. Her struggles and difficulties in setting up La
   Fronde, an all-woman daily newspaper which first appeared in December 1897. One of the first and most important steps taken toward the
   liberation of women in a male-dominated profession.

Sullerot, Evelyne. La Presse féminine. Collection Kiosque, 22. Paris:
  A. Colin, 1963. 319 pp.

   A comprehensive study on publications for a female audience in France
   up to 1848. Analysis of the taboos in each publication. Principal
   conflict studied: woman as she is presented in the press versus the
   conditions under which she lives. A historical and sociological evaluation of values as they are transmitted by the press.

IV. LITERATURE

Brée, Germaine. **Women** Writers in France: Variations on a Theme. New
  Brunswick, New Jersey: Rutgers University Press, 1973. 90 pp.

   In three concise lectures given in March 1973 at Puget Sound University, the author emphasizes the difficulties women writers encounter
   in a society dominated by male critics. The "image" of woman, created
   and perpetuated by men, has served for centuries as an obstacle to the
   honest and objective evaluation of writers from Marie de France to
   Simone de Beauvoir. Excellent notes with detailed bibliographical
   information.

Rey, Pierre-Louis. La Femme de la belle Hélène au mouvement de libération
  des femmes. Paris-Bruxelles-Montréal: Bordas, 1972. 208 pp.

   Women's role in literature as writers and as characters. Chapter 1
   gives an historical review of great female figures from antiquity to
   modern times. In the rest of the book the author presents a series of
   texts dealing with women, written by men and women. Feminist and
   antifeminist points of view from Homer to Germaine Greer. Recommended as an important reference text for a civilization course. It
   is a basic introduction yet it covers a wide variety of attitudes.
   Students interested in studying women in literature in more detail
   will find helpful references. List of discussion or paper topics.
   Bibliography of basic texts.

V. POLITICS

Cotta, Michèle. "Et pourtant elles votent," L'Express, May 8-14, 1972, p. 39.

A very short article in which the author explores the reasons why women tend to shy away from politics. Sees a slight change in this tendency since 1972 with the larger proportion of younger women voters, the increase in the number of working women, and the decreasing influence of the Church on the young.

Renard, Marie-Thérèse. La Participation des femmes à la vie civique. Paris: Les Editions Ouvrières, 1965. 175 pp.

Useful introduction to women and politics in France. Published before advent of women's liberation in France and thus does not deal with such new movements as the MLF. Composed of three parts, each followed by brief bibliography: 1) Rapid historical survey of the evolution of women's rights in France, plus a brief description of the principal women's groups in 1965; 2) Statistical data and typical cases of women's participation in French political life; 3) Analysis of a questionnaire sent to active members of the Union Civique et Sociale. (TC)

GENERAL REFERENCE

Dictionnaire des femmes célèbres. Paris: Larousse, 1969. 256 pp.

An excellent compendium of major women figures in the world.

Also refer to the bibliography appended to Professor Sayre's course outline on p. 54.

LATEST PUBLICATIONS

Parturier, Françoise. Lettre ouverte aux femmes. Paris: Albin Michel, 1974. 191 pp.

Halimi, Gisèle. La Cause des femmes. Paris: Grasset, 1974. 208 pp.

University of Massachusetts,
Amherst

Women Authors of the Twentieth Century:

A Course Outline and Commentary

by

Anne S. Kimball

A sociological, historical, and psychological investigation of the role of women as seen by twentieth-century women authors. Primary consideration given to the question of whether or not feminine literature has unique qualities which distinguish it from the masculine tradition. Among the authors to be studied: Colette, Simone de Beauvoir, Simone Weil, Elsa Triolet, Marguerite Duras, Nathalie Sarraute.

To take this course, a student had to be either a junior or a senior, and to have had twelve credits of work in the French department including two advanced courses.

List of required works for the course, in the order in which they were read:

Colette. La Vagabonde (Livre de Poche, 1910).
Simone Weil. "Réflexions sur les causes de la liberté et de l'oppression sociale" dans Oppression et liberté (1955).
———. "Lettre à une élève" dans La Condition ouvrière (1934).
———. "Les Besoins de l'âme" dans L'Enracinement (1949).
Elsa Triolet. "Les Amants d'Avignon" dans Le Premier Accroc coûte deux cents francs (Livre de Poche, 1945).
Louise de Vilmorin. Madame de (Gallimard, 1951).
Françoise Mallet-Joris. Le Rempart des béguines (Livre de Poche, 1958).
Simone de Beauvoir. Mémoires d'une jeune fille rangée (Livre de Poche, 1958).
Célia Bertin. Une Femme heureuse (Buchet-Chastel, 1958).
Françoise Sagan. Aimez-vous Brahms? (Livre de Poche, 1959).
Geneviève Gennari. Journal d'une bourgeoise (Grasset, 1959).
Nathalie Sarraute. Le Planétarium (Livre de Poche, 1959).
Marguerite Duras. Dix Heures et demie du soir en été (Gallimard, 1960).
Christiane Rochefort. Les Stances à Sophie (Grasset, 1965).
Monique Wittig. Les Guérillères (Editions de Minuit, 1968).

One book was read and discussed per week, except for "Les Amants d'Avignon" and Madame de which were both assigned for the same week. In addition to the above readings, students were required to have read Simone de Beauvoir's Le Deuxième Sexe before the course began.

These works were chosen primarily for their literary and historical importance but also because they represent a wide variety of female situations. Thus, among the heroines of the novels one finds: a young woman falling in love for the first time, the young married woman, the widow, the divorcee, the lesbian, the career woman, the society woman, and others. The plot of the novel often involves a choice made by the heroine among two or more of the roles offered her.

The first class meeting began with a brief introduction to the role played by French women authors in the literature of previous centuries, and by a broad description of the trends which seem to be developing in the twentieth century. Then there was a discussion on two topics:

1) The way the seminar was to be set up and the kind of written and oral work which would be required of the students. The students chose to have the professor lead discussions rather than to assume that responsibility themselves, because they felt that the nature of the subject matter would guarantee participation in class. It was decided that students would write two 8-10 page papers, one at midterm and one in lieu of an exam at the end of the semester. In the first paper the student was to study three of the works studied in the first half of the course in the light of one of several proposed quotes on feminine literature, written by foremost authors and critics. The following are typical examples of such quotes:

> Feminine literature has indeed, in the past, limited itself to a small number of provinces: escape to a world of dreams, the beautification of daily life through graceful art and the tenderness of a sentimental presence, and, more generally, concern with the question of happiness and with feminine subjectivity. The most touching gift of a loving woman is that of her past, of her jealously preserved treasure of childhood memories and of the world of purity and of dreams in which she grew up; she wishes her lover to share it with her and to recapture the lost paradise. Such an expression of happiness--the banished theme of modern letters--is not lightly to be cast aside. The French, who have not lost their zest for happiness through the ordeals of two world wars, have for all practical purposes exiled this theme from their literature, most of all from the comedy of Anouilh, Aymé, and others. It would be a noble achievement for women writers to restore the word and the subject to their rightful estate, in a frail and threatened world.
>   --Henri Peyre. The Contemporary French Novel (New York: Oxford University Press, 1955), p. 285.

> . . . sur la légion de femmes qui s'essaient à taquiner les lettres et les arts, il en est bien peu qui persévèrent; celles mêmes qui franchissent ce premier obstacle demeureront bien souvent partagées entre leur narcissisme et un complexe d'infériorité. Ne pas savoir s'oublier, c'est un défaut qui pèsera sur elles plus lourdement que dans aucune autre carrière; si leur but essentiel est une abstraite affirmation de soi, la satisfaction formelle de la réussite, elles ne s'abandonneront pas à la contemplation du monde: elles seront incapables de le créer à neuf. . . . Au lieu de se donner généreusement à l'oeuvre qu'elle entreprend, la femme trop souvent la considère comme un simple ornement de sa vie; le livre et le tableau ne sont qu'un intermédiaire inessentiel lui permettant d'exhiber publiquement cette essentielle réalité: sa propre personne.
>   --Simone de Beauvoir. Le Deuxième Sexe, Vol. II (Gallimard, 1949), p. 550.

The second paper was to be an <u>explication d'oeuvre</u> of a twentieth-century feminine novel not studied in this course; the student would explicate the work in the light of what she had learned in the course.

2) What the specific aims of the course should be. Using <u>Le Deuxième Sexe</u> as a basis for discussion, the class drew up a list of questions they hoped to have answered or at least elucidated during the course of the semester. Some questions were typical of the questions often asked by the Women's Liberation Movement, for example: "What is a woman and in what ways does she differ from man?"; "Are these differences imposed by society, chosen by the individual, or due to physiological characteristics?"; "Should a woman be man's inferior, his equal, or financially and intellectually independent of him?"; " Should women be working to change their role in society, either with relation to career opportunities or in the home?" Other questions were literary: "Do women authors limit themselves to certain subjects and themes?"; "Do they choose certain psychological types as their main characters or analyze them in a particular way?"; "Are women authors capable of analyzing male characters as well as they analyze their heroines?"; "Are women using literature solely as a means of improving their own situation, or are their goals purely aesthetic?" The students did not expect to address themselves directly to such questions during the semester, but rather to have them present in their minds as a kind of frame of reference adding a new dimension to a fairly typical literary treatment of the chosen novels. It was agreed, however, to have an extra, optional meeting of the class in a less formal setting after the semester was over, in order to assess the course and determine, if possible, how many of the broader questions had been answered, and how many students felt that their own lives had been materially altered by the readings.

<u>Remarks</u>

a) Texts:

It was not always possible to procure the works to be studied in this course. The works by S. Weil, Louise de Vilmorin, Célia Bertin, Marguerite Duras, and Monique Wittig all proved to be out of print, and had to be either xeroxed or put on reserve in the library.

I can think of several different interesting and exciting courses on women or women authors in French literature which would be very different from this one. But were I to give this particular course again, I would make very few changes. The one change of importance would be to eliminate Françoise Sagan from the list of authors studied. The students and I all agreed that she has not attained the literary stature reached by the other authors. I would probably substitute Albertine Sarrazin's <u>L'Astragale</u> for <u>Aimez-vous Brahms?</u> I regret also not having done something by Marguerite Yourcenar, but the subject matter of her novels does not lend itself quite as well to the content of this course.

There were no particular problems or insights arising from the fact that the course dealt with a foreign culture, since most of these students had had experience abroad. Nevertheless there were occasional debates as to whether or not situations described in certain novels could exist equally well in the United States, and whether they would pose the same problems and choices.

Only French was spoken in the classroom (and of course all the reading was done in French), but due to the advanced level of the course, no special materials were necessary.

b) Student   response:

I have always had good student participation in my classes, but I found my interaction with this class to be somewhat different than in other courses. This was due not only to the subject matter being studied, but also to the fact that all of the students and myself were women, so that it was difficult for us to be objective. Furthermore, the students were very involved in the course; they seemed to have embarked upon a personal quest--for themselves, for their life-styles, and for their identity as women. I was naturally more interested in observing this searching process than in participating in it, although it was at times a painful process to watch. However, it was difficult for me to maintain an objective distance, because I was at times tempted to speak all-knowingly from a wider range of personal experience.

Needless to say, we did not solve all the questions we had put to our-selves at the beginning of the course, although I think we made consider-able progress on some of them. I did not expect us to do more than this, and so was satisfied that this particular goal of the course had been reached. But equally interesting to me were the personal reactions of the students to the course. They felt, at the end of the semester, that the message coming from this particular set of works was both clear and pes-simistic. Most heroines chose a career and independence over love and family because they found it more important to develop themselves as peo-ple than to subordinate their desires to someone else's. And the two choices seemed to be mutually exclusive: if one chose love, one lost one's sense of identity; but if one chose a career or intellectual values, one was doomed to a life of bleak loneliness. I believe that the students felt threatened by this situation (as they sometimes seemed threatened by other aspects of the course, albeit not seriously). They clearly wanted to believe that a woman can attain both goals simultaneously, and most could not accept a commitment to one goal to the exclusion of the other. Similarly, it was often apparent in class discussions that a student was defending a certain point of view because it represented a decision she had made or was about to make, and not for purely objective reasons. Such a situation can pose problems for the professor, since it is his/her role to insist upon a certain amount of objectivity on the part of the student, and yet he/she must be careful not to tread too heavily upon sensitive areas of a student's life.

I consider this course to be a special theme course in the sense that its purpose was to study an important group of authors too often neglected, and works which offer subject matter of particular interest to women. But the fact that we studied only women authors and that we addressed ourselves to a number of broad questions concerning female identity and roles shows that it was also a feminist course. However, it was not at all our intention to downgrade men (even chauvinist authors and critics!), and I think that some of the students were relieved to discover in the first class meeting that this was the case. We were interested in constructing something of positive validity to both men and women, not in being destructive or angry.

Perhaps the most interesting development that emerged from this course was our realization that since no final conclusion could be drawn at this time we really ought to set a meeting for some time in the future. We have therefore committed ourselves to a "course reunion" to take place in ten years, at which time we will hopefully have a broader perspective from which to evaluate ourselves.

Mount Holyoke College

Claudine Guégan-Fisher   Portland State University, Portland, Ore.
Department of Foreign Languages   July 17-August 10, 1973

THE FRENCH WOMAN

An intensive three-week exploration of the nature of the French woman.
Special emphasis is given to the modern French woman, but cultural background information and a historical perspective on the evolution of the
French woman are also included. The course makes use of lectures, class
discussion, films, photographic material, French magazines, audio-visual
aids, taped interviews, and interviews of resource people from all strata
and age groups.

Format: Undergraduate and graduate students. Course taught in French
         and in English.

- The French woman and courtly love in the Middle Ages.
- The XVIIth-century hostesses, queens of the "Salons" (Marquise
    de Rambouillet, Madame de Sévigné, Madame de La Fayette).
- The XVIIIth-century frivolous coquette: her exclusion from the
    the intellectual life of public and private "cafés."
- The working woman of the industrial revolution, cf. E. Zola, Gervaise.

- The modern woman and her problems:
    - Biological aspect--French "Planning Familial" vs. Catholicism.
    - French Law--Does it protect the woman or hinder her evolution
        as an independent being?
    _ The Female at Home--the French woman 1) as lover 2) as mother.

Satirical point of view: Jacques Faizant's cartoons about Eve, his novel
    Ni d'Eve, ni d'Adam; Jean Genet, Les Bonnes.

Sociological point of view: Françoise Parturier, Lettre ouverte aux hommes.

- The French Woman's Position in the Labor Market--Her part during
    the First and Second World Wars. Nowadays: 1) work as personal
    development 2) work as a frustration.
- Feminine Press and Fashion--"Be pretty and stay young." Impact of
    advertising: Eroticism vs. Sensuality. Study of excerpts from
    the pornographic novel Histoire d'O (P. Réage), and Le Repos du
    guerrier (Ch. Rochefort).
- The French Woman and the Political World--Can she influence elections?
- Decolonization of French women--Liberation movement; "Les Etats
    Généraux de la Femme" Conference held at Versailles.
- The intellectual female--How does she cope with the norms of society?
    1) Excerpts from Simone de Veauvoir, The Second Sex 2) Experiences
    of a woman in prison: Albertine Sarrazin, L'Astragale, La Cavale
    3) Teacher/student relationship: scandal of Gabrielle Roussier,
    a teacher, falling in love with her student.
- The French Woman of the future--How could her "integration" be
    achieved--Equity rather than Equality?

Sylvie Sayre*
Department of French

Barnard College, New York City
Spring 1973

SPECIAL THEMES IN MODERN FRENCH LITERATURE:
FEMINISM

The role and struggle of women as seen by authors of the nineteenth and twentieth centuries. Readings from feminist authors and analyses of various literary idealizations of women.

Three meetings per week:

I. Historique. Lecture: O. de Gouges, Constitution.
    Historique. Lecture: Laclos, L'Education des femmes.
    Historique. Lecture: G. Sand, La Femme dans la société politique. Laclos, Les Liaisons dangereuses. Lettre LXXXI. Le thème de la ruse.

II. Jeanne Deroin, Lettre à Proudhon.
    La conception romantique: Vigny, Lettre à Eva. Michelet, L'Amour, La Femme.
    Balzac, Physiologie du mariage.

III. Baudelaire, poèmes: exposés et explication d'étudiantes.
     Flaubert, Madame Bovary: exposés et extraits.
     Maupassant, L'Inutile Beauté, Histoire d'une fille de ferme.

IV. La famille: textes de M. Deraismes et M. Pelletier.
    Zola. Types de femmes: exposés (Germinal, L'Assommoir).
    Discussion et exposés: féminisme et pacifisme, le féminisme et les révolutions.

V. CONGÉ
    Mauriac, Thérèse Desqueyroux.
    Mauriac,   "   "

VI. Saint-Exupéry, Vol de nuit (extrait).
    Colette, La Dame du photographe. Sujet de discussion: la vie quotidienne des femmes.
    Nathalie Sarraute, Tropismes X et XIII.

VII. S. de Beauvoir, Mémoires d'une jeune fille rangée (extraits et exposé).
     Ch. Rochefort, Les Stances à Sophie.
     Ch. Rochefort,   "   "   "   "

     SPRING VACATION

VIII. S. de Beauvoir, Le Deuxième Sexe, I, pp. 371-432: Le Jeune fille.
      S. de Beauvoir,   "   "   "   II, p. 54-77: La Femme mariée.
      S. de Beauvoir,   "   "   "   II, p. 204-220: La Vie de société.

IX.   S. de Beauvoir,   "   "   "   II, p. 431-454: La Femme indépendante.

      S. de Beauvoir,   "   "   "   II, p. 455-481: La Femme indépendante.

S. de Beauvoir, <u>Le Deuxième Sexe</u>, Discussion et exposés.

X.   Discussion de textes féministes récents ou exposés.
          "   "   "   "   "   "   "

       · Ch. Rochefort, <u>Les Petits Enfants du siècle</u>.

XI.   Explication de la lettre de Valérie dans <u>La Condition humaine</u>
         de Malraux.
      Exposés.
      La femme noire. Textes de Michelet, Baudelaire, et de poètes
         africains francophones.

XII.   Exposés et discussion.
      Synthèse des thèmes variés et des différentes images de la femme
         dans les textes littéraires.
      Discussion du journal tenu par les étudiantes.

XIII.   Dans une perspective historique, analyse des différents niveaux
         de la lutte féministe. Comparaison avec le féminisme
         américain.
      Discussion
      READING PERIOD/

      Travail écrit: 2 **dissertations**
                  1 journal personnel (durée à déterminer)
                  1 examen final (question préparée)

<u>Sujets d'exposés</u>

Rousseau.   <u>L'Emile</u> (livre V, "Sophie")

Stendhal.   <u>De l'Amour</u>
           <u>Lamiel</u>

Flaubert.   <u>Madame Bovary</u>

Balzac.   <u>Le Lys dans la vallée</u>

Maupassant.   <u>Une Vie</u>
            <u>Boule de suif</u>

Baudelaire.   Poèmes choisis

Dumas fils.   <u>La Dame aux camélias</u>

Colette.   <u>Gigi</u>
            <u>La Vagabonde</u>

S. de Beauvoir. <u>Mémoires d'une jeune fille rangée</u>

A. Lagroua Weil-Hallé. <u>La Grand' Peur d'aimer</u>

-- La condition de la femme qui travaille en France.

-- Lesbianisme dans la littérature française.

-- Le conditionnement des petites filles: la littérature enfantine.

-- La femme dans le cinéma français.

-- La presse féminine (comparaison entre France et U. S.).

-- La femme du Tiers Monde: (réf. Frantz Fanon, Peau noire, masques blancs, L'Algérie se dévoile, La Famille algérienne.

-- La mère: (réf. H. Bazin, Vipère au poing; Mauriac, Genitrix; Vallès, L'Enfant.)

Bibliography

General:

    Abensour, Léon. Histoire générale du féminisme (1921).

    Bardèche, Maurice. Histoire des femmes (1965).

    Bebel, August. La Femme et le socialisme.

    Engels. The Origin of the Family.

    Gennari, Geneviève. Le Dossier de la femme (1965).

    Grimal, Pierre. Histoire mondiale de la femme (3 vols.).

    Sullerot, Evelyne. Histoire et sociologie du travail féminin.

1789

    Abensour, Léon. La Femme et le féminisme avant la révolution.

    Duhet, Paule-Marie. Les Femmes et la Révolution 1789-1794 (coll. Archives Julliard).

    Sullerot, Evelyne. Histoire de la presse féminine en France (Colin 1966).

    Michelet, Jules. Les Femmes de la révolution.

    Stephens, Winnifred. Women of the French Revolution (1922).

19th century

    Abensour, Léon. Le Féminisme sous le règne de Louis-Philippe et en 1848 (1913).

    Daubié, Julie. La Femme pauvre au 19e siècle.

    Manuel, Frank. The Prophets of Paris (on Saint-Simon and Fourier).

    Sullerot, Evelyne. Histoire de la presse féminine en France.

    Thibert, Marguerite. Le Féminisme dans le socialisme français de 1830 à 1850 (1926).

    Lissagaray. Histoire de la commune.

    Michel, Louise. La Commune.

    Thomas, Edith. Pauline Roland; socialisme et féminisme au 19e siècle (Paris 1956).

    Les Femmes en 1848 (Paris P.U.F. 1948).

    Les Pétroleuses (on the Commune 1871), Trans. Women Incendiaries.

20th century

    de Beauvoir, S. Le Deuxième Sexe. (Gallimard, 1949).

    Duverger, Maurice. La Participation des femmes à la vie politique (UNESCO 1955).

    Michel, A. et G. Texier. La Condition de la Française d'aujourd'hui (Gonthier).

    Sullerot, Evelyne. Demain les femmes (Gonthier, 1965).

    La Vie des femmes (Gonthier, 1965).

    La Presse féminine (Colin, coll. Kiosque, 1966).

    Guerrand, Roger-Henri. La Libre Maternité (Casterman-poche, 1971).

    Gauthier, Xavière. Surréalisme et sexualité (Gallimard, coll. Idées, 1971).

Nahas, Hélène. La Femme dans la littérature existentielle (P.U.F.
     1957).

*An anthology, Les Femmes en France, by Sylvie Sayre and Marie Collins has just been published (New York: Scribner's, 1974). Designed for students of intermediate French, the texts trace the evolving roles of women in France from medieval times to the present day. (Eds.)

Theodore E. Braun
Department of Languages and Literature

University of Delaware
Newark, Delaware
Spring 1973

IMAGES OF WOMEN IN FRENCH LITERATURE, 1700-1900

Program:

29 January:	Introduction to course
5 February:	Prévost. Manon Lescaut
12	Marivaux. Les Fausses Confidences
19	Diderot. La Religieuse
26 February 5 March	Choderlos de Laclos. Les Liaisons dangereuses
12 March:	Beaumarchais. Le Mariage de Figaro
26	Chateaubriand. Atala
2 April:	de Musset. Les Caprices de Marianne
9 16	Flaubert. Madame Bovary
23 30	Maupassant. Une Vie
7 May:	Conclusion/Review

Three papers are due; each, about 1000 words, is to deal with the material read in the previous weeks' work. For graduate students, the third is to be a research paper written on a topic deriving from the course work and agreed upon by student and professor, 15-20 pages or longer. (Undergraduates may write a research paper for their third essay.) Students will also be responsible for leading at least one discussion group and for participating actively in discussions. (Attendance, participation and preparation are calculated into the grade.)

No examinations except for the final, a take-home exam:

Faites attention aux indications. Ecrivez des essais en choisissant DEUX des groupes de sujets proposés.

1. Choisissez (a) OU (b):
   a) La femme pécheresse et source du péché
   b) La femme, la religion, et la moralité
2. Choisissez (a) OU (b):
   a) La femme: son éducation et son rôle dans la société
   b) La femme victime
3. Choisissez (a) OU (b)
   a) La femme, l'amour, et le mariage
   b) Le mariage, la dépendance, et la liberté de la femme
4. Ecrivez un essai sur CHACUN des sujets proposés:
   a) Le féminisme au 18è siècle
   b) Les déceptions romantiques au 19è siècle

Yvonne Guers-Villate   The University of Wisconsin--Milwaukee
Department of French and Italian   Spring 1973

FRENCH WOMEN NOVELISTS OF THE TWENTIETH CENTURY

Colette.   Le Blé en herbe. Collection Folio.

Colette.   La Chatte. Livre de poche 96.

S. de Beauvoir.   L'Invitée. Livre de Poche 793.

S. de Beauvoir.   Mémoires d'une jeune fille rangée. Coll. Folio

M. Duras.   Le Square. Ed. Béque. 20th Cent. Lit. Series.

M. Duras.   Le Vice-Consul. Fol.or Livre de Poche.

N. Sarraute.   Les Fruits d'or. Livre de Poche 2638.

C. Rochefort.   Les Stances à Sophie. Livre de Poche 2801.

F. Mallet-Joris.   Le Rempart des béguines. Livre de Poche 1031.

C. de Rivoyre.   Le Petit Matin. Livre de Poche 3153.

F. Sagan.   Bonjour Tristesse. Livre de Poche 772.

V. Leduc.   La Bâtarde. Collection Folio.

Edward C. Knox
Department of French

Middlebury College
Middlebury, Vermont
Fall 1971, Spring 1974

IMAGES DE LA FEMME DE CORNEILLE A LACLOS

Texte	Exposé ou Sujet de discussion
Cinna	La féminité d'Emilie
Bajazet	Le monde de Bajazet
Les Précieuses ridicules	Le précieux et le ridicule
Le Misanthrope	Qu'est-ce qu'une coquette?
La Princesse de Clèves	L'intrigue
Le Jeu de l'amour et du hasard	Sylvia et les hommes
Manon Lescaut	L'homme et la femme
L'Ingénu	Le point de vue
La Religieuse	Le point de vue
Les Liaisons dangereuses I	Les lettres I-IV
Les Liaisons dangereuses II	Les lettres LXXXI et LXXXV

Devoir final: "Problématique de l'image féminine en littérature"

Lectures supplémentaires:

Bardèche, Maurice. Histoire des femmes. Stock, 1968.

Fauchery, Pierre. La Destinée féminine dans le roman européen du dix-huitième siècle. Armand Colin, 1972.

Ellmann, Mary. Thinking About Women. Harcourt, Brace and World, 1968.

Sister M. Hélène Messager
Department of French

College of New Rochelle
New Rochelle, New York
Fall 1972

LA FEMME DANS LE ROMAN FRANCAIS

Introduction:

Decaux, Alain. Histoire des Françaises. (Introduction)

I. La Française des origines au XVIIè siècle
Decaux, Alain. Histoire des Françaises
de La Clavière, Maude. The Women of the Renaissance

Decaux, Alain: 1. Nos Ancêtres, Les Gauloises
2. Filles de la Barbarie
Histoire des   3. La France naquit d'une Bavaroise
Françaises   4. Viragos et Cours d'amour
5. Blanches comme fleurs des prés
6. Jeanneton la paysanne, Anieuse la citadine
7. Cent ans de guerre pour les femmes
8. Deux Anne pour une Louise
9. Le siècle de Brantôme
10. Vent de Fronde pour les Dames

II. La Française au XVIIè siècle
Reynier, Gustave. La Femme au XVIIè siècle
Etude d'une oeuvre: Madame de La Fayette. La Princesse de Clèves

III. La Française au XVIIIè siècle
Wilson, R. Women of the French Revolution
Goncourt, E. La Femme au 18è siècle
Kavanaugh, Julia. Women in France during the 18th Century
Michelet, Jules. La Femme de la révolution
Hall, Evelyn. The Women of the Salons

Etude d'une oeuvre: Abbé Prévost. Manon Lescaut

IV. La Française au XIXè siècle. La Française du siècle romantique
Etude de deux oeuvres: Stendhal. Le Rouge et le Noir
Flaubert. Madame Bovary

V. La Française au XXè siècle
Clark, F. The Position of Women in Contemporary France
Patui, R. Women in the Modern World
Le Livre de l'oppression des femmes

Etude d'une oeuvre: Simone de Beauvoir. L'Invitée

Bibliography
Le Livre de l'oppression des femmes (Paris: P. Belfont, 1972)
Clark, Frances. The Position of Women in Contemporary France
Decaux, Alain. Histoire des Françaises
Goncourt, Edmond. La Femme au dix-huitième siècle
Hall, Evelyn B. The Women of the Salons

Kavanaugh, Julia. Women in France During the Eighteenth Century
de La Clavière, Maude. The Women of the Renaissance. A Study of Feminism
Michelet, Jules. La Femme de la révolution
Patui, Raphael. Women in the Modern World
Reynier, Gustave. La Femme au XVIIè siècle
Wilson, R. Women of the French Revolution

Oeuvres à étudier:

    Madame de La Fayette. La Princesse de Clèves
    Abbé Prévost. Manon Lescaut
    Flaubert, Gustave. Madame Bovary
    de Beauvoir, Simone. L'Invitée

Annabelle M. Rea
Department of Languages and Linguistics

Occidental College
Los Angeles, California
Winter (Jan.-March) 1974

LA FEMME DANS LA LITTERATURE FRANCAISE

Textes:

Madame de La Fayette. La Princesse de Clèves. Livre de Poche.

Choderlos de Laclos. Les Liaisons dangereuses. Garnier-Flammarion.

George Sand. Indiana. Classiques Garnier.

Gustave Flaubert. Madame Bovary. Livre de Poche.

Guy de Maupassant. Boule de suif. Livre de Poche.

Colette. La Vagabonde. Livre de Poche.

François Mauriac. Genitrix. Livre de Poche.

Simone de Beauvoir. Le Deuxième Sexe. Gallimard, Coll. Idées.

Marguerite Duras. Moderato cantabile. Editions de Minuit.

Sylvie Romanowski
Department of French and Italian

Northwestern University
Evanston, Illinois
Winter quarter 1972-1973

LE ROMAN ET LA FEMME

Textes:

S. de Beauvoir. L'Invitée
C. Rochefort. Les Stances à Sophie
F. Mallet-Joris. Le Rempart des béguines
M. Duras. Le Ravissement de Lol V. Stein
N. Sarraute. Tropismes

Sujets d'essais:

La solitude de la femme
Libération et prison (ou vice versa)
L'amour entre femmes
L'érotisme du point de vue féminin
L'homme avant et après le mariage
Le mariage
La femme dans la société
La société bourgeoise
L'homme vu par la femme
La lutte de l'homme et de la femme: en général, ou un aspect que vous
        préciserez
L'adolescence
Individualisme et société
La connaissance de soi
Conformisme et révolte
Images ou scènes symboliques
Le roman comme monologue intérieur

Livres mis à la réserve:

S. de Beauvoir. Le Deuxième Sexe
F. Jeanson. Simone de Beauvoir ou l'entreprise de vivre
S. Lilar. A propos de Sartre et de l'amour
_____ . Le Malentendu du deuxième sexe
N. Sarraute. L'Ere du soupçon

Format: Undergraduate and graduate students.

Edward Rossman
Department of Foreign Languages

SUNY, State University College
Geneseo, New York
Fall 1972, Fall 1973

LA FEMME DANS LA LITTÉRATURE

Textes:

A. Gide. Isabelle

_____ . La Porte étroite

C. Rochefort. Le Repos du guerrier

_____ . Les Petits Enfants du siècle

J. Anouilh. Colombe

J. Giraudoux. Electre*

F. Maurois. Thérèse Desqueyroux

F. Mallet-Jorris. Le Rempart des béguines

A. Camus. "La Femme adultère" in L'Exil et le royaume

J.-P. Sartre. "Erostrate," "Intimité," "La Chambre," "L'Enfance d'un chef," in Le Mur

_____ . Huis-Clos

_____ . Les Mouches

E. Ionesco. La Cantatrice chauve

*I plan to substitute Anouilh's Antigone for Giraudoux's Electre, since students seem to find Giraudoux hard to get into.

Edith Rostas
Department of French

Mount Holyoke College
South Hadley, Massachusetts
Spring 1972

WOMEN THROUGH FRENCH LITERATURE (Freshman Seminar)

Syllabus

1. Madame de Sévigné. <u>Lettres.</u> Nouveaux Classiques Larousse.

2. Molière. <u>Les Femmes savantes</u>. Nouveaux Classiques Larousse.

3. Marivaux. <u>Le Jeu de l'amour et du hasard</u>. Petits Classiques Bordas.

4. L'Abbé Prévost. <u>Manon Lescaut</u>. Garnier-Flammarion.

5. Balzac. <u>Une Fille d'Eve</u>. Garnier-Flammarion.

6. Flaubert. <u>Trois Contes</u>. Texte intégral, Classiques Larousse.

7. Maupassant. <u>Boule de suif</u>. Livre de Poche.

8. Gide. <u>Isabelle</u>. Ed. Elsie Pell. Appleton-Century Crofts.

9. Simone de Beauvoir. <u>Mémoires d'une jeune fille rangée</u>. Livre de Poche.

10. Monique Wittig. <u>Les Guérillères</u>. Les Editions de Minuit.

Two papers, two oral "exposés." A final synthetizing seminar: "Evolution de l'affranchissement de la femme, vue à travers les oeuvres étudiées ce semestre." Each student presented two prepared "exposés" followed by general discussion.

Janet Whatley
Department of Romance Languages

Washington University
St. Louis, Missouri
Spring 1973

LA CONDITION FEMININE

Textes:

La Fayette, Mme. de. La Princesse de Clèves
Roland, Mme. Une Education bourgeoise
Sand, George. Indiana
Colette. Chéri et La Fin de Chéri
Beauvoir, Simone de. Mémoires d'une jeune fille rangée
Duras, Marguerite. Moderato cantabile
Sarraute, Nathalie. Tropismes
Rochefort, Christiane. Les Stances à Sophie
Woolf, Virginia. A Room of One's Own
Ellmann, Mary. Thinking About Women

Two meetings per week:

I.   Introduction
     La Princesse de Clèves

II. "   "   "   "
     "   "   "   "

III. Mme. Roland
     "   "

IV. Mme. de Staël (conférence)
     Indiana

V. Indiana
    Colette

VI. Colette
    Colette

VII. de Beauvoir
     "   "

VIII. "   "
     "   "

IX. Moderato cantabile
    "   "

X. Tropismes
    "

XI. Les Stances à Sophie
    "   "   "   "

XII. Woolf
    "

XIII. Ellmann
    "

Dorothy Backer
Department of Modern Languages

Dickinson College
Carlisle, Pennsylvania
Fall 1973

WOMEN, MAKERS AND HEROINES (Fr. 364-Special Topics)

Weekly topics:
1. Troubadours and trouvères. Chrétien de Troyes. Tristan et Iseut
2. Ronsard: Les Amours. Carpe diem.
   Rabelais: Le Tiers Livre. Should Panurge marry?
3. Préciosité. The New Woman.
4. Molière, two views. The dumb wife and the bluestocking.
5. La Rochefoucauld, La Bruyère. Anti-feminist libertinage.
6. Mme. de Sévigné, Mme. de La Fayette.
7. Manon Lescaut. The grandes dames of the Salons. Mme du Deffand.
8. Laclos: Les Liaisons dangereuses. Libertine woman.
9. Constant: Adolphe. Romantic woman.
10. George Sand; Stendhal: Le Rouge et le Noir; Flaubert: Mme. Bovary.
11. Colette: Claudine à l'école.
12. Simone de Beauvoir: Mémoires d'une jeune fille rangée.
13. Sarraute, Duras.

Everyone must read:

La Princesse de Clèves   Adolphe
Manon Lescaut   Claudine à l'école
Les Liaisons dangereuses   Mémoires d'une jeune fille rangée
one novel by Sarraute or Duras
Excerpts: Troubadours, Chrétien, Tristan, Ronsard, Rabelais, précieux
     poets, La Rochefoucauld, La Bruyère, Sévigné
Everyone has already read: Molière: Les Précieuses ridicules; L'École
     des femmes; Les Femmes savantes; Dom Juan. Stendhal: Le Rouge et
     le Noir. Flaubert: Madame Bovary.

In this course I took my students, who were all advanced French
majors, on a tour through the whole of French literature, picking out
images of women, and women's responses to them. We began with the 12th-
century courts of love, and the belle dame sans merci, the queenly virgin-
goddess that women of leisure tried to emulate. This stereotype has en-
dured in literature; we found her in Ronsard's sonnets, in précieux mad-
rigals, and under many disguises up to our own day. We also encountered
Pandora, the bourgeois image of woman as nuisance and spreader of confusion, cuckolder of husbands and bane of all manly idealism. She is in
Rabelais, Molière, all satire. We discovered the sexism of the French
classical writers (La Rochefoucauld, La Bruyère). And we found that every
heroine who ever felt any genuine passion (Mme. de Clèves, Manon Lescaut,
Mme. de Tourvel, Mme de Rênal, Emma Bovary) had to be killed off in the
last chapter. We ended with the triumph of women in the successes of
Simone de Beauvoir, Sarraute, and Duras, who grapple with the continuing
problems of women, as writers and subjects.
     The course was quite a consciousness-raising event; and I think
I learned almost as much as my students did.

Eric C. Hicks
Department of French and German

University of Maryland
College Park, Maryland
Spring 1973

WOMEN IN SOCIETY, MEDIEVAL AND MODERN

(Fr. 679--History of Ideas in France)

"L'essence de la critique est de savoir
comprendre des états très différents de
celui où nous vivons."   --E. Renan

The intent of this course is to analyze the mythical centers of modern anti-feminist attitudes. It will tend to focus on a series of literary quarrels or causes célèbres in which the status of women is clearly formulated as the major issue. Some of these lie within the chronological limits of the medieval period; all are tributary to fundamentally medieval attitudes.

The plan of the course is as follows:

1. L'affaire Héloïse: Manicheism, Christian doctrine and the evils of the flesh; St. Augustine, St. Jerome, Cathari mythology; The Correspondence of Abélard and Héloise.

2. La querelle de la Rose. Women, sex, and gros mots in the Romance of the Rose (Jean de Meung); Christine de Pisan, the Church, and early Humanism: The Letters on the Rose.

3. La querelle des femmes. The elaboration of "Gallic humor": fabliaux, Renart, Les Quinze joies du mariage; Rabelais and Marguerite de Navarre.

4. Femmes savantes: la querelle des anciens et des modernes. Boileau's Satire X; Mme. Dacier.

Recommended reading:
S. de Beauvoir. Le Deuxième Sexe.
B. Friedan. The Feminine Mystique.
G. Greer. The Female Eunuch.
K. Millett. Sexual Politics.

Students will participate in establishing course format. It is hoped that oral reports will be offered on a variety of relevant topics, e.g. The Mosaic Law and the Deprecation of Women, Platonism and the Female Eunuch, The Ideal of Chastity and the Alienation of Women, Snobbery and the Female Consciousness, Boredom and Revolt, Censorship and the Forbidden Fruit, etc.

Latin and Old French would be assets to students interested in the course. Translations of the basic works will be available. Many of the shorter texts are out of print and will be made available through a common Xerox effort, not to exceed 50 pages. If there is sufficient interest from outside the department, the course may be conducted in English.

Course taught in French; Enrollment: Graduate Students.

Elaine Marks
Department of French and Italian

University of Massachusetts
Amherst, Massachusetts
Fall 1971

L'IMAGE DE LA FEMME ET DU FÉMININ DANS LA LITTÉRATURE FRANCAISE

mardi le 14 septembre: INTRODUCTION:
    I. Quelques définitions, plusieurs problèmes:
        A. Qu'est-ce qu'une femme? Faits et théories.
        B. Qu'est-ce que le féminin?
        C. Qu'est-ce qu'une image?
    II. La littérature française: absence et présence de la femme et
       du féminin:
        A. Auteurs.
        B. Personnages littéraires.
        C. Personnages historiques.
        D. Couvents, cours d'amour, salons . . .
        E. Le deuxième genre: "la."
   III. La structure du cours:
        A. d'Iseut à Winnie.
        B. A partir de Combray.
jeudi le 16 septembre: Féminisme et Anti-féminisme en France de Dieu à
   J.-J. Rousseau:
      La femme sous l'ancien régime:
      Lectures: Simone de Beauvoir, Le Deuxième Sexe: "Destin" et
                "Histoire."
      Extraits: La Sainte Bible, Le Roman de la Rose, Le Jeu d'Adam,
              textes sur la Vierge, Christine de Pisan, Le Procès de
              Jeanne d'Arc, Mlle de Gournay, Poulain de la Barre,
              Fénelon, les "philosophes," Rousseau.
mardi le 21 septembre: Féminisme et Anti-féminisme en France du Code
   Civil à Simone de Beauvoir:
      Lectures: Simone de Beauvoir, Le Deuxième Sexe: "Histoire."
      Extraits: Le Code Civil, Rimbaud.
jeudi le 23 septembre: La France:
      Lectures (extraits): La Chanson de Roland, Eustache Deschamps,
           Charles d'Orléans, Du Bellay, Ronsard, d'Aubigné, Chénier,
           Robespierre, Michelet, Henri de Régnier, Aragon, De Gaulle.
mardi le 25 septembre: Images:
      Lectures (extraits): Cantilène de Sainte Eulalie, Marie de France
           Laustic, Aucassin et Nicolette, Le Roman de Tristan et
           Iseut.
jeudi le 30 septembre: Images:
      Lectures: Le Roman de Tristan et Iseut.
mardi le 5 octobre: Images:
      Lectures (extraits): Guillaume de Machault, Villon.
jeudi le 7 octobre: Images
      Lectures (extraits): Marot, Labbé, Scève, Du Bellay, Ronsard.
mardi le 12 octobre: Images:
      Lectures (extraits): La Fontaine. Molière, Les Femmes savantes.
jeudi le 14 octobre: Images:

Lectures: Molière, Les Femmes savantes.
Extraits: Racine.
mardi le 19 octobre: Images..
Lectures: Racine, Phèdre.
jeudi le 21 octobre: Images:
Lectures: Madame de La Fayette. La Princesse de Clèves.
mardi le 26 octobre: Images:
Lectures: Madame de La Fayette, La Princesse de Clèves.
Extraits: Madame de Sévigné.
jeudi le 28 octobre: Images:
Lectures: Laclos, Les Liaisons dangereuses.
mardi le 2 novembre: Images:
Lectures: Laclos, Les Liaisons dangereuses.
jeudi le 4 novembre: Images:
Lectures: Balzac, La Fille aux yeux d'or.
Extraits: Les "romantiques."
mardi le 9 novembre: Images:
Lectures: Baudelaire, Les Fleurs du mal.
jeudi le 11 novembre: Images:
Lectures: Baudelaire, Les Fleurs du mal.
mardi le 16 novembre: Images:
Lectures: Flaubert, Un Coeur simple.
jeudi le 18 novembre: Images:
Lectures (extraits): Les "Symbolistes."
mardi le 23 novembre: Images:
Lectures: Proust, Combray.
mardi le 30 novembre: Images:
Lectures: Proust, Combray.
jeudi le 2 décembre: Images:
Lectures (extraits): Valéry, Claudel.
mardi le 7 décembre: Images:
Lectures: Colette, Chéri, Sido, La Maison de Claudine.
jeudi le 9 décembre: Images:
Lectures (extraits): Les "surréalistes."
mardi le 14 décembre: Images:
Lectures: Anouilh, Antigone.
jeudi le 16 décembre: Images:
Lectures: Beckett, Oh les beaux jours!
mardi le 21 décembre: Conclusion: Programmes provisoires . . . . .

Sister Mary Ann Quinn
Department of Modern Languages

Anna Maria College
Paxton, Massachusetts
Spring 1973

WOMEN IN FRENCH LITERATURE

A discussion of woman, love, and suffering in the works of representative French authors, including the myths of femininity and the revelations of existential literature.

I. Characteristics of Women:

"The ideal woman will be she who incarnates most exactly the OTHER capable of revealing him to himself." The Second Sex, p. 236.

"There are some women who love and stay selfish through it all." Cousin Bette, p. 50.

All page references below refer to Simone de Beauvoir, The Second Sex, trans. and ed. by H. M. Parshley. New York: Bantam Books, 1961.

Situation and Character, pp. 562-591.

Justifications, pp. 592-638.

Toward Liberation--The Independent Woman, pp. 639-689.

II. Renowned French Women:

History through the Middle Ages to the 18th Century, pp. 89-100.

Since the French Revolution, pp. 100-118; pp. 118-128.

Women in Existential Literature

a. Origins of feminine literature--Marie de France
b. Beginning of women's struggle--Christine de Pisan
c. Toward the glorification of women--Renaissance
d. Women, all-powerful, create "La Préciosité"
e. The century of two friends: Mme. de Sévigné and Mme. de La Fayette
f. The reign of women
Mme. de Staël
George Sand
Comtesse de Noailles
Colette

III. Dreams, Fears, Idols, pp. 166-185.
Myth and Reality, pp. 237-247.
The Myth of Women in:
Stendhal. pp. 223-233. The Red and the Black, The Charterhouse of Parma
Balzac. Cousin Bette

Laclos. Les Liaisons dangereuses.

Zola. Thérèse Raquin.

Montherlant, pp. 185-200.

Claudel, pp. 209-216.

Breton, pp. 217-223.

Summary, pp. 233-237.

Colette. Gigi and selected writings.

Gide. Madeleine.

Proust. Remembrance of Things Past.

Mauriac. The Desert of Love.

Nathalia Sarraute.

Françoise Sagan.

Marguerite Yourcenar.

Simone Weil.

IV. Women of America and France:

See: Saturday Evening Post, F18, 1961.

V. Course Requirements:

a. A character study of Valérie in Cousin Bette or Madame Bovary in Madame Bovary, or Manon Lescaut, or Phèdre, or Prouhèze in Le Soulier de satin, or Gigi, or Madeleine, or Thérèse Raquin, or Mme. Arnoux in Sentimental Education, or Nadja, or Maria Cross in The Desert of Love, or Odette in Proust.

b. Questions: Who better knows and describes women? A man or a woman?
Is there really a problem or a case?
Is the French woman any different from another?
Etc.

Emile Langlois
Department of French

Mount Holyoke College
South Hadley, Massachusetts
January Term, 1973
(approximately 3 weeks)

EVER READ A FRENCH-CANADIAN NOVEL?

List of novels read:

Gabrielle Roy. Bonheur d'occasion

Marie-Claire Blais. Une Saison dans la vie d'Emmanuel

Anne Hébert Kamouraska

Jacques Godbout. Salut Galarneau*

*Included as an example of Canadian humor. Would choose instead another novel, written by a woman, next time; for example, Germaine Guèvremont, Le Survenant.

Conducted in French.

Gale Hilary Nigrosh
Department of Romance Languages

Clark University
Worcester, Massachusetts
January Term 1973

CHRISTIANE ROCHEFORT: FRENCH SISTER IN STRUGGLE

Required reading:

Christiane Rochefort. Le Repos du guerrier

Christiane Rochefort. Les Stances à Sophie

Christiane Rochefort. Les Petits Enfants du siècle

Christiane Rochefort. Printemps au parking

Additional optional readings:

Simone de Beauvoir. Le Deuxième Sexe

Germaine Greer. The Female Eunuch

Articles from current French periodicals (Réalités, Le Nouvel Observateur, Elle, Lui, L'Express)

Marie Collins   Rutgers University, Newark, New Jersey
Department of Foreign Languages   Spring 1973

SEXUAL POLITICS IN THE NOVEL AND DRAMA (Fr. 312)

Required readings:

Molière. School for Wives, trans. Wilbur.

Laclos. **Les Liaisons dangereuses**

Stendhal. The Red and the Black

Flaubert. Madame Bovary

Balzac. Cousin Bette

Zola. Germinal

Mauriac. Thérèse

Anouilh. Antigone

Simone de Beauvoir. The Mandarins (if possible) and excerpts, The Prime
    of Life

Three meetings per week:

I.   Molière
II.   Laclos
III.   "
IV.   Stendhal
V.   "
VI.   "
VII.   Flaubert
  Spring recess
VIII.   Flaubert
IX.   "
X,   Zola
XI.   "
XII.   "
XIII.   Mauriac
XIV.   **Anouilh**

Lynne L. Gelber   Skidmore College
Department of Modern Languages and   Saratoga Springs, New York
    Literatures   Fall 1974

WOMEN IN FRANCE SINCE THE REVOLUTION

The course has a three-fold goal. The syllabus includes, first of all, works by women writers in an attempt to ascertain if there is a female sensibility. Second, it will focus on women characters, those of both male and female authors to compare attitudes toward women in a given period. Third, it will contain historical and sociological texts to enable class discussion to include the real as well as the literary place of women and to facilitate some evaluation of the influence of society on literature by, for, and about women.

Basic Required Bibliography:

Albert Guérard. France, A Modern History. Ann Arbor, 1959. pp. 213-439.
Mme. Roland. The Private Memoirs, ed. E. G. Johnson. Chicago, 1900.
Mme. de Staël. Mme. de Staël on Politics, Literature, and National Character, ed. Morree Berger. New York, 1964.
_____. Corinne.
George Sand. Indiana
Stendhal. Lamiel or The Ways of the Heart. New York. 1929.
Flaubert. Madame Bovary.
Balzac. The Curé of Tours.
Colette. Gigi, Julie de Carneilhan, Chance Acquaintances. New York, 1952.
de Beauvoir. Memoirs of a Dutiful Daughter. New York. 1959.
Claudel. Tidings Brought to Mary.
Sagan. Bonjour Tristesse.
Duras. Moderato Cantabile.
Sarraute. The Planetarium.

Additional sources:

Vigman, Fred. Beauty's Triumph. Boston, 1966.
Stewart, John Hall. A Documentary Survey of the French Revolution, New York, 1951.
Lettres de Napoléon à Joséphine, ed. Léon Cerf. Paris, 1928.
Abrantès, Laure Junot. Memoirs of Napoleon, His Court and Family.
Masson, Frédéric. Napoléon et l'amour. Paris, 1933.
Brinton, C. C. A Decade of Revolution, 1789-1799. New York, 1934.
Lehmann, Andree. "France," in Women in the Modern World. pp. 220-246. New York, 1967.
Dobson, Austin. Four Frenchwomen, New York, n.d.
Stephens, W. Women of the French Revolution. London, 1922.
Wilson, R. McNair. Women of the French Revolution. London, 1936.
Herold, S. C. Mistress to an Age. New York, 1958.
Jaeck, Emma. Mme. de Staël and the Spread of German Literature. New York, 1915.
Wood, John. Sondages, 1830-1848, Romanciers français secondaires. Toronto, 1965.
Cachard, Henry, ed. The French Civil Code, revised ed. Paris, 1930.

Balzac. _The Lily of the Valley_.

Zola. _Nana_.

Thomas, Edith. _The Women Incendiaries_. New York, 1966.

Yale French Studies, "Women Writers." No. 27, 1961.

Portnoy, Harold, ed. _La Femme aujourd'hui_. Paris, 1971.

de Beauvoir. _The Second Sex_. New York, 1953.

_____. _The Coming of Age_. New York, 1972.

Nahas, Hélène. _La Femme dans la littérature existentielle_. Paris, 1957.

Machard, Raymonde. _Les Françaises_. Paris, 1945.

Bertaud, Jules. _La Jeune Fille dans la littérature française_. Paris, n.d.

Sarraute, Nathalie. _L'Ere du soupçon_. Paris, 1956.

Gillian C. Gill   Northeastern University, Boston
Department of Modern Languages   April–June 1973

CHERCHEZ LA FEMME: WOMEN AS SEEN BY GREAT FRENCH
NOVELISTS OF THE EIGHTEENTH AND NINETEENTH CENTURIES

Required Texts (to be read in the original or in English translation):

Madame de La Fayette	La Princesse de Clèves
L'Abbé Prévost	Manon Lescaut
Choderlos de Laclos	Les Liaisons dangereuses
Stendhal	Le Rouge et le Noir
Balzac	La Cousine Bette
Flaubert	Madame Bovary
Zola	Nana

Suggested Reading on Feminist Issues:

Betty Friedan	The Feminine Mystique
Kate Millett	Sexual Politics
Germaine Greer	The Female Eunuch
Virginia Woolf	A Room of One's Own and Three Guineas

The course will also included Xeroxed passages for close analysis from:

Le Grand Cyrus

Moll Flanders

Clarissa

La Nouvelle Héloïse

Émile

La Religieuse

and from the works of Madame de Staël.

Lygia Johnson　　　　　　　　　　California State College, Sonoma
Department of Foreign Languages　　Rohnert Park, California
　　　　　　　　　　　　　　　　　　Fall 1973

IMAGES OF WOMEN IN FRENCH LITERATURE (Fr. 313)

The focus of the course is women's search for identity and self-realization in modern society and the effects of women's rising expectations to achieve full self-definition. We shall also examine the problems of modern life: The changing relationship between the individual and society, the breakdown of traditional values, the disintegration of the individual, and other related issues.

Reading list:

 Colette, The Vagabond　(On reserve)

 Simone de Beauvoir, The Woman Destroyed (Fontana)

 Madame de La Fayette, The Princess of Clèves (Signet)

 Marguerite Duras, The Ravishing of Lol Stein (Grove)

 Violette Leduc, Ravages (Panther)

 Françoise Sagan, Bonjour Tristesse

 George Sand, Selections from Intimate Journal

 Nathalie Sarraute, Tropisms (Braziller)

 Albertine Sarrazin, Runaway (Grove)

 Marie-Claire Blais, A Season in the Life of Emmanuel (Grosset
  and Dunlap)

Selected poetry of Christine de Pisan, Louise Labé, Edith Boissonnas, Anne Hébert, Joyce Mansour, Anne Sylvestre, and others.

Madeleine G. McDermott
Modern Language Department

Towson State College
Baltimore, Maryland
Fall 1973

WOMEN IN FRENCH LITERATURE

The basic reading list for this course, taught in English, included:

Mme. de La Fayette. The Princess of Clèves in H. Peyre, Seven French Novels. Popular Library.

Molière. The Learned Ladies. Random House.

Racine. Phaedra. Appleton-Century.

Beaumarchais. Marriage of Figaro. Appleton-Century.

Chateaubriand. Atala, René. Signet.

Flaubert. Madame Bovary. Signet.

Zola. Germinal. Signet.

Marks, Elaine. French Poetry from Baudelaire. Dell.

Claudel. Tidings Brought to Mary. Gate-Regnery.

Beauvoir. The Prime of Life. Lancer.

Mallet-Joris. The Paper House. Curtis.

Marthe Rosenfeld   Indiana University at Fort Wayne
Department of Modern Foreign Languages   Fall 1973

WOMEN IN FRENCH LITERATURE (F. 408)

Sophomore standing or consent of instructor. Readings of works by
such writers as Racine, Flaubert, Mauriac, Anouilh, Giraudoux, Simone de
Beauvoir, Duras, and Robbe-Grillet. Lectures, discussions, and reports on
the changing image of woman from the seventeenth century to the present.
Analysis of the themes, imagery, and the language as they relate to the
feminine condition. Eligible for the cultural option. Conducted in English.

List of texts:

Racine.	Phaedra. Trans. by Robert Lowell (Farrar, Straus and Giroux)
Flaubert.	Madame Bovary. Trans. P. De Man (A Norton Critical Edition)
Mauriac.	Thérèse. Trans. G. Hopkins (Noonday)
Anouilh.	Five Plays. (Mermaid Drama Book)
de Beauvoir.	The Prime of Life. Trans. P. Green (Lancer Books)
Duras.	Four Novels. (Grove Press)
Robbe-Grillet.	Two Novels (Jealousy and In The Labyrinth) (Grove Press)

Dates	Texts	Assignments
9/4	Madame Bovary	Part I
9/6	" "	Part II, pp. 1-88
9/11	" "	pp. 88-134
9/13	" "	pp. 134-185
9/18	" "	pp. 185-225
9/20	" "	Finish reading Madame Bovary and the last two critical essays.
9/25	Thérèse	Chapters 1-4
9/27	"	" 4-7
10/2	"	" 7-11
10/4	"	Finish reading Thérèse
10/9	Antigone	pp. 3-27
10/11	"	Finish reading Antigone

MIDSEMESTER REPORT (will be announced)

Dates	Texts	Assignments
10/16	Phaedra	Act I
10/18	"	Act II
10/23	"	Act III
10/25	"	Acts IV and V
10/29	The Prime of Life	pp. 9-67
11/1	" " " "	Finish chapter I
11/6	" " " "	Chapter II
11/8	" " " "	Chapter III
11/13	Moderato Cantabile	Chapters I-V
11/15	" "	Finish reading Moderato Cantabile

Dates	Texts	Assignments
11/20	The Square	Chapter I
11/27	" "	Chapters II and III
11/29	Jealousy	pp. 39-65
12/4	"	pp. 66-93
12/6	"	pp. 93-121
12/11	"	Finish reading Jealousy
12/13		

Outside reading: At least two chapters in Simone de Beauvoir's work
The Second Sex.

Patricia Ward
Department of French

Pennsylvania State University
University Park, Pennsylvania
Winter Term 1974

WOMEN IN MODERN FRENCH LITERATURE (French 198)

This is an experimental course in translation to permit students who are interested in French culture and in changing views of women to examine portraits of women in nineteenth- and twentieth-century French literature; both male and female writers will be discussed. Special attention will be given to the social context of literature to see whether the roles of women in society are reflected in imaginative writings. In addition, literary problems such as "tone" and "point of view" will also be considered with reference to the characterization of women.

Though lectures, occasionally by guest lecturers, will be given and three films will be shown, most class time will be given to discussion of assigned readings and students will be expected to participate. In addition to tests on January 28 and February 27, students will read one book outside of class and hand in a brief essay on it during the week of February 18.

Course fulfills University requirement in the Humanities. Optional work in French.

Textbooks:

        Anouilh. Five Plays. Volume I. Hill and Wang
        Balzac. Cousin Bette. Penguin
        Baudelaire. The Flowers of Evil. New Directions
        de Beauvoir. The Second Sex. Bantam.
        Colette. Earthly Paradise. Farrar, Straus and Giroux.
        Duras. Hiroshima mon amour. (Text for the film) Grove.
        Flaubert. Madame Bovary. Modern Library.
        Mauriac. Thérèse. Noonday.
        Zola. Thérèse Raquin. Penguin.

Calendar
Week
December 7 - Introduction - Women and Social Change
        10 - Films - Française 63, Colette
             The Romantic Ideal - Selected Poems
        17 - Typology - Cousin Bette

January 4 - Cousin Bette
         7 - Baudelaire*
        14 - Disappearance of the Romantic Ideal - Madame Bovary
        21 - Heredity and Environment - Thérèse Raquin
        28 - Test
             Revolt and the Bourgeois Marriage - Thérèse
                 (Mauriac, pp. 1-133)

February 4 - 20th-century Views of Mythic Prototypes - Antigone, Eurydice
                 (Anouilh, pp. 1-120)

February 11 - The Woman Writer - Colette*
          18 - Showing of Resnais's film--<u>Hiroshima mon amour</u>
               Discussion of Duras's text for the film
               Outside reading reports due
          25 - Beauvoir and Contemporary Feminism, <u>The Second Sex</u>*
               Test

*Readings in the text to be assigned in class.

Suggested Outside Reading:

de Beauvoir. <u>Les Mandarins</u>. (tr. <u>The Mandarins</u>, Meridian paperback)
     <u>Mémoires d'une jeune fille rangée</u>. (tr. <u>Memoirs of a Dutiful Daughter</u>,
     Cleveland, World Publishing Co.) <u>Une Mort très douce</u>. (tr. <u>A Very
     Easy Death</u>, Warner PB)
Colette. <u>La Vagabonde</u>. <u>Sido</u>.
Duras. <u>Four Novels</u>. (<u>The Square</u>, <u>Moderato Cantabile</u>, <u>Ten-Thirty on a
     Summer Night</u>, <u>The Afternoon of Mr. Andesmas</u>, Evergreen)
     <u>Un Barrage contre le Pacifique</u>. (tr. <u>The Sea Wall</u>)
Gide. <u>La Porte Etroite</u>. (tr. <u>Strait is the Gate</u>, Vintage PB)
Leduc, Violette. <u>La Bâtarde</u>. (Tr. <u>The Bastard</u>, Dell PB)
     <u>Thérèse et Isabelle</u>.
Rochefort, Christiane. <u>Les Petits Enfants du siècle</u>. (tr. <u>Children of
     Heaven</u>) <u>Les Stances à Sophie</u>. (tr. <u>Cats don't Care for Money</u>)
Sand. <u>Indiana</u>.
Sarraute, Nathalie. <u>Tropismes</u>. (tr. <u>Tropisms</u>, Braziller PB)
de Staël. <u>Corinne</u>.
Wittig, Monique. <u>Les Guérillères</u>.

Abensour, Léon. <u>La Femme et le féminisme avant la révolution</u>. Paris:
     E. Leroux, 1923.
_____. <u>Le Féminisme sous le règne de Louis-Philippe et en 1848</u>.
     Paris: Plon, 1913.
_____. <u>Histoire générale du féminisme</u>. Paris: Delagrave, 1921.
Chombart de Lauwe, Marie-José, et al. <u>La Femme dans la société; son image
     dans différents milieux sociaux</u>. Paris: CNRS, 1963.
d'Eaubonne, Françoise. <u>Histoire et actualité du féminisme</u>. Paris:
     A. Moreau, 1973.
Gauthier, Xavière. <u>Surréalisme et sexualité</u>. Paris: Gallimard, 1971.
Nahas, Hélène. <u>La Femme dans la littérature existentielle</u>. Paris:
     PUF, 1957.
Stephens, Winnifred. <u>Women of the French Revolution</u>. London: Chapman
     and Hall, 1922.
Sullerot, Evelyne. <u>Histoire de la presse féminine en France</u>. Paris:
     Colin, 1966.
_____. <u>Women, Society and Change</u>. World University Library. New
     York: McGraw Hill, 1971.
Thibert, Marguerite. <u>Le Féminisme dans le socialisme français de 1830 à
     1850</u>. Paris: M. Giard, 1926.
Thomas, Edith. <u>Pauline Roland, socialisme et féminisme au 19e siècle</u>.
     Paris: M. Rivière, 1956.
_____. <u>Les Femmes en 1848</u>. Paris: PUF, 1948.

_____. Les Pétroleuses. Paris: Gallimard, 1963.

Vigman, Fred K. Beauty's Triumph. Boston: Christopher Publishing House, 1966. (Development of feminist thought in England and France from the Renaissance to modern times).

Mary Ellen Connell   University of Kansas
Department of French and Italian   Lawrence, Kansas
                                                Spring 1974

IMAGES OF WOMEN IN FRENCH LITERATURE (Fr. 400)

The Course: This is not a literature course, nor a feminist course,
                 nor a history course, nor a sociology course, but one
                 which ideally should call upon all these disciplines.
                 During this semester we shall read works by both men and
                 women from several periods of French literature ranging
                 from the Middle Ages to the 1960's. By focusing on the
                 images of women present in these works, we shall attempt
                 to analyse the various roles, myths, and stereotypes of
                 women in French literature and to relate these images to
                 the social and historical setting in which they were cre-
                 ated. What we discover regarding the roles of women may
                 not be accurate in a real or scientific sense but it will
                 be true in a psychological one. Writers, whether male or
                 female, are conditioned in their attitudes toward women
                 by their own society and culture and these cultural values,
                 as well as the writer's subjective perceptions, are bound
                 to be reflected in their depiction of women.

                 Because we are engaging in a new sort of critical analysis,
                 the insights of the students are just as valid, if not
                 more so, than those of the instructor who may well be in-
                 fluenced by years of traditional (male-oriented?) study
                 of these texts. It is therefore imperative that all stud-
                 ents read and reflect upon the assigned text before coming
                 to class so that they may contribute to discussions.
                 Class participation and attendance will count heavily in
                 determining the final grade.

The Syllabus: The course syllabus is far from ideal. Unfortunately the
                 greatest criterion in selecting texts has been simply what
                 is available in translation. Many, many works relevant
                 to this course have never been translated or are out of
                 print. This is particularly true of those by women writ-
                 ers. In order to correct the imbalance imposed by such a
                 syllabus, students will be required to do an individual
                 project. Details may be found following the reading
                 schedule.

Required Texts: Brians, Paul, ed. Bawdy Tales from the Courts of Medi-
                 eval France. New York: Harper Torchbooks, 1973.

                 Bentley, Eric, ed. The Classic Theatre Vol. IV: Six
                 French Plays. Garden City, N. Y.: Anchor Books, 1961.

                 Peyre, Henri, ed. Seven French Short Novel Masterpieces.
                 New York: Popular Library, 1965.

                 de Laclos, Choderlos. Les Liaisons dangereuses. Harmondsworth, Middlesex: Penguin Books Ltd., 1972.

Colette. Earthly Paradise. New York: Farrar, Straus and Giroux, 1966.

Mallet-Joris, Françoise. The Paper House. New York: Curtis, 1972

Duras, Marguerite. Four Novels. New York: Grove Press, 1965.

Sarrazin, Albertine. Astragal. New York: Grove Press, 1968.

Reading Schedule

Mon., Jan. 21: Lecture: Medieval Attitudes Toward Women

Wed., Jan. 23: Troubadour Poetry, "La Châtelaine de Vergi" (hand out)

Mon., Jan. 28: Andreas Capellanus, The Art of Courtly Love: Part I RESERVE and "The Knight of the Sword," Bawdy Tales

Wed., Jan. 30: Capellanus, The Art of Courtly Love: Part II RESERVE and "The Lady Who Was Castrated," "Auberée, the Old Bawd," "Aloul," "The Sacristan Monk," "The Lay of the Lecher," Bawdy Tales.

Mon., Feb. 4: Molière, "The School for Wives," Tartuffe and Other Plays, (ed. Frame) RESERVE and de la Rochefoucauld, Maxims (hand out)

Wed., Feb. 6: Quiz

Mon., Feb. 11: Lecture: Women and the Aristocratic Ideal

Wed., Feb. 13: Corneille, "The Cid," Classic Theatre

Mon., Feb. 18: de La Fayette, "The Princess of Clèves," Seven French Short Novels

Wed., Feb. 20: Racine, "Phaedra," Classic Theatre

Mon., Feb. 25: Lecture: Mme. de Maintenon and the Education of Women Assignment: xeroxed article "Female Education" from Lewis, Splendid Century RESERVE

Wed., Feb. 27: Lesage, "Turcaret," Classic Theatre

Mon., Mar. 4: Laclos, Les Liaisons dangereuses

Wed., Mar. 6: Laclos, Les Liaisons dangereuses

Mon., Mar. 18: Quiz

Wed., Mar. 20: Lecture: 19th-Century Male Writers Discover a New Subject: Women. Assignment: Balzac, "The Girl with the Golden Eyes," Seven French Short Novels

Mon., Mar. 25: Guest Lecture by Dr. Fernande De George on Baudelaire Assignment to be announced

Wed., Mar. 27: Flaubert, "A Simple Heart," Seven French Short Novels and Maupassant, "Rosalie Prudent," "The Chair Mender," "Saved," The Portable Maupassant (ed. Galantière) RESERVE

Mon., Apr. 1: Maupassant, "Yvette," Seven French Short Novels and Becque, "La Parisienne," From the Modern Repertoire (ed. Bentley) RESERVE

Wed., Apr. 3: Guest Lecture by Beth Lindquist on the Feminist Movement in 19th-Century France

Mon., Apr. 8: Colette, Earthly Paradise, Part I, Childhood

Wed., Apr. 10: Colette, Earthly Paradise, Part II, Marriage and Literary Apprenticeship

Mon., Apr. 15: Easter Vacation

Wed., Apr. 17: Colette, Earthly Paradise, Part V, The Pure and the Impure

Mon., Apr. 22: Lecture: Women and Society in Contemporary France
Assignment: Mallet-Joris, The Paper House

Wed., Apr. 24: Mallet-Joris, The Paper House

Mon., Apr. 29: Duras, Four Novels   Assignment: Selected readings to be announced.

Wed., May 1: Sarrazin, Astragal

Mon., May 6: Discussion

A third quiz approximately 1 1/2 hours in length will be given during the regularly scheduled final examination period.

Individual Project: Students will be required to do an individual project during the course of the semester which will count for one quarter of the final grade. The topic of the project should be decided in consultation with me by February 11. Projects are due May 1. The project may take several forms; following is a list of some possibilities.

A translation of a hitherto untranslated work or works accompanied by a short critical analysis.

A study of the images of women in selected works by a single male writer or group of writers (ex. Molière, Jean-Jacques Rousseau, the Romantic poets, Jean-Paul Sartre) or by a female writer (alas, no group of women writers springs to mind).

A study of the images of women in a particular genre (ex. the fabliaux, Surrealist poetry, Theatre of the Absurd).

A study of a female archetype in one or several periods of French literature (ex. the young girl, the unmarried woman, the castrating female, etc.).

A study of a woman's life in relation to literature.

There exists a category of women whose writing is, to a greater or lesser degree, secondary in importance to their lives; women who have, in effect, lived their art (ex. Ninon de Lenclos, Mme. de Staël, George Sand, Simone de Beauvoir).

Janice S. Green
Department of Romance Languages

Tufts University
Medford, Massachusetts
Fall 1973

THE FEMININE IMAGE IN FRENCH LITERATURE (French 191B)

Book list

Simone de Beauvoir.   The Second Sex   (Bantam)
J. Bédier. Tristan and Iseult   (Vintage)
Molière. The School for Wives Trans. Wilbur   (Harcourt, Brace)
Flaubert. Madame Bovary   Trans. Steegmuller   (Mod. Lib.)
Balzac. Cousin Bette   (Penguin)
F. Mauriac. Thérèse   (Farrar, Straus)
Marguerite Duras. Four Novels   (Grove)

Substitute list (If you have already studied one of the above, please
substitute from the following list.)

Chrétien de Troyes. Cliges or Lancelot, Knight of the Cart
Molière. Précieuses ridicules
Madame de La Fayette. The Princess of Clèves
Emile Zola. L'Assommoir
Balzac. Père Goriot
Simone de Beauvoir. The Mandarins, or Memoirs of a Dutiful Daughter

Supplementary reading

Students will be expected to read at least one novel, etc., in addition to those appearing on the book list.

Syllabus (subject to revision)

Two meetings per week:

Week I.   1)   Mythology of feminine image, Courtly love

              2)   Tristan and Iseult

Week II.   1)   "   "   "

              2)   Feminine image of the Renaissance (Montaigne,
                         Louise Labbé)

Week III.   1)   School for Wives

              2)   "   "   "

Week IV.   1)   Feminine image of the 18th century (Rousseau,
                         Mme. Roland)

Week V.   1)   Madame Bovary

              2)   "   "

Week VI.   1)   "   "

              2)   "   "

Week VII.	1)	Pot-pourri
	2)	Cousin Bette
Week VIII.	1)	" "
	2)	" "
Week IX.	1)	" "
	2)	" "
Week X.	1)	Duras. The Square
	2)	Duras. Moderato cantabile
Week XI.	1)	" "
	2)	Second Sex
Week XII.	1)	" "
	2)	" "
Last class		A day to draw conclusions

The course is conducted in a lecture/discussion format and student responsibility includes a journal, a term paper, and a final exam of sorts. The journal must be kept throughout the semester and represents the student's reactions (objective, subjective, critical, analytical, creative, etc.) to the readings and class discussions.

Dr. Green has offered versions of this course as a Winter Study Project (WS 101) in 1972 and as a course in French, Spring 1974 (192D). The description of the Winter Study Course reads:

> Consideration of a number of works will reveal that women have traditionally been depicted by French writers from the Middle Ages to the present in the extremist terms of either idealization or misogyny, or more plainly, as either ange or bête. The resultant protest of women writers from Louise Labbé to Simone de Beauvoir leaves no doubt as to the unjustness and unacceptability of these two attitudes. Readings in French or in English, discussions (in English), paper or oral presentation.

She reports that response has been enthusiastic and that the course will again be offered in English, Fall 1974, with the book list somewhat altered as follows:

Tristan and Iseult.
Mme. de La Fayette. The Princess of Clèves.
Flaubert. Madame Bovary.
Zola. L'Assommoir.
Colette. Chéri.
Mauriac. Knot of Vipers.
Duras. Moderato Cantabile and The Square
de Beauvoir. The Second Sex.

We are including some materials used in the course, all translated by
Dr. Green.

To Those who say that it is not good for women to be educated

I marvel at the thinking of those men who do not permit their
daughters, wives, or female relatives to acquire knowledge lest their
morals be corrupted. From this you can plainly see that all judgments
made by men are not founded on reason, and that these men are wrong, for
one cannot assume that knowledge of the moral sciences (ethics, history,
philosophy) which teach the virtues, can corrupt morals. On the contrary,
there is no doubt that they are improved and uplifted. How then can one
believe that the person who studies good lessons and doctrines will be
corrupted? Such a thing can neither be said nor defended.

I do not say that it is good for women to study the sciences of
magic or other forbidden areas, for it is not for nothing that the holy
Church has removed them from common usage, but that women are corrupted
from attaining knowledge of the good is unbelievable. . . .

Le Livre de la Cité des Dames
Christine de Pisan, 1405

Excerpts from the Memoirs and Letters of Madame Roland

Letter to a friend announcing her impending marriage

I see a new horizon, happiness is smiling upon me, and my position
is changing. Deeply moved, but without being intoxicated, I contemplate
my destiny with eyes at once peaceful and brimming with tears. Touching
and multiple duties are going to fill my heart and my every instant. I am
no longer this isolated being deploring her uselessness. Austere resignation, proud courage, which sustain strong souls through misfortune, will
be replaced by the pure and modest enjoyments of the heart. As the cherished wife of a man I respect and love, I shall find my felicity in the
inexpressible charm of contributing to his happiness. In short, I am marrying M. Roland. The contract is signed, the announcements will be made
Sunday, and before Lent I am his.

Thoughts of a young girl on the destiny of woman (Memoirs)

I felt, after those excursions (Sunday outings and social functions)
an unbearable emptiness, an uneasiness, and a disgust which made me pay
dearly for the pleasures of my vanity. Accustomed to reflecting, to analyzing my sensations, I painfully searched for the causes of these unpleas-
ant feelings and my philosophy was fully exercised.

Is it truly in order to shine in public, like flowers in a garden,
to receive useless praise, that people of my sex are trained in virtue,
that they acquire talents? What signifies this extreme desire for pleasure
which devours me, and which does not give me happiness even while it would
seem to be sufficient. What matter the curious glances, the compliments
softly murmured, from people I don't even know, people whom I would perhaps scarcely esteem if I knew them. Do I exist then to spend my existence in frivolous matters, in tumultuous feelings? Ah! Without doubt I

have a better destiny; this admiration which inflames me for all that is beautiful, wise, great and generous, teaches me that I am called to practice it. The sublime and pleasurable duties of wife and mother will one day be mine; it is to render me capable of fulfilling them that my young years must be employed. I must study their importance, I must learn, through ruling my own inclinations, how one day to direct those of my children.

Letter to a male friend, the biologist, who claimed the biological superiority of the male

You were not mistaken about the claims of your sex. . . . But even then you have not endangered your position, for I do not intend to challenge it. . . . For what are the deference and consideration your sex shows toward mine if not the regard the powerful have for the weak, which they honor and protect at the same time? When you speak like masters, you immediately make one think that you can be resisted, and go even further than that, your strength not withstanding. Do you pay us homage? It is like Alexander treating his female prisoners as though they were queens, even though they remain aware of their dependence. Perhaps only in this respect does our civilization follow nature; the law keeps us constantly under your thumb, and usage grants us in society all the small honors. In action we count for naught; in appearance we are everything.

Do not imagine, therefore, that I delude myself about what we can demand or expect. I believe, I would not say more than any woman, but as much as many, in the superiority of your sex in every respect. In the first place, you have strength, and everything that goes with it results from it: courage, perseverance, wide horizons and great talents. It is up to you to make the laws in politics as it is to make the discoveries in science. Govern the world, change the surface of the globe, be proud, terrible, clever, and learned. You are all that without our help, and through all that you are bound to be our masters. But without us you would not be virtuous, loving, loved, or happy. Keep therefore all your glory and authority. As for us, we have and wish no other supremacy than that over your morals, no other rule than that over your hearts. I shall claim nothing beyond that. It often angers me to see women disputing privileges which illbefit them. And even the name of author, whatever the circumstances may be, strikes me as ridiculous when applied to them. No matter what their facility may be in some respects, they should never show their learning or talents in public.

Mme. Roland speaks of her marriage in retrospect, after thirteen years
(Memoirs)

. . . If marriage was, as I thought, a strict bondate, a partnership in which the woman took upon herself the responsibility of two people's happiness, was it not better that I put my talents and my courage to this honorable task rather than continue in the isolation in which I lived? I must here dilate upon the very sensible reasons which, I believe, decided me; I was not, moreover, moved by the train of thought which was the fruit of meditation, but only by what experience had permitted me to observe. I became the wife of an honest man whose love for me increased the more he knew me. My marriage was a rational one and there was nothing that tempted me away from it. In the devotion I gave to it, there was more spontaneity than calculation. By force of considering nothing but my partner's happiness, I soon perceived that there was something lacking in mine. I never for one instant ceased to think my husband one of the most estimable men alive, and one to whom I would always be proud to belong; but I often observed the lack of gaiety, and felt that a dominating character, added to the fact that he was twenty years my senior, made too great a disparity between us. When we lived in retirement, the hours were sometimes difficult to endure; were we in company, I found myself well liked by other people, some of whom might have come to mean too much to me. I submerged myself in work with my husband, another extreme measure which had its drawbacks. I accustomed him never to doing without me for anything in the world, or for one instant, and I wore myself out.

He made me his copyist and his proofreader. I performed this task with a humility at which I cannot help smiling . . . but it came from the heart. I so frankly respected my husband that I readily believed he knew better than I, and I was so afraid that a shadow might darken his countenance, so strongly did he hold to his opinions, that it was only after quite a time that I gained sufficient confidence to contradict him.

Excerpts from La Nouvelle Héloïse

Julie's marriage

[Julie's father speaks] I know the fantasy, unworthy of a well-born girl, which you nourish in your heart: it is time to sacrifice to duty and integrity a shameful passion which dishonors you and that you will satisfy only at the cost of my life. Listen once and for all to what a father's honor [he has promised her in marriage to a man she doesn't love] and your own demand of you and judge for yourself. . . . You see how much all you might tell me is now irrelevant: see if your preferences, which a sense of decency denies, or some fleeting passion of youth can ever be weighed against a daughter's duty and the compromised honor of a father. . . .

Julie's description of her wedding

. . . I was led to the church like an impure victim who defiles the sacrificial rites.

Arrived at the church, I felt, upon entering, a kind of emotion I had never experienced. I don't know what terror seized my soul in this simple and august place, filled with God's majesty. A sudden fright made me shiver; trembling and ready to faint, I could scarcely drag myself to the foot of the altar. Far from recovering, I felt my anxiety increase during the ceremony . . . I imagined that I saw the instrument of Providence and that I heard the voice of God in the minister gravely pronouncing the holy liturgy. The purity, the dignity, the sanctity of marriage, so clearly set forth in the words of the Bible, its chaste and sublime duties, so important to the happiness, order, peace, and perpetuation of humanity, so agreeable to fulfill; all this made such an impression on me that I seemed to experience an unexpected inner revolution. An unfamiliar power seemed suddenly to correct the disorder of my feelings and to re-establish them according to the law of duty and of nature. . . .

I envisaged the sacred bond that I was going to form as a new state which would purify my soul and return it to its duties.

After the ceremony

I saw that, to think of you [her lover, Saint-Preux], I had no need to forget I was the wife of another. In telling myself how dear you were to me my heart was moved, but my conscience and my senses were tranquil and I knew that from that moment I was truly changed. What a torrent of pure joy inundated my soul! What a feeling of peace, lost for so long, re-vived this heart blighted by ignominy, and spread throughout my being a new serenity. I felt myself reborn; I was beginning a new life.

On marriage [Julie's words]

One does not marry to think solely of one another, but to fulfill jointly the duties of society, prudently to govern the household, to raise the children wisely. Lovers see only each other, think incessantly of each other, and all they can do is love each other. For the married couple with so many obligations, this is not enough.

The harvesting of the grapes at the estate of Julie and her husband [described by Saint-Preux]

. . . It [agriculture] is the first vocation of man; it recalls to the mind pleasant ideas and to the heart all the charms of the golden age. The imagination does not remain sterile at the sight of the plowing and the harvests. The simplicity of the pastoral farm life is always moving . . . how charming to see the good and wise managers [Julie and her husband] make of the cultivation of their lands the instrument of their good deeds, amusements, pleasures; pouring with full hands the gifts of Providence; nourishing all that surrounds them, man and beast, with the good which fill their barns, their cellars, their lofts; gathering abundance and joy about them, making of the work which enriches them a continuous celebra-tion! One forgets his century and his contemporaries and is transported to the age of the patriarchs. One desires to put his hands to work, to share in the rustic labors and happiness. Oh time of love and innocence, when women were tender and modest, when men were simple and lived happily. Oh Rachel, charming girl so steadfastly loved, happy was he who to obtain you never regretted his fourteen years of bondage. Oh sweet pupil of Naomi! No, never did beauty reign more absolutely than in the midst of country toil. It is there that the graces are enthroned, adorned by sim-plicity, animated by gaity, and adored by all.

Invocation to women [by Saint-Preux]

Women! Women! Precious and fatal objects adorned by nature for our torture, who punish when confronted, pursue when feared, whose hate and love are equally harmful and who can neither be sought nor avoided with impunity. . . . Beauty, charm, attraction, inconceivable being or dream, abyss of pain and pleasure! Beauty, more terrible to mortals than the element in which you were born, unhappy he who surrenders to your deceptive calm! It is you who produce the tempests which torment the human species. Oh Julie! Oh Claire! How dearly you sell me that cruel friendship which you dare to boast of! I have lived in the storm, and it is always you who roused it. But what diverse agitations you have made my heart feel! Those of Lake Geneva are unlike those of the waters of the vast ocean. The first has only sudden, brief waves, never forming a long pattern. But on the sea, tranquil in appearance, one feels oneself lifted, carried softly and far by the slow waters; one feels motionless and yet arrives at the ends of the earth.

Jean-Jacques Rousseau, 1761

Excerpt from La Prudence de la chair

Since the time that women have claimed to be equal to men, men declare that there are no longer any women. In any case, no more real women.

But, in fact, what is a real woman?

It is enough to listen to men talking among themselves to know that young girls are not yet women, that mothers are no longer women, and on the other hand, that single women, free women, women who work, resourceful women, business women, right-thinking women, none of these are real women. Without counting those exquisite creatures whom nature has ill-endowed and whom we call saints.

One is obliged to admit that when men evoke the idea of a real woman, they are thinking, consciously or not, of that charming and cursed type called by Molière "mon petit museau" [my little face, slang], in other words the liars, the false, the betrayers, the cruel ones, in brief the poisoners and the dishonorable.

Now, one of the sociological phenomena of the twentieth century is precisely the disappearance of this sort of woman, and the men who have spent centuries complaining about "those beautiful masks" are going to have, God willing, centuries to regret their loss.

Never daring to admit that their instincts are less noble than their ideas, men often proclaim desires not in accord with their profound tastes. As a result of repeating to women that it was too bad that they were foolish, frivolous, inconsequential, futile, illogical and untruthful, they ended up by persuading themselves that they detested in their female companions exactly those faults which, in the course of the millennia, had given them most happiness.

But happiness, like good health, is a possession discovered only when lost.

Actually, one of the dramas of the modern couple, and not the least one, is that women, while changing their life, are in the process of changing their soul and of becoming honest. One would imagine that men would be the beneficiaries of such a marvelous transformation. . . . In reality, they are the victims.

Freed of the thousand feminine faults which obscured their minds, women finally see the world as it is, beginning with their lord and master

and having become honest, they no longer want or need to lie, many men
are discovering with consternation that they are not the witty, noble and
generous beings they imagined themselves. Thanks to the new frankness of
their women, they are learning little by little that they are often boring,
monotonous, petty, and idiotic, almost always pompous and repetitive, giving interminable lectures on no matter what subject, believing they know
everything better and never tolerating contradiction, in short, learning
that their pretensions in all matters far exceed their abilities.

Nevertheless, today as always women ask only to admire their men,
but on condition that they are admirable, just as they ask only to love
them on condition that they are lovable. . . . Why would an honest and im-
partial woman say to a mediocre man that he is a genius or to a cad that
he is charming?

How would men, readily tender and sensitive, not regret the blessed
era when, to better deceive them, their adored mistresses repeated all day
long that they were of all men the handsomest, the most intelligent, the
strongest, and the most loved? How can one hold it against them when they
search desperately about them for one of the last little deceivers who
will help them to preserve the flattering image they have forged of themselves since childhood, and if they declare in a fit of temper that other
women are not real women. . . .

In reality, the more truthful women become, the less real they are
in the eyes of men!

Françoise Parturier, 1963

Excerpts from Les Jeunes Filles

On Happiness

Happiness for a man is the satisfaction of vanity. . . . Vanity is
the man's dominating passion. Almost all men would voluntarily go without
eating and drinking for an entire day if, by so doing, he could in the
course of that day succeed in achieving some satisfaction of his vanity.
. . . For the man it is less a question of being happy than of making people think he is. A young doctor from an isolated country region, recently
married, said cleverly: "I am extremely happy. But one must have someone
to tell it to." Most men would like nothing better than to have the happiness of the sage. Basically this is what they want, just as they all
look forward to retirement. But no one would believe they were happy;
people would think they had given up or were incapable, and thus they set
out on a different track, make themselves seem important, busy themselves
in ridiculous and visible activity, make many phone calls, and soon a day
of happiness becomes for them a day wherein they have made many phone calls,
that is, a day in which they have been very important. . . .

The woman, on the other hand, develops a positive concept of happiness. While the man is more active, the woman is more alive. She will
not ask, as would the young man, "What do you mean by living?" She has no
need of explanations. Living, for her, is feeling. Women would rather be
consumed in flames than be extinguished, be devoured rather than dis-
dained. . . .

Happiness for a woman is a clearly defined state of being, endowed with a personality and a particularity, a substantial and living reality, powerful, sensitive. A woman will tell you that she's happy as she'll tell you that she's warm or cold . . . she will prefer even a happiness which she knows to be shortlived to none at all.

The one acceptable destiny for a woman is a happy marriage. Thus she depends on the man, and knows this from her earliest years. . . . The young boy knows that his future will be what he wants it to be; the young girl knows that her future will be what a man wants it to be . . . while the woman creates her happiness from the happiness of her husband, men are scarcely concerned with making their wives happy. A public figure who risks sacrificing his career, an industrialist who risks sacrificing a part of his capacity for work in order to make a woman happy (for example, by marrying her), this is rare.

A woman who is happy, who loves and is loved, asks nothing more. A man who loves and is loved needs something more . . . marriage is a gift from the man to the woman, since she has a basic need for marriage and he does not.

The woman is made for one man, man is made for life and for all women.

Montherlant

Marguerite Duras talks about The Square (excerpt from an interview)

In my opinion The Square is a political conversation. I don't know how you see it. It's the story of a human being (a maid) situated on the lowest rung of the social ladder, corresponding politically speaking to the "lumpen proletariat." Because of her condition or her situation, she is the living example of what Marx meant when he outlined his theory of need. This girl has, in reality, created her own revolution, and at the same time, become in a way a revolutionary doctrinaire. But in an empirical sense. The dialogue which creates The Square is consequently very special, an extra-ceremonious dialogue, absolutely anti-realistic. And this is why I have been criticized--stupidly in any case. I say stupidly because I wrote the dialogue that way intentionally. For the two characters in The Square (the traveling salesman and the maid), who are part of the lowest echelon of society, have never had the possibility of expressing their thoughts, even in generalities. I have created a very special language for them, concise, almost theatrical, with a moderation appropriate to the circumstances.

Angela M. Jeannet
Department of French and Italian

Franklin and Marshall College
Lancaster, Pennsylvania
Fall 1972, Fall 1973

FROM COURTLY LOVE TO THE SECOND SEX:
WOMEN IN FRENCH LITERATURE (Fr. 7)

The aim of the course is to help participants understand how French writers have constructed the female image from the XIIth century to the XXth, under the stimulus of changing cultural patterns. A critical reading of well-known texts will add new dimensions to the readers' self-awareness and to their sensitivity to the essential problems of Western civilization. It will also increase their appreciation of literature, viewed as living expression of human experience.

Lectures and discussion are in English. Texts are read in translation. Evaluation is based on two brief take-home exams (25% of the grade each) and on one term paper (50%).

French 7 satisfies the Humanities requirement. If taken, by pre-arrangement, as French 43, it may be included in the requirements of a French major.

Syllabus :

Texts marked (PUR) are to be purchased.

I week	Introduction to the course: Literature and the image of woman
	Lecture: A new mythology for the Western world
	Readings: S. de Beauvoir--The Second Sex (PUR)
	(Introduction, Chapters IX and XI)
	Bédier--Romance of Tristan and Isolde (PUR)
	Chrétien de Troyes--Yvain
II week	Lecture: The respectability of misogyny
	Readings: Molière--The School for Wives (PUR)
	The Learned Ladies (PUR)
III and IV weeks	Lecture: Passion and the female hero
	Readings: Racine--Andromache (PUR)
	Phèdre (PUR)
	de La Fayette--The Princess of Clèves (PUR)
	Stendhal--The Red and the Black (PUR)
V week	Lecture: Princess and fairy godmother
	Readings: Perrault--Fairy Tales (PUR)
VI week	Lecture: Woman as the ultimate object
	Readings: Rousseau--Emile (Book V)
VII week	Discussion session
	Readings: Laclos--Dangerous Liaisons (PUR)
	de Sade--Justine (PUR)
VIII and IX weeks	Lecture: The prisoner
	Discussion of term paper topics
	Readings: Balzac--Eugénie Grandet (PUR)

97

Flaubert--Madame Bovary (PUR)

X and XI weeks	Lecture: Readings:	Woman looks at herself de Sévigné--Selections Sand--Selections Colette--Earthly Paradise: Sido, Wedding Day, Monsieur Willy, Motherhood: "I was forty . . .", Under the Blue Lantern: "It has taken me a great deal of time . . ." Colette--Short Novels: Chéri Duras--Four Novels: Moderato Cantabile (PUR)
XII week	Lecture: Readings:	The female condition and its mirrors Zola--Selections Genet--Selections The Balcony (PUR)
XIII week		Term papers to be handed in. Students must make copies of an extract to be distributed to the whole class. Discussion: Woman in contemporary French culture
XIV week		Discussion of term papers and evaluation of the course

Readings required of the French 43 students (in addition to the ones on
the French 7 list which may or may not be read in translation):

    Racine--Phèdre (PUR)
            Andromaque (PUR)
    de la Fayette--La Princesse de Clèves (PUR)
    one work by Colette
    one work by Simone de Beauvoir (or part of one work)
    one work by Mallet-Joris

Jeffry Larson   University of Wisconsin-Milwaukee
Department of French and Italian   Spring 1973

IMAGES OF WOMEN IN FRENCH FICTION
(Honors Seminar 400-383)

After reading and discussing Simone de Beauvoir's The Second Sex to provide a conceptual framework, we will study portrayals of women and their situations in outstanding works of French fiction, from Guinevere in the courtly romances of the Middle Ages to François Mauriac's Thérèse Desqueyroux. Most of the works are by men and deal with love, marriage, and adultery; some are anti-feminist.

Discussion will not be limited to the common thematic material, but will involve the evolution of narrative form. No particular literary or historical background is required; opportunity will be provided for students to learn more about French literary history, but this will not be one of the main emphases of the course.

Students will be asked to make at least one oral and one written presentation about selected aspects of the works under study, in addition to a final exam.

Reading list:

S. de Beauvoir. The Second Sex
  Chrétien de Troyes. Arthurian Romances (Erec and Enide and Lancelot)
Anonymous. Fabliaux
Mme. de La Fayette. The Princess of Clèves
Diderot. The Nun
C. de Laclos. Les Liaisons dangereuses
H. de Balzac. Eugénie Grandet
Stendhal. The Red and the Black
Flaubert. Madame Bovary
F. Mauriac. Thérèse

Syllabus:

	Tuesday	Thursday
1/16, 18	Introduction	S. de Beauvoir, The Second Sex Parts I-III (extr.)
1/23, 25	The Second Sex, Pt. IV	The Second Sex, Pt. V
1/30, 2/1	The Second Sex, Pts. VI, VII, and interview (7)*	Chrétien de Troyes, Erec and Enide
2/6, 8	Chrétien de Troyes, Lancelot or the Knight of the Cart	Chrétien de Troyes (and courtly love?): cf. E. Auerbach, Mimesis, Ch. 6, esp. pp. 140-42
2/13, 15	Fabliaux (selections)	Fabliaux (selections); cf; E. Auerbach, Mimesis, Ch. 10, esp. pp. 250-61
2/20, 22	Mme. de La Fayette, The Princess of Clèves	
2/27, 3/1	Diderot, The Nun	Diderot, "On Women" (15)*
3/6, 8	Laclos, Les Liaisons dangereuses	

3/13, 15 Les Liaisons dangereuses
3/20, 22 Balzac, Eugénie Grandet
3/27, 29 Stendhal, The Red and The Black
4/3, 5   The Red and The Black
4/10, 12 Flaubert, Madame Bovary
4/17, 19 Madame Bovary
5/1, 3   F. Mauriac, Thérèse
5/8, 10   Thérèse, and J.-P. Sartre,   Conclusion
          "François Mauriac and
          Freedom" (32)*
5/16, Wednesday, 3:00 p.m.   Final exam

*numbers refer to reserve list bibliography

Reserve list:

A. General Literary History
   1. E. Auerbach. Mimesis*
   2. G. Brereton. A Short History of French Literature.**
   3. L. Cazamian. A History of French Literature.
   4. M. Turnell. The Art of French Fiction.
   5. _____. The Novel in France.
B. Women and Love
   6. D. de Rougemont. Love in the Western World.
   7. A. Schwartzer. "The Radicalization of Simone de Beauvoir." (in-
      terview) Ms, I, no. 1 (July 1972), pp. 60-63, 134.
   8. K. Thomas. "The Double Standard," The Journal of the History of
      Ideas, 20 (1959), pp. 195-216.
C. Medieval
   9. Andreas Capellanus. The Art of Courtly Love.*
  10. J. Frappier. "Chrétien de Troyes," Ch. 15 in Arthurian Litera-
      ture in the Middle Ages. Ed. R. S. Loomis, pp. 157-191.**
  11. R. S. Loomis. The Development of Arthurian Romance, Ch. 4.**
  12. J. C. Moore. Love in Twelfth-Century France.**
  13. P. Noble, "The Character of Guinevere in the Arthurian Romances
      of Chrétien de Troyes," Modern Language Review, 67 (1972),
      524-535.
D. Seventeenth and Eighteenth Centuries
  14. Mme. de La Fayette. La Princesse de Clèves. Ed. K. B. Kettle.**
  15. D. Diderot. "On Women," in Dialogues, Tr. F. Birrell, pp. 185-196.
  16. P. Brooks. The Novel of Worldliness (from Mme. de La Fayette to
      Stendhal; consult index).
  17. French Literature and Its Background. Ed. J. Cruickshank. Vol.
      3, The Eighteenth Century.**
  18. P. Gay. "Three Stages on Love's Way: Rousseau, Laclos, Diderot,"
      Ch. 5 in The Party of Humanity.
  19. V. Minogue. "'Les Liaisons dangereuses': A Practical Lesson in
      the Art of Seduction," Modern Language Review, 67 (1972),
      775-786.
  20. J. S. Munro. "Studies in Sub-Conscious Motivation in Laclos and
      Marivaux," Studies on Voltaire and the 18th Century, 89 (1972),
      1153-1168.
  21. V. Mylne. The Eighteenth-Century French Novel.**

22. R. Niklaus. A Literary History of France. Vol. 3: The Eight-
    eenth Century.**
23. J. W. Scott. "The 'Digressions' of the 'Princesse de Clèves,'"
    French Studies, 11 (1957), 315-322.

E. Nineteenth and Twentieth Centuries
24. G. Flaubert. Madame Bovary
25. Stendhal. On Love.*
26. Stendhal. Ed. V. Brombert.**
27. A. Fairlie. Flaubert: Madame Bovary.**
28. R. Girard. Deceit, Desire, and the Novel (on Stendhal, Flaubert,
    et al.; consult index).
29. Flaubert: A Collection of Critical Essays. Ed. R. D. Giraud.**
30. F. W. J. Hemmings. Balzac: An Interpretation of "La Comédie
    Humaine."**
31. H. Levin. The Gates of Horn (from Balzac to Proust).
32. J.-P. Sartre. "François Mauriac and Freedom," in Literary
    and Philosophical Essays.

* In the bookstore
** Has bibliography

Mary Lou Lovette
Foreign Language Department

Wilkes College
Wilkes-Barre, Pennsylvania
Fall 1972, Fall 1973

FEMININE PERSPECTIVES IN FRENCH LITERATURE (French 261 and 397)

It is the aim of this course to inquire into the attitudes toward women expressed by men and women of French letters from the Middle Ages to the present day. Readings are selected which shed light on such questions as: the woman as an instrument of man's salvation, the education of women, the woman as artist, power and dominance in the social relationship between the sexes, convent life, dowry, marriage, women as business and political pawns, and the political implications in a patriarchal society of woman as the inferior or second sex. This implies an inquiry into the various feminist initiatives resulting either from a different moral and cultural value system (such as that resulting in the movement of the "Précieuses") or from misogynic attacks such as that which set off the century-long "Querelle des Femmes." Perspectives on these and other related questions will be studied in works by Jean de Meung, Christine de Pisan, Rabelais, Montaigne, Molière, Diderot, Rousseau, Mme. de Staël, Stendhal, Flaubert, Baudelaire, Gide, Colette, Mauriac, Simone de Beauvoir, Marguerite Duras, Albertine Sarrazin, Monique Wittig, and others. The readings can vary appreciably each time the course is offered due to the abundance of pertinent material available. In addition to an analysis of the prevailing attitudes toward women as apprehended in the literature of France, equal emphasis is given to the study of the female and problems peculiar to her sex, using Simone de Beauvoir's The Second Sex as point of departure.

Evaluation consists of a mid-term, a final exam, and a project. In keeping with the principle that learning should not be separated from action, much flexibility is permitted regarding the project; it need not be a paper and it can be a combined endeavor of two or more students.

The course is to be taught in English in order to give all interested students an opportunity to enroll. Readings will be in translation unless the student is capable of and prefers reading the originals. French is not a prerequisite.

Justification for approval of this course: since there is no other Female Studies course offered at Wilkes, since studies of this nature have assumed considerable importance and prestige throughout the country since 1970, and in view of the fact that the request for this type of course has come about from student demand, it is urged that French 261 be approved. Our appeal is also based on the principle of academic freedom (academic freedom in this case implying an available forum) and the concept of a liberal arts education. We submit that no education is truly liberal that excludes the contributions of women. Most of our students, after four years of study, will earn a diploma never having read, in course-related assignments, a work written by a woman (a survey probing the question might prove interesting).

Syllabus and texts:

Basic text: The Second Sex, Simone de Beauvoir, Translated by H. M.
               Parshley. New York, Bantam Press, 1970.

Readings: François Mauriac. _Thérèse_
                Albertine Sarrazin. _Astragal_
                Racine. _Andromache_
                Lorris and Meung. _Romance of the Rose_
                Abbé Prévost. _Manon Lescaut_
                Monique Wittig. _Les Guérillères_
                Molière. _School for Wives_
                Denis Diderot. _The Nun_

Part A - Based on _The Second Sex_.   Part B - Based on readings.

A.   I.   Facts and Myths vis à vis the Female

               Biology
               The Psychoanalytic Point of View
               History
               Dreams, Fears, Idols

      II. Woman's Life Today

               Childhood
               Sexual Initiation
               The Lesbian
               The Married Woman
               The Mother
               Social Life
               Prostitutes and Hetaerae
               The Woman in Love
               The Mystic

     III. Toward Liberation

               The Independent Woman

B.   Feminine Perspectives in Literature.

Suzanne Relyea   The University of Massachusetts, Boston
Department of French--College I   Fall 1973

THE FEMININE PRESENCE IN FRENCH LITERATURE (Fr. 271)

Everyone should attend one:

(a) lecture (obligatory for everyone): Tuesday, 3:30-4:45

(b) discussions (chose one): Wednesday, 10:40-11:30
                              Thursday,   9:30-10:45
                              Thursday,   3:30-4:45
                              Friday,   9:30-10:25

We will be reading selected literary texts from the Middle Ages to the 20th century by men and women writers whose work shows significant consciousness of the formalization of gender roles in art and society. There will be specific emphasis on the evolution of various "feminine" roles as they relate to the social and literary contexts we examine. Each student is responsible for:

(1) a 1000-word paper (5 typed pages) on a subject of his/her choice--to be discussed with the teacher beforehand and due Wednesday, November 21, at the latest.

(2) a 10-minute oral exposé (in discussion section) related to current course reading.

(3) a final exam on the reading and the ideas touched on in the course.

Readings:

Tristan et Iseut (Modern French), ed. Donald Stone, Prentice Hall, 1966.

Denis de Rougemont. Love in the Western World

Chrétien de Troyes. Erec
                     Yvain   in Arthurian Romances

Mme. de La Fayette. The Princess of Clèves (in Seven French Short Novel
                                            Masterpieces)

J.-J. Rousseau. Emile or Education

Stendhal. The Red and the Black

Flaubert. Madame Bovary

Simone de Beauvoir. The Second Sex

Janet Aldis. Mme. Geoffrin, Her Salon and Her Times.

Nancy Mitford. Mme. de Pompadour

Recommended (highly, and available in the bookstore):

Dan Wakefield. Going All the Way

104

Nancy Reeves. <u>Womankind: Beyond the Stereotypes</u>

Elaine Showalter, ed. <u>Women's Liberation and Literature</u>

Susan Koppelman Cornillon, ed. <u>Images of Women in Literature</u>

Topical Outline:

Introduction: The notion of stereotype and stereotypical thinking.
  Dan Wakefield. <u>Going All the Way</u> (not required)
  Denis de Rougement. <u>Love in the Western World</u>
  Nancy Reeves. <u>Womankind: Beyond the Stereotypes</u> (not required)

1. Courtly love: the stylization of sexual roles.
  - Tristan et Iseut: "role contracts."
  - Chrétien de Troyes. <u>Erec</u>, <u>Yvain</u>
  - Madame de La Fayette. <u>The Princess of Clèves</u>

2. Women born of men.
  Stendhal. <u>The Red and the Black</u>
  Flaubert. <u>Madame Bovary</u>

3. Education by role.
  a. The female mentor
    Mme. de Sévigné. <u>Letters</u>
   The male mentor
    J.-J. Rousseau. the <u>Emile</u>
  b. The woman intellectual
    Janet Aldis. <u>Mme. Geoffrin</u>
    Nancy Mitford. <u>Mme. de Pompadour</u>
    Simone de Beauvoir. <u>The Mandarins</u>

4. The Education of roles: women in the first person.
  a. "We": the subject of couples
    Marguerite de Navarre. <u>The Heptameron</u>
  b. "I": female identity
    Simone de Beauvoir. <u>The Second Sex</u> (I)
  c. "We": female consciousness
    Simone de Beauvoir. <u>The Second Sex</u> (II)

Conclusion: Hypothesis for an on-going literary process:
  Stereotype--Integration--Whole
    Elaine Showalter (ed.). <u>Woman's Liberation and Literature</u>
    (not required)
    Susan Koppelman Cornillon (ed.) <u>Images of Women in Literature</u>
    (not required)

Mara Vamos
Department of Modern Languages
    and Literatures

Fairleigh Dickinson University
Rutherford, New Jersey
Spring 1973, Fall 1973

THE LITERARY TREATMENT OF WOMEN

SYLLABUS

Session and Date	Lecture and Discussion	Assigned Reading	Student Reports
September			
1. Friday 7	Intro: Archetypes and Stereotypes		
2. Tuesday 11	The Love Story: Then and Now	Tristan and Iseult / Romeo and Juliet	
3. Friday 14	Woman as Mystery	Manon Lescaut (excerpts)	
4. Tuesday 18	The Fallen Woman	Camille	
5. Friday 21		Camille	
6. Tuesday 25	The Masochistic Heroine	Portuguese Nun (excerpts)	
7. Friday 28	The Willing Victim	Story of O	de Sade, Justine
October			
8. Tuesday 2		Story of O	
9. Friday 5	Man as the Victim of Love	Carmen	"Women in Art"
10. Tuesday 9		Carmen	
11. Friday 12	Oral reports and discussion		"Women in Adv." Dramatic Presentations "Women in the Theatre"
12. Tuesday 16	MID-TERM EXAM		
13. Friday 19	The Adulteress, French-style	Mme. Bovary	"Women in Music"
14. Tuesday 23		Mme. Bovary	"Biology is not Destiny"
15. Friday 26		Mme. Bovary	
16. Tuesday 30	The Adulteress, Russian-style	Anna Karenina	"The Multiple Roles of Women"

November

17.	Friday 2	The Adulteress, Russian-style	Anna Karenina	
18.	Tuesday 6		Anna Karenina	
19.	Friday 9	Castrating Bitches: Wives and lovers	Hedda Gabler	"Psychology of Women"
20.	Tuesday 13	Castrating Bitches: Mothers and mistresses	Portnoy's Complaint	
21.	Friday 16		Portnoy's Complaint	
22.	Tuesday 20	Brainy Bitches	Molière, Learned Women	"Professional Women"

Thanksgiving recess

23.	Tuesday 27	Oral reports and discussion		
24.	Friday 30	Independent Women	Molière, The Misanthrope	Contemporary works (e.g., Love Story, The Bell Jar, Sheila Levine Is Dead . . .
25.	Tuesday 4	Libertine Women	Les Liaisons dangereuses (excerpts)	
26.	Friday 7	Sympathy--or Tea?	A Doll's House	
27.	Tuesday 11	Bernard Shaw's "New Woman"	Mrs. Warren's Profession	
28.	Friday 14	Open House		
		FINAL EXAMS		

Assigned Reading:

The Romance of Tristan and Iseult. J. Bédier, ed.

Dumas Fils, Alexandre. Camille

Flaubert, Gustave. Madame Bovary

Ibsen, Henrik. A Doll's House
                Hedda Gabler (optional)

Mérimée, Prosper. Carmen
                Colomba (optional)

Molière. The Misanthrope
       The Learned Women

Réage, Pauline. Story of O

Roth, Philip. _Portnoy's Complaint_

Shaw, Bernard. _Mrs. Warren's Profession_

Tolstoy, Leo. _Anna Karenina_

Recommended women writers (for term papers)

Jane Austen	Mme. de La Fayette	Christiane Rochefort
Simone de Beauvoir	Rosamond Lehmann	George Sand
Emily Brontë	Doris Lessing	Alix Kates Shulman
Alba de Céspedes	Katherine Mansfield	Gertrude Stein
Colette	Mary McCarthy	Virginia Woolf
Isak Dinesen	Flannery O'Connor	
George Eliot	Dorothy Parker	

Course requirements:

1. Mid-term exam covering material discussed to date.

2. Final exam covering texts assigned, student reports, and outside reading.

3. ONE PAPER of about TEN pages, to be submitted no later than Tuesday, December 4, on one of the following themes:

   a. Did women writers reflect the male view of women?

   b. Did women writers show woman's experience in a different light than male writers?

   c. Is there a difference between the way women and male writers view the relationship of "love"?

   d. Is the novel by a woman, analyzed in your paper, innovative?

   Please note: A list of "Recommended Women Writers" is attached. You may choose any writer or any work for your paper, provided your paper deals with a woman writer. With my approval, you may discuss a writer other than the ones listed, and/or select a theme other than the ones suggested above.

4. ONE ORAL REPORT thematically relevant to the course. Please choose any field you are interested in--literature, art, sociology, anthropology, psychology, etc.--and submit for my approval the work you wish to present to the class, as well as two/three alternate dates when you prefer to make your presentation. The report should be limited to 15 minutes.

Martha Everett
College Seminar Program

Yale University
New Haven, Connecticut
Spring 1973, Spring 1974

FEMININE NARCISSISM: STUDIES IN LITERARY SELF-CONSCIOUSNESS

This course will respond to the ways in which literature traditionally perceives the feminine self merely as an echo (see Ovid, Metamor-
phoses, Book III) of male narcissism. It will focus on analyses of autobiographies and autobiographical novels by female writers with a view to
determining the effect of distinctively female psychology on the self-
consciousness associated with the autobiographical genre. We will consider the ways in which traditional psychological and critical concepts
must be expanded or modified in order adequately to describe the products
of female creativity. Because such works cannot be discussed without a
consideration of the cultural context in which the authors wrote, the seminar will concentrate on literature produced in Paris in the first half
of the twentieth century. Supplementary readings and brief topics for investigation will include consideration of the presentation of women and of
the problems of autobiography in the works of Proust and Sartre, and analyses of the rhetoric of some texts of the women's liberation movement.

In general the course will meet for one one-hour session and one
two-hour session each week. The one-hour meeting will be the instructor's
presentation of the biographical facts, cultural context, and a general
discussion of the works of the author. The two-hour meeting will include
presentation by a student of an oral report, on one particular facet of the
readings for the week, which will then be elaborated and discussed at
length. One oral report, one short paper, and one term paper (which may
be an expansion of the short paper) are required. Class participation is
stressed. Reading knowledge of French is helpful but not a prerequisite,
since all the basic texts and many of the supplementary ones are available
in translation. Students are also asked to keep a journal.

Course Outline:

I. Introduction
    1) Introductory lecture: problems of narcissism and autobiography--
    traditional views.
    2) The Journal of Marie Bashkirtseff: an introduction to the prob-
    lems of female narcissism.
    3) Lecture on theories of feminine psychology.

II. Colette: Between Mother and Child
    1) General introduction: biographical facts, cultural milieu, sum-
    mary of her work.
    2) Analyses of selected passages from the autobiographical writings
    together with autobiographical projections in Claudine at School, The
    Vagabonde, and Chéri.
    3) The search for personal and literary purity: The Pure and the Im-
    pure, discussed in terms of the works listed above.
    4) Colette and Proust: temporal problems in autobiography.

III. Gertrude Stein: Objective Autobiography

1) General introduction: biographical facts, cultural milieu, discussion of her theories of writing.
2) The Autobiography of Alice B. Toklas and Everybody's Autobiography: third-person autobiography related to theories of feminine psychology.
3) Two: The Story of Gertrude Stein and Her Brother: repetition and transformation.

IV. Simone de Beauvoir: Existentialism and Women
1) General introduction: biographical facts, cultural milieu, summary of her work, presentation of the feminine existential dilemma in The Second Sex.
2) Triangular structure in Simone de Beauvoir's works: analyses of passages from the Memoirs in conjunction with She Came to Stay and The Woman Destroyed.
3) Discussion of the works listed above in comparison with Sartre's The Words.

V. Violette Leduc: Prisons and Homosexuality
1) General introduction: biographical facts, cultural milieu, summary of her other novels.
2) Psychological prisons in La Bâtarde and In the Prison of Her Skin.
3) Comparison with selected passages from the writings of Jean Genet.

VI. Anaïs Nin: Autobiography and the Illusions of Freedom
1) General introduction: biographical facts, cultural milieu, summary of her work.
2) Labyrinths and the search for personal and literary freedom: analyses of selected passages from the Diaries together with The Four-Chambered Heart and Seduction of the Minotaur.

VII. Conclusion: Women's Liberation and Literature
1) Discussion of the literary criticism in The Second Sex and Sexual Politics; the rhetoric of the women's liberation movement.

Readings:

Marie Bashkirtseff.	The Journal of Marie Bashkirtseff
Colette.	The Earthly Paradise, selections
_____.	The Vagabond
_____.	Claudine at School
_____.	Chéri
_____.	The Pure and the Impure
Gertrude Stein.	Two: The Story of Gertrude Stein and her Brother
_____.	The Autobiography of Alice B. Toklas
_____.	Everybody's Autobiography
Simone de Beauvoir	Memoirs, selections
_____.	She Came to Stay
_____.	The Woman Destroyed
Violette Leduc	La Bâtarde
	In the Prison of Her Skin
Anaïs Nin.	Diaries, selections
_____.	The Four-Chambered Heart
_____.	Seduction of the Minotaur

Supplementary readings:

Marcel Proust.   Remembrance of Things Past, selections
Jean-Paul Sartre.   The Words
Simone de Beauvoir.   The Second Sex (Introduction, chapters on narcissism,
                            chapters on literature)
Kate Millett.   Sexual Politics (Chapters on literature)
Female Sexuality (Translation of Recherches psychanalytiques nouvelles
    sur la sexualité féminine)

(Usual assignment: about 300 pages per week. Some of the texts listed
above are quite short.)

Dorin Schumacher
Comparative Literature Program

University of Pittsburgh
Pittsburgh, Pennsylvania
Winter Term 1971-1972

LITERARY AND SOCIAL VIEWS OF WOMEN (CLP 120)

Possible approaches to feminist criticism, emphasizing experimental forms that some women develop in an effort to express female consciousness and experience.

I   Introduction

    A. Theoretical uses of literature: Simone de Beauvoir, The Second Sex; Kate Millett, Sexual Politics

    B. Situation of the woman writer: Virginia Woolf, A Room of One's Own

    C. Feminist criticism: applications to literature

II   Images of women in literature by men

    A. André Gide, The Immoralist

    B. André Malraux, Man's Fate

    C. William Faulkner, As I Lay Dying

III Images of women in literature by women

    A. Marguerite Duras, L'Amante anglaise

    B. Nathalie Sarraute, Tropisms; Susan Sontag, "Nathalie Sarraute and the Novel," Against Interpretation

IV   The Black woman

    Maya Angelou, I Know Why the Caged Bird Sings

V   The theme of lesbianism

    Violette Leduc, La Bâtarde

VI   Woman as critic

    Jill Johnston, Marmalade Me

VII Images of woman in pornography

    Pauline Réage, The Story of O; Susan Sontag, "The Pornographic Imagination," Styles of Radical Will

VIII Woman as poet

    Gertrude Stein, Writings and Lectures 1909-1945

Barnard College.

Donna C. Stanton, Department of French, reports, "In the Spring of 1974, and hopefully every year thereafter, I plan to offer a course at Barnard in the French department (taught in French, and therefore neither interdepartmental nor interdisciplinary) which will be entitled: FEMALE AND FEMINISM. I intend to stress three themes in particular: the mythic image of the female, the dilemma of the modern woman, and the rise of feminism through the examination of literary works from Romanticism to the present. Among the authors to be studied are: Sand, Baudelaire, Flaubert, Becque, Colette, Breton, Mauriac, Montherlant, de Beauvoir, Sarraute, Roche-fort, and Leduc."

Tatiana W. Greene, Department of French, repeated a course in Fall 1973: FRENCH WOMEN WRITERS (French 44). A literary and cultural study of poets, writers, and influential groups, with emphasis on Marguerite de Navarre, Louise Labé, the "Précieuses," Madame de Sévigné, Madame de La Fayette, the eighteenth-century Salons, Madame de Staël, Marceline Desbordes-Valmore, Sand, Colette, de Beauvoir, Duras, Rochefort. Pre-requisite: Masterpieces of French literature (or its equivalent). Course is also open to non-majors.

Beaver College.

Benkt Wennberg, Department of Foreign Languages, gave a different focus to an existing course: MAJOR WRITERS IN FRENCH, I: FROM THE BEGINNINGS TO 1789 (French 31), taught in French, Soph.-Jr. level, and considered it a very successful revamping of the old stand-by "Major Writers in French." The course was given in Fall 1972. Mr. Wennberg also offered a Freshman Seminar in Spring 1971, LOVE--VARIATIONS ON A THEME studied in the Romance of the Rose, Don Quixote, and Sons and Lovers.

Boston College.

Betty T. Rahv, Department of Romance Languages and Literatures, of-fered a course in Spring 1974, WOMEN IN FRENCH LITERATURE OF THE 20TH CENTURY (taught in English translation): MYTH AND REALITY OF CONTEMPORARY WOMAN AS HEROINE AND AS AUTHOR.

Erich Neumann, Amour and Psyche	Breton, Nadja
M. Duras, Moderato Cantabile	Claudel, Tidings Brought to Mary
N. Sarraute, Tropisms	Colette, Gigi
Giraudoux, Electra	Mauriac, Thérèse
Anouilh, Antigone	de Beauvoir, The Second Sex

Carnegie-Mellon University (Pittsburgh, Pa.):

Michel Fougères, Department of Modern Languages and Literatures, taught a course WOMEN AND WOMEN'S LIB IN FRENCH LITERATURE in Spring 1973. (He reports that the course will be retitled WOMEN AND FEMINISM at the suggestion of a student.) Course given in French.

The City College, CUNY:

Gisèle Corbière Gille, Department of Romance Languages, taught a course in translation Fall 1973, WOMAN IN FRENCH LITERATURE, a study of representative French women writers with emphasis on the aspect of their works dealing with women's concerns. For more information see Appendix A.

Cornell University .

N. Furman, Department of Romance Studies, offered a course in Spring 1973, WOMEN IN FRANCE IN THE XIXTH CENTURY. The course was taught in French.

Davis and Elkins College.

David W. Seaman, Division of Humanities, gave a course for Spring 1974, THE FRENCH WOMAN. Examination of the role, status, and achievements of women in France, from the Medieval Courts of Love to the Romantic hero-ines, concluding with the condition of women in modern France. Both lit-erary and historical figures are considered: Marie de France, Madame de Pompadour, Madame Bovary, George Sand, Simone de Beauvoir, Catherine Deneuve, others. Course in English but "French majors will do some read-ings and write papers in French."

Fairleigh Dickinson University.

In addition to the course listed on p. 106 f. f., Mara Vamos, Department of Modern Languages and Literatures, also gave a course, THE IMAGE OF LOVE IN FRENCH LITERATURE, in Spring 1974. The course "explored ambivalent atti-tudes towards women." Readings from authors of the twelfth to the twentieth century.

Fordham University.

Diane Butturff, Department of Romance Languages, offered an under-graduate course, IMAGE OF THE WOMAN IN MODERN FRENCH LITERATURE, in Spring 1973.

King's College (Wilkes-Barre, Pa.).

Diane L. Cook, Department of Foreign Languages and Literatures, taught an independent study course entitled WOMEN WRITERS IN FRENCH LITERATURE, in the 1973 Summer Session. "While most of the works were read in English, a few were read in French." In Fall 1973 and in Spring 1974 she offered an inter-disciplinary women's studies course in the Honors Program. The title of the seminar: WOMEN'S STUDIES: AN EXAMINATION OF TRADITIONAL AT-TITUDES TOWARDS WOMEN AND CONTEMPORARY FEMINIST VIEWS.

University of Maryland.

Leonora Cohen Rosenfield, Department of French and Italian, gave a graduate seminar LA FEMME DANS LA LITTERATURE FRANCAISE--HISTORY OF IDEAS, WOMEN IN FRENCH LITERATURE, 1661 TO THE PRESENT, during Spring 1974. From the course description: "Books by women writers of France from the 17th through the 20th centuries are read along with works by both sexes about woman and her struggle for her rights--political, legal, marital, educational, and economic." Ms. Rosenfield also chaired a sectional program for the American Society for 18th-Century Studies (ASECS) "Women's Place in 18th-Century Intellectual Life." The meeting was held at the University of Pennsylvania, April 25, 1974.

Montclair State College (Upper Montclair, N. J.).
      Kay Wilkins, Department of French, taught a course, IMAGES OF WOMEN
IN FRENCH LITERATURE, Spring 1973. The course was given in English and
has been offered as a humanities elective or as an alternative to the
French language requirement.

University of Oregon.
      Lilian R. Furst, Department of Romance Languages, taught a graduate
and upper division seminar THE PORTRAYAL OF WOMEN IN THE FRENCH NOVEL,
1750-1950, Spring 1973. Texts read in French. Ms. Furst hopes to teach
this topic as a Comparative Literature course "in the near future extend-
ing into English, German, American, and Italian literatures."

Portland State University (Portland, Oregon).
      Claudine Guégan-Fisher, in addition to the course listed on p.50 ff.
also offered a course WOMEN IN FRENCH LITERATURE, a study of literary
figures from the twelfth to the twentieth century. The course was offered Winter 1973. "Half of the term was devoted to Marie de France,
Marguerite de Navarre, The Seventeenth Century and the Women of the
"Salons" and of "Préciosité," Madame de Sévigné, Madame de La Fayette,
Madame de Staël, George Sand, La Comtesse de Noailles. The other half
of the term focussed on modern writers: Colette, Simone de Beauvoir,
Françoise Parturier, Nathalie Sarraute, Marguerite Duras, Violette Leduc.
The social and cultural impact of these writers was discussed as well as
their themes and their comments on women."

University of Rhode Island (Kingston, R. I.).
      Edward Benson taught a course SEX-ROLE CONFLICT IN RECENT FRENCH
LITERATURE, Fall 1972 (undergraduate), team-taught with a colleague from
the English department, Karen Stein. (In English).

University of Rochester.
      Fernande Gontier, Department of Foreign and Comparative Literature,
taught an evening course, THE FEMALE CHARACTER IN THE 20TH CENTURY FRENCH
NOVEL, in Spring 1973. The course was taught in French.

Saint Joseph College (West Hartford, Conn.).
      Susan Clark, Department of French, taught a course, WOMEN IN LITERA-
TURE in Fall 1972. Texts read: Montaigne, Essais; Molière, Les Femmes
savantes; Madame de Sévigné, Lettres; Marivaux, Le Jeu de l'amour et du
hasard; Prévost, Manon Lescaut; Constant, Adolphe; Flaubert, Madame Bovary; Mauriac, Thérèse Desqueyroux.

SUNY (State U. of N. Y.) Binghamton.
      Hela Michot-Dietrich, Department of Romance Languages and Literatures,
reports a course, Fall 1973, LA FEMME DANS LE ROMAN NATURALISTE. The course
is described as "a study of major novels by Emile Zola, Edmond and Jules
de Goncourt, and others. The role of women as treated by these authors
will be especially scrutinized, and the reasons why the majority of these
authors' protagonists are women will be examined closely. Readings and
lectures in French. Course open to any student with sufficient knowledge

of French."

SUNY, Stony Brook.

Harriet R. Allentuch, Department of French and Italian, taught a graduate (M.A. level) free seminar Fall 1972 on the topic IMAGES DE LA FEMME DANS LA LITTERATURE FRANCAISE. The course "was very successful; it was taught in French and half the class were native speakers." In fall 1973, Ms. Allentuch taught a course on the undergraduate level on women in French Literature covering all centuries (in English).

Elizabeth P. Riggs plans to offer a graduate seminar, THE CULT OF WOMAN IN MEDIEVAL FRENCH LITERATURE. This course will explore "the position of women in the Middle Ages in France as reflected in the literature of the period" (in English).

Vassar College.

The Department of French reports the following courses:

Fall 1972   Freshman Seminar on women writers
Fall 1973   LA FEMME AU XVIIIe SIECLE--Special Studies Seminar.
                 Adrienne D. Hytier.
Fall 1974   LA QUERELLE DES FEMMES AU MOYEN-AGE--Special Studies Seminar
All courses taught in French

Wesleyan University.

Michael C. Danahy, Department of Romance Languages and Literatures, will offer a course, WOMEN IN FICTION during 1974-75. The characteristics of the novel will be discussed in conjunction with the various fictitious roles and functions made up for women: La Princesse de Clèves, Manon Lescaut, Cousine Bette, Madame Bovary, Nana.

During 1973-74 a course was co-taught by Ms. Meyer and Mr. Danahy, FEMININE ROLES IN FRENCH AND RUSSIAN LITERATURE. "The purpose of the course is to show how a set of critical concepts may be applied to quite diverse works of narrative fiction. The current interest in women's role in society will be discussed in relation to images of French and Russian women which will be presented in paired fictional works. The theme of the Woman Question, cast in the perspective of four centuries of the French and Russian traditions will be used as a means to reveal literary devices. Authors to be studied will include Balzac, Flaubert, Zola, Dostoevsky, Pushkin, Tolstoy, Nabokov, and Solzhenitsyn."

University of Wisconsin--Milwaukee.

Martine D. Meyer, Department of French and Italian, reports "the following are courses with a focus on women which are being taught currently (Spring 1973) in this department":
    1) A LITERARY GENRE: NOVELS WRITTEN BY WOMEN. Taught in French
    2) Honors Seminar: Studies in the French novel in translation,
        IMAGES OF WOMEN IN FRENCH LITERATURE. Taught in English.

Appendix A

Gisèle Corbière Gille   The City College, CUNY
Department of Romance Languages   Fall 1973

WOMAN IN FRENCH LITERATURE

A study of representative French women writers with emphasis on the aspects of their works dealing with women's concerns.

Outline:

Historical background: the battle of the sexes.

Woman in Medieval French Literature:
Héloïse's letters to Abélard.
Marie de France and her lais.*
Béatrix de Die (poems).
Péronnelle d'Armentières.
Christine de Pisan (Epistle to Cupid).

Woman in 16th-C. French Literature:
Marguerite de Navarre's Heptameron.
Catherine d'Amboise.
Pernette du Guillet.
Louise Labé (Sonnets, Debate between Folly and Cupid, Epistle to AMCDBL).
Marie de Gournay.

Woman in 17th-C. French Literature:
Madeleine de Scudéry (Clélia).
Comtesse de Suze
Marie-Catherine de Villedieu (her short stories).
Antoinette Deshoulières.
Marie-Catherine d'Aulnoy
Marquise de Sévigné and her letters.
Mme. de La Fayette (Princess of Clèves).

Woman in 18th-C. French Literature:
The letter writers: Mme. du Deffand, Mme. du Châtelet, Mlle. de
    Lespinasse.
The story tellers: Mme. de Villeneuve, Mme. de Tencin, Mme. de
    Charrière.
Mme. Roland: her memoirs.

Woman in 19th-C. French Literature:
Mme. de Staël and Corinne.
Mme. de Krüdener.
George Sand.
Marceline Desbordes-Valmore and other poets: Amable Tastu, Delphine
    de Girardin, Louise Ackerman, Anaïs Ségalas, Louise Michel, Marie
    Nizet.

Woman in 20th-C. French Literature:
Simone de Beauvoir and The Second Sex.

117

Anna de Noailles.
Colette.

Format: Course conducted in English. All students had reading knowledge
of French.

*These and other poems from: Jeanne Moulin, <u>La Poésie féminine</u>, 2 Vols.
 Seghers-Melior , 1971.

SPANISH STUDIES

"El casamiento engañoso": Marriage in the Novels of María Luisa Bombal, Silvina Bullrich, and Elisa Serrana

by

Marcia L. Welles

There exists a poetic tradition of the marriage-song known as the epithalamium, written in honor and celebration of a wedding. In Edmund Spenser's "Prothalamion," an outstanding example of this genre, the espoused may look forward to joy, contentment, and offspring. If there existed such a tradition in prose narration, the three novels here discussed would have to be classified as an "anti-epithalamium." In the novels of two Chilean authors, La última niebla (1935) by María Luisa Bombal and Chilena, casada, sin profesión (1963) by Elisa Serrana, as well as in Bodas de cristal (1951) by the Argentine Silvina Bullrich, harmony has become discord, and peace has deteriorated into anxiety. Praise of marriage has not, however, turned into a denunciation of the institution. Although there is an implicit questioning of social values, the authors are not radicals. They do not formulate a general solution to the problem of marriage in the upper-class stratum of society. The interest of each novel lies rather in the individual revelations of each feminine protagonist.

These are psychological novels of self-interpretation which portray the nuances of feeling. The difficulty of explaining such subtleties is stated by the narrator of Bullrich's novel: "There are times when I would like to be very intelligent in order to know exactly what name to give certain reactions."[1] In the narratives there is a scarcity of metaphor or simile, and their use is limited to the clarification of complex emotional reactions. Mental states are made concrete by means of comparison to a physical sensation. For instance, in La última niebla emotional pain is personified as a biting animal. "And I gather my forces to resist its assault but the pain arrives, and it bites me, and then I scream, I scream slowly so that no one can hear."[2] In Bodas de cristal anxiety is compared to the sensation of a gnawing rat. "I awakened feeling that something like a rat was going in circles inside my mind . . . ." Teresa, of Chilena, casada, sin profesión, defines the relief of confiding in someone as being "like a menstruation, necessary, painful and normal, which restored her femininity to her, which finished a cycle."[3]

These novels are primarily first-person narratives. La última niebla is strictly a narrated monologue. Bodas de cristal, though principally from a personal "I" perspective, does shift to the point of view of other characters, namely those of the husband and his mistresses. In Chilena, casada, sin profesión the narrator Teresa functions both as an "I" in the italicized portions of the text and as a third-person "she", creating an interesting interaction between the self and the objectified self. The effect of this choice of discourse is what Amado Alonso, in his analysis of La última niebla, calls the "structural role of the accessories,"[4] in which "no descriptive detail is merely informative, much less is it a documentation of the objective realm, but rather each one functions as an element of interior life."[5] This technique of "represented perception,"[6] as it is named by the critic Paul Hernadi, emphasizes not the event but the reaction to the event. If there had been an omniscient author the effect would have been quite different, because, as he "pretends to know everything about everything, his discourse appears to deal with actual 'things' rather than certain 'facts' which, on specific occasions, may become manifest about those things to a mind."7

Because these are novels of introspection, their plots cannot be described in terms of the action. Their plot-type is "indexical" rather than "distributional," the characters and atmosphere being the principal ingredients of the meaning.8 In terms of the affective state of the narrator, each of the three novels follows an equivalent plot sequence, which can be condensed into a three-step series in which each step is a response to the previous one. In each novel the illusion of the idea of marriage is succeeded by a reaction of disillusion, and this reaction in turn is followed by the attempt of the protagonist to seek an alternative to disillusion. The first two steps of the series are presented as inevitable ones in which the protagonist is a passive subject. It is in the last step that the core of the meaning of each novel lies. At this point the protagonist is faced with the necessity of choosing among possible alternatives and becomes, for the first time, an agent. Each protagonist chooses a different alternative.

In La última niebla the narration commences just after the marriage has taken place. Daniel, the husband of the unnamed narrator, informs the servants that "my cousin and I were married this morning."9 The action thereafter unfolds in the present tense. In Bodas de cristal and Chilena, casada, sin profesión memory is the principal narrative medium. In Bodas de cristal the likewise unidentified narrator reconstructs, in an imaginary few minutes upon awakening the morning after the anniversary celebration, her fifteen years of married life. Teresa, the narrator of Serrana's novel, waiting in a hotel en route from Katmandu to New Delhi to rejoin her second husband after a lengthy separation, reflects upon her life since the moment of her first marriage at nineteen years of age. The temporal perspective in the novels of Bullrich and Serrana establishes a contrast between the present "I" and the past "I" of the reflections,10 and in both cases the time preceding marriage is remembered with nostalgia for the lost happiness. In Bodas de cristal the narrator recalls that during her courtship "life was easy, days were happy, nights were agitated by vague desires which we tried to halt through continuous parties. We were moving, smiling, towards an inevitable end: marriage." Teresa remembers the feeling of plenitude she experienced upon meeting her future husband, Ignacio. "Everything was perfect: life, she herself, and all objects; the table, the flowers and the entranceway. They harmonized. She was satisfied with letting herself feel, happiness and anguish, a subtle touch, a pair of eyes, a voice, and life was hers."11

After the marriage has taken place, the unhappiness which ensues is actually stated in Bodas de cristal and symbolized in the other novels. The solitude and boredom experienced by the wife in Bodas de cristal during her pregnancy cause her to feel regretful about her new role. "At times it seemed to me that I had been deceived. I had changed my large house, my irresponsible and active life, my full days, for that small apartment, those long afternoons, that servant who grumbled: 'Madam doesn't know how to give orders.'"[12]   In La última niebla and Chilena, casada, sin profesión atmospheric details serve as "objective correlatives"[13] which indicate an affective state. In La última niebla the first sentence of the novel serves as an atmospheric index: "The storm of the previous night had dislodged roof-tiles from the old country house. When we arrived, the rain was leaking in all the rooms" (p. 37). The rooms are cold, and the bride shivers, wrapped in a shawl which a servant, not her husband, has sympathetically tossed over her shoulders. The mist and the silence begin encroaching upon her. The image of mist becomes the presiding symbol of the novel. Amado Alonso interprets its symbolic significance as referring to the protagonist's dreamlike state, in which she is unable to distinguish between fantasy and reality.[14] While this is certainly true, it has a larger contextual meaning, for it is associated with immobility, stagnation, and ultimately with death.[15] The narrator's first reaction to the mist is one of fear. In Chilena, casada, sin profesión Teresa returns after the honeymoon to her husband's house and finds it cold and inhospitable. When she suggests a heater, Ignacio refuses her request, saying that "I like the cold. I suffocate in heated houses."[16]

The disappointment with marriage is expressed in all the novels as a feeling of emptiness. Each protagonist has viewed marriage as her life's project, and this has proven to be a delusion.

In La última niebla the protagonist's life is one of meaningless habit in which she functions like a robot. The monotony and inevitability of such habitual action are expressed in a series of short parallel phrases, all beginning with an adverb of time and followed by the verb in the future, indicating probability: "Tomorrow we will return to the country. The day after tomorrow I will go to church in the village, with my mother-in-law. Later, during lunch, Daniel will talk to us about the farm chores . . . . And the day after will be the same, and within a year, and within ten . . . ." (pp. 54-55).[17]

In Bodas de cristal and Chilena, casada, sin profesión the word "emptiness" appears several times. When Teresa's husband voices his total disenchantment with her she feels that "the emptiness was total, the solitude profound, like the night, like the nothingness around her." After a brief period of illusion, the sensation recurs during her second marriage to the diplomat, Lucho. "The consumption of whiskey, the number of dinners and the flattery increased. The emptiness increased." In Bodas de cristal the wife recalls her loneliness during her pregnancy. "And now until evening my solitude, my emptiness."[18]

Images of desolation also appear to express radical solitude. In Bodas de cristal the narrator describes "that great desert which the world had become for me since Luis remained so distant, . . ." and Teresa, of Chilena, casada, sin profesión, admits that "sometimes I dream that they leave me alone in a desert or in a sea, I don't know, and I awaken without having known it; in the nightmare they all leave without me."[19]

At this point in the novels, the solitude and boredom oblige each narrator to seek a change in her situation.

In Bombal's novel the escape from boredom is at first withdrawal in the form of abandonment to fatigue. "My tiredness is so extreme that instead of answering I prefer to collapse into an armchair." The arrival of

Regina, the brother-in-law's wife, who is having an affair, crystallizes the narrator's anxiety into sexual desire. Regina is the narrator's counterpoint. From her first encounter with Regina she senses her own lack. The sight of Regina's disordered hair is a reminder of her own graceless braided hairstyle which her husband has forced her to adopt in imitation of his deceased first wife. Regina's passionate existence is a constant reminder of her own dreariness and stagnation.

At first the narrator's only alleviation comes in the form of narcissistic sublimation by bathing in a pool where "tepid currents caress and penetrate me. Like silky arms the aquatic plants encircle my body with their long roots. The fresh breath of the water kisses the nape of my neck and rises to my forehead." Later, Regina's lover, upon returning from hunting, tosses a yet warm and bleeding wild pigeon into the narrator's lap. The connection between this action and her own rape fantasy can be seen in her response of fear combined with excitement, described as attraction to Regina's lover.

During a visit to the city, the narrator is presented with the opportunity for action. She takes a walk by herself at night, meets a man and returns to his home with him. Only during this brief encounter with a lover is she free from the threat of the mist. "The night and the mist can flutter in vain against the windowpanes; they will not succeed in infiltrating one single particle of death into this room." After this experience her existence acquires meaning. Henceforth the monotony of her life is replaced by a state of dynamic tension, alternating between memory and hope. She savors the remembrance of her lover, and anticipates the future which now seems full of possibilities.

This action of the narrator's is successful. In spite of some moments of anxiety and doubt as to the reality of the occurrence, she has a focus for her imagination, which is a defense from the lifelessness around her. Eventually she retraces her steps and returns to the house where she had been with her lover. There she learns that he had died fifteen years ago and also that he had been blind. It is the fact of his blindness which destroys her, for she realizes that not even he had appreciated her youth and beauty. With the collapse of this last vital illusion, she succumbs to the tedium of the reality around her, decides to follow her husband, and explains that "I follow him in order to complete an infinity of trivial chores; in order to perform an infinity of pleasant frivolities; in order to cry out of habit and smile out of duty. I follow him in order to live correctly, in order to someday die correctly."[20]

In Bodas de cristal the narrator also finds herself in an unhappy marital situation. Her husband, Luis, is cold, egotistical, and constantly unfaithful to her. Although she does, as a means of revenge, have an ephemeral experience with a lover, this does not prove to be an authentic solution. Her critical action is a decision to non-action in the form of resignation. She explains, in general terms, that "rebellion provokes us against the whole world and also against ourselves; resignation, on the other hand, at least leaves us at peace with ourselves." The purpose of her life as a wife is described as preservation of the family and its traditions since "for us that's what life is: the family. We like familiar faces, familiar places, the repetition of themes . . . ."

This endorsement of woman as a maternal, unchangeable being corresponds to textual images which reveal the presence of the archetypal concept of the Great Mother. For example, in the observation that "understanding between a man and a woman seems as difficult to me as between a whale and a giraffe,"[21] the ground of the metaphor is the maternal impression of roundness, greatness, and stability[22] created by the whale, in contrast to that of agility and speed suggested by the giraffe. In other metaphors water and earth are personified into male and female agents respectively, water being the active, fecundating agent. His wife says of Luis, "You were always the river, I was always the bank of the river," and another character generalizes that "Argentine women . . . have something akin to that mighty resignation of the land or the sea, but the men possess that blind fury of the rain that beats them or of the waves that, when they embrace, bruise, overturn, toss us breathless onto the sand."

The decision of the wife in Bodas de cristal also succeeds in providing her with an alternative to despair. At the end she feels rewarded for her tolerance by the fact that, in spite of all the difficulties, the marriage has survived and the relationship with Luis promises to improve, for "now that he is aging I see him returning slowly towards me."[23]

In Chilena, casada, sin profesión the protagonist adopts the most fundamental course of action. Neither her first marriage to Ignacio, who dies in an airplane crash, nor her second marriage to Lucho, the diplomat, is satisfactory. The alternative chosen by Teresa is to attempt to free herself by struggling inward. This is truly a "novel of formation."[24] The maturity which the character achieves in her passage from illusion to reality is represented by the fact that, while at the beginning of the novel, at age nineteen, she is playing the part of a leper in a play, by the end of the novel, at age thirty-six, she is in an actual leper colony in Nepal, though not herself a leper. Her struggle for inner peace and self-knowledge is a slow and painful one. The first step occurs as an awareness of the outside world, especially of nature. There are no landscape descriptions in the first part, which takes place in Chile. In the second part, which coincides with Teresa's arrival in New Delhi, the impressions of the city and landscape become intensely vivid, and colorful images proliferate. Then brief encounters with gurus help her to find relief from her mutilated sense of self. Her visit to the leper colony in Katmandu is decisive, for there, with the guidance and love of the teacher of the colony, she finally experiences, through abandonment of self to cosmic unity, an inner peace and strength. This is expressed with images of fertility: "The seed germinates within me, a small and fertile grain of the heights. I do not know how to produce or to reap, but I am pleased by the sensation of spiritual fertility that I experience and I feel myself impregnated."[25]

These are not thesis novels. They share, however, certain themes of conflict which have the cumulative effect of an indictment of society. The conflicts may be designated as follows: the conflict between self and role; the conflict between woman and man; the conflict between individual and society.

Because self-concept and role identity are closely interrelated, the loss of a significant role can produce a damaged self-esteem.[26] A woman's principal role is that of wife (and mother). In order to assume the role of wife a woman must be selected, and the basis of selection is principally her beauty. In the novels, the mirror represents the women's concern with self as a desirable object whose prime value, beauty, is continually threatened by age. In La última niebla the narrator looks in the mirror, and undoing her hair, notices that "my hair is growing darker. Each day it will grow even darker. And before it loses its brilliance and lustre, there will be nobody who says that I have beautiful hair." Later, although she detects signs of aging, she does not feel the same anguish because she has known love. The narrator of Bodas de cristal also examines herself in the mirror. "I looked at myself in the mirror. I could see only my disheveled hair without any gray, my neck with some wrinkles which, while from there not discernible, I knew well, my upper arms somewhat heavier; my breasts, less taut, no longer raised the silk of the nightgown with such insolence."[27] She comforts herself with the fact that her husband is ten years older than she.

In each novel the role identity of the narrator as wife is invalidated by her husband's lack of esteem. This results in a very negative concept of self. The narrator of Bodas de cristal admits her lack of self-assurance and constant need for praise. "I still asked myself, after fifteen years of marriage, if Luis looked upon me as a pretty woman or simply as his wife" for "in order to live I need praise as much as I need air." The crisis of identity is extreme in La última niebla. At one point the narrator reacts to her own sensation of non-being by insisting that "I exist, I exist . . . and I am lovely and happy! Yes. Happy! Happiness is no more than possessing a young, slim, and agile body."[28] The fact that she is beheld by her lover grants her existence. Therefore, upon learning of her lover's blindness, she is annihilated. This narrator's concept of self is so diminished that she exists only as seen by another.[29]

Teresa, of Chilena, casada, sin profesión, fails in her role as wife and as mother, for she loses a baby and cannot have more children. She seeks alternative role definitions for herself, but feels totally insufficient. A painter urges her to express her own personality in her sketches, whereupon she responds that "I don't have any personality . . . it's not very interesting." When she does charity work in a hospital she apologizes to the doctor that "I'm not good for very much, really I'm good for nothing." Unable to find any suitable alternatives she admits complete failure. "My anguish is my failure. I have achieved nothing, either in the spiritual or human realm, and I began life full of spiritual and human graces. I am a failure."[30]

A larger theme appearing in the novels is the conflict between a woman's world and a man's. The disparity between them is seen to be so great that a perfect relationship of harmony and understanding seems impossible. The narrator of Bullrich's novel concentrates on the different perceptual awareness between herself and Luis, generalizing it to be a generic difference between male and female. A woman's time sense is different. In contrast to a man's more cosmic vision, she enjoys the perfection of a moment. She writes that "I would have liked for that day to have been complete, perfect; I would have liked to prolong it. Luis, on the other hand, considered it finished. Always, during the course of our life, he dampened my enthusiasm for perfecting the moment, for reaching a plenitude. . . ." A woman's imagination is richer, while a man is more intent on the present reality. "He enjoys things and moments, and not the anticipation of things and moments. When he chooses an object, when he relishes a view it is because he has them before his eyes; I, on the other hand, have little by little sketched that object, that view in my imagination; later I look for what most resembles what I have imagined."[31]

Serrana's novel stresses man's egocentricity and lack of compassion. Teresa's first husband, Ignacio, will not help a friend in financial difficulty, and Teresa draws a check from her own funds. Her second husband, Lucho, is irritated by her concern for the problems of a servant girl. There is also a linguistic dimension to the separation between male and female. Teresa comments ironically on the authoritative arrogance with which men speak. "Teresa admired the rich Spanish language and the assurance of the opinions of the Latin Americans; that abundant verbiage made her feel deficient, and the paradoxical, graceful, lyrical phrases stupefied her; also the ease with which they synthesized their explorations of the racial and mystic marrow of India." Both of these issues point to the larger problem of the individual in a society in which expectations and values are distorted.

Societal expectations of women are rigidly defined. In La última niebla Daniel considers that his wife is fortunate to be married to him, for it has saved her from the dreaded alternative of being an "old maid." In Bodas de cristal Susanna, one of Luis' mistresses, exemplifies the problem of the lack of preparation for any role outside that of marriage. Married to an alcoholic, she cannot divorce him because she has no way of supporting herself and her daughter. In contrast to her brothers, she was neither educated nor did she inherit money. She eventually commits suicide. In Chilena, casada, sin profesión Teresa's project in life had been to be a good wife and mother, and when this fails there is no other vocation with which to replace it. "That's the way it was. She had not foreseen another opening, another possibility, beyond love, maternity, a home. Direction and vocation coming from men; emotional stability also. . . . Unsuccessful love, frustrated motherhood, works without substance, no fountain of life. She wished to seize upon something, she desired it so desperately that she experienced anguish."[32]

The contrast between the male and female points of view carries an implicit condemnation of a society where the masculine values of aggression and ambition have dominated over the traditionally feminine values of compassion and understanding. Teresa knows that Lucho's goal is financial success and social acceptance. She sees these desires fulfilled, his conscience untroubled at having caused the suicide of an Indian girl. "Success, importance, money. He lived. I saw him live, certain of his body, of his sex, of his soul and future. He was a happy man. Profoundly happy." Her alienation from him is complete, and she decides to separate from him. In Bodas de cristal one of the female characters comments bitterly that "I have often heard it said that women have no soul. Some religious maintain this. If by soul one means coldness, a lack of scruples, the neglect of all responsibility that does not bear a signature, duplicity, the knack for making various women miserable at the same time, in this case I admit that the soul of man is unable to be equalled."[33]

It can be seen in these novels that the myth of the married woman as depicted in Fray Luis de León's La perfecta casada (1583) is still

127

operative today. The three narrators had believed that their most sacred aim was marriage and childbearing, accepting Fray Luis's statement about women: "And since God granted them neither the ingenuity required by important business, nor the strength necessary for war and farming, let them assess themselves for what they are and content themselves with their lot, let them tend to the house and move within its sphere, since God created them for that alone."[34] María Luisa Bombal, Silvina Bullrich, and Elisa Serrana commence their novels with this illusion and slowly unfold the reality of the situation. The traditional structure of marriage no longer fulfills the needs of a modern woman, but the society does not provide the necessary alternatives.

                                        Barnard College
                                        New York City

Notes

[1]Citations from Silvina Bullrich's Bodas de cristal are to the 3d ed. (Buenos Aires: Editorial Sudamericana, 1959), p. 138. Translations are my own.

[2]Citations from María Luisa Bombal's La última niebla are to the 5th ed. (Buenos Aires: Editorial Andina, 1970), p. 88. Translations are my own.

[3]Citations from Elisa Serrana's Chilena, casada, sin profesión are to the 4th ed. (Santiago de Chile: Editorial Zig-Zag, 1964), pp. 137, 218. The italicized portions of the novel are indicated by a single underline. Translations are my own.

[4]Amado Alonso, "Aparición de una novelista," Nosotros, 3 (June 1936), 245. "Papel estructural de lo accesorio."

[5]Ibid., 248. "Ninguna nota descriptiva representa una mera información, ni mucho menos una documentación de lo objetivo, sino que cada una es un elemento del vivir interior."

[6]Paul Hernadi, "Dual Perspective: Free Indirect Discourse and Related Techniques," Comparative Literature, 24 (Winter 1972), 41.

[7]Ibid., 43.

[8]Seymour Chatman compares distributional and integrative functions, or units of narrative meaning, as follows: "Distributional functions are cardinal functions, or functions tout court: a character buys a gun; later he shoots it off. Integrative functions, or indices, on the other hand, refer 'upward' to the characters or the atmosphere. . . ." See Seymour Chatman, "New Ways of Analyzing Narrative Structure, with an Example from Joyce's Dubliners," Language and Style, 2 (Winter 1969), 5.

[9]Bombal, p. 37.

[10]The difference in the identity of the autobiographical first person is noted by Jean Starobinski, "The Style of Autobiography," in Literary Style: A Symposium, ed. Seymour Chatman (New York: Oxford University Press, 1971), p. 290.

[11]Bullrich, pp. 25, 15.

[12]Ibid., p. 29.

[13]Term used by Carlos Bousoño, Teoría de la expresión poética, 4th ed. (Madrid: Editorial Gredos, 1966), p. 166.

[14]Bombal, p. 37; Alonso, p. 250.

[15]Lynette Seaton, "La creación del ensueño en La última niebla," Armas y Letras, 8, No. 4 (1965), p. 44, points out that "la falta de amor, falta de color y de sentimiento llega a componerse en la forma de una niebla que amenaza ahogarla." Cedomil Goic, "La última niebla: Consideraciones en torno a la estructura de la novela contemporánea," Anales de la Universidad de Chile, 121, No. 128 (1963), p. 76, disagreeing with Alonso's interpretation, says that "la función específica de la niebla es representar lo

ominoso, la presencia de las potencias hostiles del mundo."

[16] Serrana, p. 20.

[17] Bombal, pp. 54-55.

[18] Serrana, pp.18, 116; Bullrich, p. 29.

[19] Bullrich, p. 120; Serrana, p. 75.

[20] The quotations in the previous paragraphs are from Bombal, pp.39, 48, 57, 103.

[21] Bullrich, pp.144, 146, 36.

[22] According to Erich Neumann, these qualities correspond to the elementary, as opposed to the transformative, character of the feminine: "As elementary character we designate the aspect of the Feminine that as the Great Round, the Great Container, tends to hold fast to everything that springs from it and to surround it like an eternal substance." See Erich Neumann, The Great Mother. An Analysis of the Archetype, trans. Ralph Manheim, 2d ed., Bollingen Series, 47 (Princeton: Princeton University Press, 1955; reprinted 1963), p. 25.

[23] Bullrich, pp.172, 158, 166.

[24] Term used by Wolfgang Kayser, Interpretación y análisis de la obra literaria, 4th ed., rev. by María D. Mouton and V. Carcía Yebra (Madrid: Editorial Gredos, 1961), p. 485. Translation is my own.

[25] Serrana, p. 232.

[26] For a discussion of this point see Pauline B. Bart, "Portnoy's Mother's Complaint," Trans-action (Nov.-Dec. 1970), revised and reprinted as "Depression in Middle-Aged Women," in Women in Sexist Society. Studies in Power and Powerlessness, eds. Vivian Gornick and Barbara K. Moran (New York: Basic Books, Inc., 1971), p. 172.

[27] Bombal, pp. 45-46; Bullrich, p. 15.

[28] Bullrich, pp.34, 35; Bombal, p. 43.

[29] This narrator's need to be admired and desired coincides with Jean-Paul Sartre's description of the "masochistic attitude," in which the self becomes wholly a "being-as-object" as apprehended by the Other. Because it is an attitude doomed to failure, it causes anguish. See Jean-Paul Sartre, Being and Nothingness, trans. Hazel E. Barnes (New York: Washington Square Press, 1953), pp. 491-93.

[30] Serrana, pp.53, 66, 170.

[31] Bullrich, pp. 34-35, 36.

[32] Quotations in the previous paragraphs are from Serrana, pp.115, 79.

[33] Serrana, p. 202; Bullrich, p. 56.

[34] Fray Luis de Léon, Obras (Madrid: Compañía de impresores y libreros del Reino, 1885), III, 502. Translation is my own.

The "Protesta femenina" in Latin America

by

Margaret P. Stanley

Virtually all students of Hispanic literature have at least a super-ficial familiarity with the seventeenth-century Mexican poet, dramatist, and scientist, Juana de Asbaje y Ramírez, better known as Sor Juana Inés de la Cruz. Many must identify on M.A. and Ph.D. exams the writer who is admiringly referred to as "Phoenix of America" and "Tenth Muse." It is perhaps not common knowledge, however, that Sor Juana voiced the first "protesta femenina" in Latin America and that another less well-known wom-an poet, Alfonsina Storni, voiced it anew in the early years of our own century. Both women express in their poetry some of the same feminist concerns which are so widely debated today.[1]

Sor Juana, who is generally conceded to be the greatest literary figure of colonial times in Mexico, was unmistakably a prodigy. She learned to read at the age of three. She heard that the sciences were taught in Mexico City and at the age of seven was tormenting her mother to dress her as a boy and send her to the home of a relative in the city so that she could attend the university. The request denied, she began to teach herself. She set herself goals, and if she failed to achieve her goal for a given day she cut off four or five finger lengths of hair as punishment for her stupidity.

Sor Juana was noted socially more for her beauty and charm than for her intelligence and was invited to the viceregal court to serve as lady-in-waiting to the wife of the viceroy. However, she soon became the in-tellectual leader of the court, and the viceroy was so amazed by her geni-us that he assembled a group of forty outstanding scholars to question her on their particular fields. She defended herself admirably. At the age of sixteen she entered a religious order; apparently dissatisfied, she left after three months but entered another order two years later and re-mained there until her death. The order was not so strict that she could not receive friends, and she made of the convent a kind of literary cen-ter. In spite of her prestige, she suffered the criticism of the world and the Church. People contended that literature was unsuited to a woman --much less a nun. She eventually sold her library of 4,000 books and dis-posed of her astronomical instruments. Even after that, though, she could not refrain from studying. Every time she saw a child's top spin or an egg fry she would begin to try to deduce the applicable law of physics.[2]

Most of the literary historians and critics who have written about the poetry of Sor Juana have tried to explain the theme of love in her po-etry. Some think love for her was purely imaginary. Others are sure that she experienced a tragic love affair that drove her to the convent. The German critic Ludwig Pfandl psychoanalyzed her through her writings and concluded that the loves she speaks of are projections of her own narcis-sism and of her fixation on the paternal figure.[3] Some critics see her verbal attacks on men as a renunciation of her femininity.

When we read her poetry from a feminist point of view, we can see that Sor Juana defends and affirms woman and thus affirms herself. She affirms the equality of capacities of men and women. She regrets not

being a man because in Mexico in the seventeenth century--as elsewhere
then and to a large extent now--women simply could not do the things men
could. She went to the convent because it was a way of being free, of having time and privacy to pursue her many intellectual interests, a way of
retaining her individuality. There was quite simply no man in her society
with whom she could have lived and still been free, and the only available
options were marriage and the convent.

We can see in Sor Juana's poetry an expression of revolutionary sensibility. In some well-known <u>redondillas</u> she speaks out against traditions
and myths that enslave women, such as the cult of virginity and the double
standard:

> Stupid men, who unreasonably attack women, without seeing
> that you are the cause of the very thing you blame;
> if with unparalleled ardour you make love to their disdain, why
> do you expect them to act virtuously when you incite them to sin?[4]

> (Hombres necios, que acusáis
> a la mujer sin razón,
> sin ver que sois la ocasión
> de lo mismo que culpáis;
>
> si con ansia sin igual
> solicitáis su desdén,
> ¿por qué queréis que obren bien
> si las incitáis al mal?)

She makes a point women are still trying to make today:

> Who is most to blame in a guilty passion, the woman who falls
> when she is begged, or the man who begs when he has fallen
> (on his knees)?
> Oh, which is most to blame, although both have done wrong,
> the woman who sins for payment, or the man who pays for the sin?

> (¿Cuál mayor culpa ha tenido
> en una pasión errada,
> la que cae de rogada,
> o el que ruega de caído?
>
> ¿O ciál es más de culpar,
> aunque cualquiera mal haga,
> la que peca por la paga
> o el que paga por pecar?)

In another poem Sor Juana describes her own inner conflict this way:

> I am my own executioner, and I am my own prison,
> Who would think that the pain and the one who suffers pain
> would be the same thing?

> (De mi misma soy verdugo,
> y soy cárcel de mí misma,
> ¿quién vio que pena y penante
> una propia cosa sean?)[5]

132

Sor Juana was in a sense her own executioner; she created her own misery by daring to pursue the intellectual activity open to men and forbidden to women. Her poetry expresses very well the conflicts and frustrations felt by women then and now.

Not until the twentieth century do we find another woman writer who voices feminist concerns. A Latin American literary historian wrote in 1942 that "one of the most interesting single events in this contemporary period is the emergence of women in the realm of Spanish American letters. . . . Spanish America boasts a good number of distinguished twentieth-century poetesses."[6] Their poetry is not, however, feminist in the sense that it contains social or political implications. As Carmen Rosenbaum pointed out, "They used their newly-won freedom for expressing their thoughts more openly, for giving vent to their emotions--womanly thoughts and emotions that had, perhaps, long lain dormant, merely awaiting an opportunity to be freely articulated."[7] In this group Alfonsina Storni stands out as the exception who voices truly feminist concerns.

Alfonsina was born in Switzerland but moved to Argentina at a very early age. She was considered something of a radical in her time because she joined an itinerant theatrical company at the age of thirteen. At the age of twenty she had an illegitimate child whom she referred to as a "fruit of lawless love" and reared by herself. She frequented gatherings of writers at a time when it was not considered proper for a woman to form part of these circles, and she was criticized for her daring. She committed suicide in 1938 at the age of forty-six by hurling herself into the Río de la Plata.

The theme of oppression of women runs throughout her poetry. In a poem called "Peso ancestral" (Ancestral Weight), she says that her mother told her that the men of her family did not cry. Saying that, her mother shed a tear and it fell on the poet's mouth and was full of poison:

> Weak woman, poor woman who understands,
> I knew the pain of centuries upon drinking it.
> Oh, my soul cannot support
> All its weight.

> (Débil mujer, pobre mujer que entiende,
> dolor de siglos conocí al beberlo.
> Oh, el alma mía soportar no puede
> todo su peso.)[8]

No poet has expressed in a more moving way the tragic effects of sex stereotyping which is destructive of men and women alike. In the poem "Bien pudiera ser" (It Well Might Have Been) Alfonsina says that the women of her family have been silent, but that at times she saw in her mother fleeting indications of a desire to liberate herself from the confines of a male-dominated society; but these quickly changed to an expression of profound bitterness. Now the poet bears the weight:

> And all that, mordant, broken, mutilated,
> all that was locked up in her soul,
> I think that without wanting to I have freed it.

(Y todo eso mordiente, vencido, mutilado,
todo eso que se hallaba en su alma encerrado,
pienso que sin quererlo lo he libertado yo.)9

In a poem called "La que comprende" (She Who Understands) Alfonsina
describes a woman who is kneeling before a Christ figure, the weight of an
enormous sadness in her eyes and in her breast the weight of the child
about to be born. And she prays, "Father, may my child not be born female" (Señor, el hijo mío que no nazca mujer).

Like Sor Juana, Alfonsina cries out against the injustice of the
double standard in a poem called "Tú me quieres blanca" (You Want Me
White). She says to her lover that he can demand that she be pure when
he has cleansed himself of his egotism. Bitterness leads to irony and
anger. In the poem "Hombres pequeñitos" (Miserable Little Men) Alfonsina
vents her hostility toward men:

> I don't understand you either, but meanwhile
> open the cage, for I want to escape;
> miserable little man, I loved you half an hour,
> don't ask more of me.

> (Tampoco te entiendo, pero mientras tanto
> ábreme la jaula, que quiero escapar;
> hombre pequeñito, te amé media hora,
> no me pidas más.)10

The central theme of Alfonsina Storni is rebellion, rebellion against
the restricting bonds of convention of her sex and of the man's world of
Buenos Aires. She struggles with the conditioned feminine instinct to
surrender and her determination to remain free. Like Sor Juana she feels
at times totally frustrated with her role in life:

> I am the one who always lives her
> life incomplete . . .
> the one to whom things were given only partially in life.

> (Yo soy la que incompleta
> vive siempre su vida . . .
> que todo a medias se te dio en la vida.)11

She triumphs in the end, however, Unlike Sor Juana, Alfonsina did
not retreat and give in to society's demands. In her own criticism of her
work she recognizes some defects but concludes that she has to agree with
the current opinion: "Soy una gran poetisa" (I am a great poet).12 Alfonsina thus affirms herself as a woman and as a poet.

Since Alfonsina wrote, women have made significant gains socially
and politically in some Latin American countries, but feminist concerns
have no powerful literary voice. Hopefully women writers will pick up the
trail blazed by Sor Juana and Alfonsina and verbalize for their country-
women today's "protesta femenina."

Louisiana State University

Notes

[1]It is interesting to compare the "protesta femenina" in Latin America with the "querelle des femmes" in France as described by Germaine Brée in Women Writers in France: Variations on a Theme (New Brunswick: Rutgers University Press, 1973). As Sidonia Carmen Rosenbaum points out in Modern Women Poets of Spanish America (New York: Hispanic Institute, 1945), p. 20, "the course of women in literature has followed almost identical patterns everywhere."

[2]Sor Juana Inés de la Cruz, Respuesta a Sor Filotea de la Cruz, ed. Abreu Gómez (Mexico: La Voz nueva, 1929).

[3]Ludwig Pfandl, Sor Juana Inés de la Cruz, la décima musa de México (Mexico: Universidad Nacional Autónoma de México, 1963).

[4]Both the Spanish and the English translation come from the Penguin Book of Spanish Verse, ed. J. M. Cohen (Baltimore: Penguin, 1966), pp. 311-314.

[5]Poesías completas, ed. Ermilo Abreu Gómez, 2nd. ed. (Mexico: Ediciones Botas, 1948). The translations of this and all other poems which follow are mine.

[6]Arturo Torres-Ríoseco, The Epic of Latin American Literature (Berkeley and Los Angeles: University of California Press, 1961; originally printed in 1942), p. 120.

[7]Rosenbaum, p. 11.

[8]Languidez (Buenos Aires: Meriodión, 1959). First pub. 1920.

[9]Irremediablemente (Buenos Aires: Meriodión, 1957). First pub. 1919.

[10]Ibid.

[11]Ocre (Buenos Aires: Editorial Babel, 1925).

[12]Quoted by Rosenbaum, p. 227, from "Autodemolición," in Repertorio Americano, San José, Costa Rica, June 7, 1930.

Three Peninsular Novelists Comment on the Spanish Woman

by

Joan Cain

The information included in this article has not as yet been the subject matter of a course. It is the result of interviews with three Spanish women novelists whose work as women was one of my primary concerns. I asked each of them for her opinion regarding the role of women in to-day's world.

Carmen Kurtz, the oldest and most cosmopolitan of the three, be-lieves that the Spanish woman who wishes to play a specific role in her contemporary society is free to do so, but that most Spanish women, at least those of the middle class, choose not to do so. She feels that the Spanish man counts on this lack of interest and concern on the part of women. If a man knew that his wife would react to his behavior, he would govern himself accordingly, and life would be different. In the opinion of Señora Kurtz, the Spanish concept of marriage must change; it will do so only when women become as strong as men.

Marta Portal, a research scholar as well as a novelist, recognizes that women suffer a disadvantage, no matter what their social class or type of work may be. She believes, however, that the situation will change and that women will have achieved their ultimate goal when one speaks or writes not of the man or the woman, but of the person.

It is noteworthy that the protagonists in Marta Portal's 1966 prize-winning Planeta novel, A tientas y a ciegas, and in her last novel, Ladridos a la luna, are women. Their characters are developed by means of an interior monologue. Through it the reader becomes acquainted with other persons. The two women resemble each other, but the heroine of the second novel, published in 1970, has a much more complex personality.

Señora Portal introduced me to a possible text for a course in Spanish on women: Mujeres de España by Alyette Barbier. Published by Masson et Cie in France it consists of a series of readings about women followed by questions for student use.

The third novelist, Concha Alós, has concerned herself much more with women of the Spanish working classes, doubtless because she herself is a product of that group. Of the three authors interviewed, it is she who speaks the language of the movement for women's rights in Spain.

There existed in Barcelona not too long ago a periodical entitled Diario feminino. Concha Alós thought it ridiculous when she was asked to contribute articles. The response of working-class women, however, made her continue to do so until the newspaper ceased to exist. Señora Alós showed me a letter which had moved her greatly from a woman reader who scarcely knew how to write. She also provided me with copies of several articles, among them "Sus labores," "Y sin novio," and "Vencer y llorar." Señora Alós has written similar articles for La Vanguardia. At the time I visited her she was working on a Spanish translation of a revolutionary Italian feminist document.

Of these three writers Concha Alós is obviously the only one in-

volved in a Spanish feminist movement. How extensive it is or whether it
can even be considered such is unknown to me. All three women, however,
are cognizant of the new role of Spanish women and each is anxious to
play her part.

University of Southwestern Louisiana

Hispanic American Fiction and Drama Written by Women: Suggested Readings

by

Gabriela Mora

Designers of courses on Hispanic literature and on the problems of women can select from numerous works by Spanish and Latin American authors. The selection will depend on whether the literature of both Spain and Hispanic America are included and whether men as well as women writers are to be considered. The instructor who prefers working exclusively with material from Spain has a good point of departure in María del Pilar Oñate's El feminismo en la literatura española (Madrid: Espasa Calpe, 1938) and in Isabel Calvo's Antología biográfica de escritoras españolas (Madrid: Biblioteca Nueva, 1954). One must bear in mind, however, that many suitable works like La Celestina, La perfecta casada, Yerma, or La casa de Bernarda Alba are used in standard survey courses, and their inclusion would be a repetition limiting the opportunity to study more recent authors.

As for male writers, we see no disadvantage in including their works if these truly offer new insights into the problems of women. For example, some of Miguel de Unamuno's essays such as "A una aspirante a escritora" and "Nuestras mujeres" in Soliloquios y conversaciones (Buenos Aires: Espasa Calpe, 1942) can stimulate fruitful discussions. In courses based on the literatures of Spain and Latin America, novels like Cinco horas con Mario by Miguel Delibes (Barcelona: Destino, 1966) and Boquitas pintadas by Manuel Puig (Buenos Aires: Destino, 1966)--splendid presentations of ignorant bourgeois women with all the prejudices that enslave them and their men--can be effectively used in analyzing the situation of women in present-day societies.

The study of works by men, however, perpetuates the neglect that women writing in Spanish have suffered for so long, a situation made intolerable by the recent emergence in Latin America of so many high quality women publishing fiction, drama, and poetry. Therefore, we will restrict our suggestions to Hispanic American women writers and concentrate on prose fiction and drama published in this century. We will attempt to select those writers of recognized literary value and those works that in some ways illuminate aspects of the woman's world. As in any selection of this kind we cannot be comprehensive, and in all probability some names worthy of consideration have been omitted.

For the writers in the following bibliography the place and date of birth will be given whenever possible. Information about editions will refer to the first edition unless otherwise noted.

FICTION

Aguirre, Margarita (Chile, 1925). Her novel El huésped won the Argentinean prize Emecé for 1958. La culpa (Santiago: Zig-Zag, 1964) depicts the corruption of the upper class in Chile and portrays the fate of a girl who has been raped and is thrown out of her home by her father, a rich, brutal landowner. Although not Aguirre's best novel, it is of interest because of the problems treated.

Bombal, María Luisa (Chile, 1910) is one of the best known authors of Latin America. She has had an extraordinary influence on other writers since the publication of La última niebla (Buenos Aires: Sur, 1935), a poetic dreamlike story of unrequited love. Her second novel La amortajada (Buenos Aires: Sur, 1938. Trans. The Shrouded Woman, New York: Farrar and Straus, 1948),is a dead woman's recollection of her life and loves. Her well-written short story "El árbol" has a protagonist somewhat similar to Ibsen's Nora, and it has been reprinted in several anthologies. One of the many recent editions of La última niebla (Buenos Aires, Ed. Andina, 1971) includes "El árbol" and two other stories by Bombal. A warning: the translation The House of Mist (New York: Farrar and Straus, 1948) is not La última niebla. Apparently urged by the publisher, Bombal added new episodes, replaced the unhappy ending with a happy one, and transformed the moving, poetic original into sentimental mush.

Brunet, Marta (Chile, 1897-1967) is another woman writer with an established literary reputation in Latin America. She was awarded the Chilean National Prize of Literature in 1961. The works of Brunet usually portray strong peasant women who, despite living in male-dominated societies, manage to exert a powerful influence within the confines of the traditional family. María Rosa Flor del Quillén (1927) and Humo hacia el sur (1946) are cases in point. María Nadie (1957) describes the life of a young telephone operator suffering the pain of an unhappy love affair who comes to a provincial town only to be driven away by petty gossip. Brunet's short story "La soledad de la sangre" is a masterpiece about the lonely married life of a sensitive woman tied to a brutal man. All these works are found in Brunet's Obras completas (Santiago: Zig-Zag, 1963).

Bulrich, Silvina (Argentina, 1915) is a very prolific novelist and author of best sellers in her country. A strong advocate of women's rights, a passionate critic of bourgeois society, a destroyer of myths about love and marriage, her major works are very apt for a course dealing with women. Mañana digo basta (Buenos Aires: Sudamericana, 1968), Bodas de cristal and Un momento muy largo in Tres novelas (Buenos Aires: Sudamericana, 1966) illustrate very well her dominant themes. Bulrich's "Nota autobiográfica" published in Entre mis veinte y treinta años (Buenos Aires: Emecé, 1970) is a good introduction to her biography.

Castellanos, Rosario (Mexico, 1925) is one of the best writers of Hispanic America today. Besides being an excellent poet, she is also an accomplished novelist and essayist. Her novels Balún-Canán (Mexico City: Fondo de Cultura Económica, 1957. Tr. Irene Nicholson, New York: Vanguard, 1959) and Oficio de tinieblas (Mexico City: Joaquín Mortiz, 1962) have contributed to raising the literary quality of fiction portraying the lives and psychologies of Indians in a society dominated by whites and mestizos. Los convidados de agosto (Mexico City: Biblioteca Era, 1964) is a series of short stories about life in a provincial town where women are the principal victims of traditions and prejudices. The story that gives the book its title is a moving description of a spinster desperate to find a man. In Ciudad real (Jalapa: Universidad Veracruzana, 1960)--a powerful indictment against social injustices--the short story "Modesta Gómez" is a terrifying example of how poverty can deprive people (women in this case) of compassion and humanity. Album de familia (Mexico City: Joaquín Mortiz, 1971) includes four stories that question marriage, "good motherhood," and other relationships and roles with subtle irony and humor.

Dolujanoff, Emma (Mexico, 1922). Her novel La calle de fuego (Mexico City: Universidad Nacional Autónoma de México, 1966) focuses on two young male friends neglected by their rich, ill-suited parents. The portrayal of the mothers, empty persons addicted to love affairs and alcohol, should generate student discussion in a course on women.

Gallardo, Sara (Argentina, 1934). Her first novel Enero (Buenos Aires: Sudamericana, 1958) is a poignant and poetic story of a young, frightened girl made pregnant by a man she hardly knows and then has to marry. Eisejuaz (Buenos Aires: Sudamericana, 1971) portrays the saint-like agonies of an Indian, and although not directly related to women's problems the book deserves attention for its quality.

Garro, Elena (Mexico, 1920) is an excellent dramatist, novelist, and short story teller. Her novel Los recuerdos del porvenir (Mexico City: Joaquín Mortiz, 1963. Tr. L. C. Simms, Recollections of Things To Come, Austin: University of Texas Press, 1969) compares well with the best recent Latin American narratives. The book combines brutal reality and poetic fantasy, recreating a period of Mexican history where one of the social ills is the economic and emotional dependency of women whose lives have not been altered by the Revolution. The same poetic quality is found in La semana de colores (Jalapa: Universidad Veracruzana, 1964), a collection of short stories. One of them, "La culpa es de los Tlaxcaltecas," is a small literary gem that fits well into a course linking good writing and women's problems.

Guido, Beatriz (Argentina, 1924) is a well-known contemporary novelist. Her books depict the decadence and corruption of the upper class under Peron's regime of the fifties. La casa del ángel (Buenos Aires: Emecé, 1955. Tr. Joan C. Mac Lean, The House of the Angel, New York: McGraw-Hill, 1957) and El incendio y las vísperas (Buenos Aires: Losada, 1964. Tr. A. D. Towers, End of a Day, New York: Scribner, 1966) are provocative books about love and politics.

Hernández, Luisa Josefina (Mexico, 1928) is a renowned dramatist and prolific novelist. El valle que elegimos (Mexico City: Joaquín Mortiz, 1965) and La noche exquisita (Jalapa: Universidad Veracruzana, 1965) deal with the personal problems of artists, some of them lesbians and homosexuals. We prefer La plaza de Puerto Santo (Mexico City: Fondo de Cultura Económica, 1961), a delightful story describing life in a small town. Women and men are not romanticized in this novel, and their human frailties are observed with subtle humor and irony rarely found in books critical of society.

Lombardo de Caso, María (Mexico, 1905-1964) received favorable reviews for
La culebra tapó el río (Jalapa: Universidad Veracruzana, 1962), a
short novel about an Indian child living under miserable conditions
in a Mexican village. Una luz en la otra orilla (Mexico City: Fondo
de Cultura Económica, 1959) is a somewhat melodramatic but exciting
story of women at the mercy of men who are heartless criminals.

Lynch, Marta (Argentina, 1924), preoccupied with love and politics, is a
frank and perceptive observer of erotic experiences of women. La
señora Ordóñez (Buenos Aires: Sudamericana, 1967), a novel about a
middle-aged woman living in Peronist Argentina and enslaved by her
passion for a younger man, reveals some nontraditional aspects of
marriage and motherhood. Cuentos de colores (Buenos Aires: Sudamericana, 1970) is a collection of short stories in which women's sexuality is a dominant theme. Among them "Domingo por la tarde," "La
pieza de alquiler," and "Cuentos de colores" are splendid vehicles
for the discussion of women's problems. El cruce del río (Buenos
Aires: Sudamericana, 1972) is a novel divided in two parts. In the
first a guerrilla fighter recalls the episodes of the ambush in
which he is killed. The magnificent second half, told by the mother
of the young man, shows a strong, good-humored, earthy woman of the
lower middle class learning to survive without a man and eventually
becoming a political activist.

Parra, Teresa de la (Venezuela, 1890-1936). Her novel Ifigenia was published in Paris in 1924 and has been reprinted several times (an in-
expensive edition---Caracas: Monte Avila, 1972). The book tells of
an eighteen-year-old girl who, because of economic and social pressure, has to marry a man she despises. Written in the first person,
the style imitates very well the language of an educated, upper-class
young lady who feigns sophistication to cover her inabilities and
fears.

Poniatowska, Elena (Mexico, 1933) is one of the most successful journalists of her country. Her reputation as a novelist was established
with Hasta no verte Jesús mío (Mexico City: Biblioteca Era, 1969,
now in its 12th edition), a powerful portrayal of the miseries of a
poor, illiterate, generous woman whose courage to survive has nothing to do with the traditional image of the "weaker" sex. The book
is also an unusual document about customs, prejudices, and events
of Mexican history.

Serrana, Elisa (Chile) writes novels that sell well, perhaps because of her
ability to narrate extramarital affairs of women searching for satisfaction beyond social and economic status. Her protagonists belong
to the Chilean upper class, and their empty lives reveal deep social
malaise even though the author may not have intended to write social
criticism. Las tres caras de un sello (1960), Chilena, casada, sin
profesión (1963) and Una (1964), novels published by Zig-Zag (Santiago), make easy reading.

Traba, Marta (Argentina, 1930, resides in Colombia). Originally a critic
of art, she is rapidly becoming a well-known novelist. Las ceremo-

nias del verano (Buenos Aires: Jorge Alvarez, 1966) won the Casa de las Americas Prize for novels in 1966. This work and the short stories included in Pasó así (Montevideo: Arca, 1968) expose the painful struggles of poor, sensitive women to survive in sordid surroundings.

Some other works of fiction related to women's problems are:

Amor, Guadalupe (Mexico). Yo soy mi casa. Mexico City: Fondo de Cultura Económica, 1957.

Canto, Estela (Argentina). Isabel entre las plantas. Buenos Aires: Falbo, 1966.

Díaz Lozano, Argentina (Honduras). Peregrinaje. Santiago, Chile: Zig-Zag, 1946.

Dueñas, Guadalupe (Mexico). Tiene la noche un árbol. Mexico City: Fondo de Cultura Económica, 1958.

García Iglesias, Sara (Mexico). Exilio. Mexico City: Fondo de Cultura Económica, 1957.

Silva, Clara (Uruguay). El alma y los perros. Buenos Aires: Compañia General Fabril Editora, 1971.

DRAMA

Latin American dramatists, whether men or women, find it difficult to publish their plays. Therefore, several works that could be useful for women's studies are available only in mimeographed form seldom found outside the countries in which they originated. With this in mind we will consider those women playwrights whose dramas are more accessible and have some relevance to the subject of women.

Aguirro, Isidora (Chile, 1919) has had many successfully produced plays in Chile. From her first period of light comedies, Carolina (Teatro chileno actual, Santiago: Zig-Zag, 1966) is a one-act play about a lovely, somewhat scatterbrained girl going on vacation, fearful she has left the kitchen stove lighted. This piece was translated and published in Best Short Plays 1959-1960 (Boston: Beacon Press, 1966). Later, inspired by the epic realism of Brecht, Aguirro began writing plays of social protest. These are best exemplified by Los papeleros (Mapocho, II, No. 4, 1964) in which the leader of a revolt against an abusive boss is a woman.

Bidart Sanzi, Blanca (Uruguay) has two published plays dealing with women: Nacarina and Una mujer está bordando (both in one volume, Montevideo: Ed. Letras, 1946). Nacarina concerns a spiritual girl of happy disposition who does not fit the narrow reality of her native town and falls victim to the jealousy of the villagers.

Gambaro, Griselda (Argentina), a distinguished writer of fiction, is the best known female dramatist of her country today. Her plays El desatino (Buenos Aires: Instituto del Teatro, 1965) and Los siameses (Buenos Aires: Ed. Insurrexit, 1967) deal with the problems of individual freedom and the cruelty of man. William I. Oliver, who

142

translated El Campo says of Gambaro's plays: "I was stunned by their brutality and vigor, their economy of means, and their cruel, almost Strindbergian assessment of life. Miss Gambaro shows promise of becoming one of the most powerful playwrights in Latin America." (Voices of Change in the Spanish American Theater, Austin: University of Texas Press, 1971, p. 49. This anthology includes Gambaro's The Camp).

Garro, Elena (Mexico, 1920) is one of the outstanding dramatists in contemporary Mexico. Her short plays Andarse por las ramas, Los pilares de doña Blanca, and Un hogar sólido published in Un hogar sólido (Jalapa: Universidad Veracruzana, 1959) mark an important evolution of the Mexican theater from a pure naturalistic mode to a more poetic and symbolic one. The one-act play La señora en su balcón in Teatro Breve Hispanoamericano (Madrid: Aguilar, 1970) presents a woman at different ages—8, 20, 40, and 50 years—facing the same problem of alienation until she commits suicide.

Hernández, Josefina (Mexico, 1928) is one of the most prolific and best-known dramatists in her country. Her plays have been praised for their sobriety and lack of sentimentality. Los frutos caidos in Teatro mexicano del siglo XX, III (Mexico City: Fondo de Cultura Económica, 1957), her most celebrated work, succeeds in creating an oppressive atmosphere of hopelessness in which the protagonist—an unhappy remarried divorcée—is afraid to love again. Los huéspedes reales in Teatro mexicano del siglo XX, IV (Mexico City: Fondo de Cultura Económica, 1970) used the Electra complex as a major theme in a portrayal of two ill-matched couples. The Mulatto's Orgy, a play with impressive theatrical possibilities, was translated and published in English by William I. Oliver in Voices of Change in the Spanish American Theater (Austin: University of Texas Press, 1971).

Lehman, Marta (Argentina, 1922-1965). Her plays are published in Teatro (Buenos Aires: Farbo, 1966). Of this collection, Lázaro, perhaps the best work, is a well-constructed piece about fidelity and the differences between generations. El secreto, a one-act play with a contrived ending, has two possessive women, a mother and her daughter-in-law, facing the suicide of their son/husband. The other plays seem more suitable for the cinema than for the stage because of their interior monologues and many scene changes.

Requena, María Asunción (Chile) generally writes about historical subjects. Fuerte Bulnes in Teatro, No. 5 (Teatro Experimental de la Universidad de Chile, 1955) and Ayayema in Teatro chileno (Madrid: Aguilar, 1970) have to do with the struggle to colonize Magallanes, Chile's most southern province. The play El camino más largo, still unpublished, was inspired by the life of Ernestina Pérez, the first woman physician of Chile.

Roepke, Gabriela (Chile) is another good dramatist with few plays published. Una mariposa blanca in Teatro chileno (Santiago: Zig-Zag, 1966), a poetic one-act fantasy about an old woman looking for a memory in the lost-and-found department of a store, has been printed in English in <u>Best Short Plays 1959-1960</u> (Boston: Beacon Press, 1960). Also published are three one-act plays written in the mode of the theater of the absurd under the title <u>Martes 13</u> (Mapocho, No. 22, 1970). Among several other works presented with success in Chile but available only in mimeographed form is <u>Juegos silenciosos</u> (1959). This fine play portrays three frustrated spinsters whose social prejudice and lack of money drive them to plot a crime.

Sandor, Malena (Argentina, d. 1968). Her works were collected in <u>Teatro completo</u> (Buenos Aires: Ed. Talía, 1969). Several of Sandor's plays have been successfully staged, but they do not read well today. An ardent advocate of women's rights, her pieces such as <u>Una mujer libre</u>, <u>Tu vida y la mía</u>, and <u>Yo me divorcio papá</u>, have women struggling to maintain their independence and dignity, but the 'message' is too obvious, and there is no poetry nor subtlety to be found in them.

Vilalta, Maruxa (born in Barcelona, 1932, but a long-time resident of Mexico). Preoccupied with social issues, Vilalta follows the theater of the absurd in <u>Cuestión de narices</u> in <u>Teatro mexicano del siglo XX</u>, V (Mexico City: Fondo de Cultura Económica, 1970), a protest against wars, and in <u>Esta noche amándonos tanto</u> (Mexico City: Organismo de promoción internacional de la cultura, 1970), an attack on the selfish, bourgeois concept of marriage. <u>Un país feliz</u>, written in a more realistic vein, denounces political dictatorship. This play has been published in <u>5 obras de teatro</u> (Mexico City: Secretaría de Educación, 1970) with four other works one of which, <u>Un día loco</u>, is a monologue by a woman telling of her dreams and the dullness of her everyday life.

Some other plays related to women's problems are:

Algarra, María Luisa (Mexico). <u>Los años de prueba</u>. <u>Concurso Nacional de Teatro</u>, <u>Obras premiadas 1954-1955</u>. Mexico City: Instituto Nacional de Bellas Artes.

Castillo Ledón, Amalia (Mexico). <u>Una comedia</u>. <u>Cuatro siglos de literatura mexicana</u>. Mexico City: Ed. Leyenda, 1946.

Guzmán, Julia (Mexico). <u>Quiero vivir mi vida</u>. <u>Teatro mexicano contemporáneo</u>. Mexico City: Ed. Sociedad General de Autores de Mexico, No. 12·, n.d.

Ocampo, María Luisa (Mexico). <u>La virgen fuerte</u>. <u>Teatro mexicano contemporáneo</u>. Mexico City: Ed. Sociedad General de Autores de Mexico, No. 20, 1943.

Urueta, Margarita (Mexico). <u>El señor perro</u>. <u>Teatro mexicano del siglo XX</u>, V. Mexico: Fondo de Cultura Económica, 1970.

The City College of The University of New York

Maryellen Bieder
Department of Romance Languages

Syracuse University
Syracuse, New York
Spring 1974

IMAGES OF THE WOMAN IN THE SPANISH NOVEL, 1880-1920

Designed to offer the undergraduate Spanish major a look at the
range of female "types" and the social alternatives presented in the
Spanish novel, this course introduces students to female characters
created by what critics generally concede to be the masters of the traditional Spanish novel. Within the limits of the readings, the course attempts to capture the major literary presentations, from the naturalistic
determinism of Emilia Pardo Bazán's Los pazos de Ulloa to the popular
legend à la Valle-Inclán in Flor de santidad. The options available to
a strong female character by the social context of the novel are contrasted in Misericordia, La tía Tula, El mundo es ansí, Tristana, and
Memorias de un solterón. These novels confront the student with the
variety--and inherent limitations--of the female image but there is no
attempt to establish rigid compartmentalization of these images.

Mildred Boyer
Foreign Language Education Center

University of Texas
Austin, Texas
Fall 1973

WOMEN WRITERS OF HISPANIC LITERATURE

Spn. 385M, Studies in <u>Spanish</u> Literature since 1700,

    Crosslisted with:

Spn. 380K, Studies in <u>Spanish American</u> Literature since 1700.

    This course will strive toward an inclusive view of the contribu-
tion of women to Spanish and Spanish American creative literature.

    The precursors, Santa Teresa de Jesús (1515-1582) and Sor Juana Inés
de la Cruz (1651-1695), will be dealt with as well as outstanding nine-
teenth- and twentieth-century figures: Fernán Caballero, Rosalía de Castro
Emilia Pardo Bazán, Carmen Laforet, and Ana María Matute for Spain; Gertrudis Gómez de Avellaneda, Alfonsina Storni, Gabriela Mistral, and Rosario
Castellanos for Latin America.

    Works will be examined both as literature and as creations by women
in an Hispanic society: that is, the class will attempt to define what, if
any, is the effect of the "condición de mujer" in the artistic production
of these writers.

    Each student will prepare a term project (paper and oral presenta-
tion) on one female writer.

Prerequisite: graduate standing in Spanish. Qualified minorities (including men) welcome.

Sara E. Cohen
Department of Hispanic and
  Italian Studies

SUNY
Albany, New York
Spring 1974

TWENTIETH-CENTURY SPANISH WOMEN WRITERS

Elena Quiroga. <u>Viento del Norte.</u> Barcelona: Colección Ancora y Delfín 58

Gabriela Mistral. <u>Desolación</u>. Austral

Ana M. Matute. <u>Primera Memoria</u>. Barcelona: Ancora

Carmen Laforet. <u>Nada</u>. Oxford University Press

Alfonsina Storni. <u>Antología Poética</u>. Austral

Rosario Castellanos. <u>Album de familia</u>. Joaquín Mortiz. Mexico

Carmen Conde. <u>Derribado arcángel</u>. Madrid: Colección Literatura Arte

Víctor García   Antioch College
Department of Foreign Civilizations   Yellow Springs, Ohio
    and Languages   Spring 1973

CONTEMPORARY LATIN AMERICAN WRITING

(Translated from the original)

I. Course description

This course will first focus on the social problems and political
implications envisaged by these women writers. Secondly, it will emphasize the role played by Latin-American women in their respective societies.
Thirdly, the social and historical causes which have contributed to their
oppression will be analyzed: the feudal system of colonization, the In-
quisition and the Catholic church, machismo, etc. Finally, the literary
value of each work will be studied with respect both to form and content.

II. Requirements

Full participation will be required. The students must read all the
works assigned each week. Each student will present an oral report on a
selected topic of his/her choice always related to the theme under discussion. Finally, each student will write an evaluation of the course.

III. Asignaciones semanales (una reunión de tres horas):

1a. semana: Introducción: La sociedad indígena; la influencia española;
     La Colonia; La Inquisición; Sor Juana Inés de la Cruz; La indepen-
     dencia.

2a. semana: Aves sin nido de Clorinda Matto de Turner, "La mujer en
     Perú" (leer artículos en reserva). "El machismo en Hispanoamérica."

3a. semana: Poemas escogidos de Juana de Ibarbourou, Las Lenguas
     de diamante (de la misma autora) (Reporte oral).

4a. semana: Poemas escogidos de Alfonsina Storni, Poemas escogidos de
     Delmira Agustini, "El gaucho en la Argentina," "La mujer en la Argen-
     tina" (leer artículos en reserva). Eva Perón (Reporte oral).

5a. semana: Poemas escogidos de Gabriela Mistral (Premio Nobel de litera-
     tura, 1945). Reporte oral. La mujer en Chile (artículos en la
     reserva).

6a. semana: La amortajada de María Luisa Bombal, El cepillo de dientes
     (1er acto) de Jorge Díaz. Allende y la mujer en Chile.

7a. semana: "Máscaras mexicanas" de El laberinto de la soledad (Capítulo
     II de Octavio Paz). "Los hijos de la Malinche" de El laberinto de
     soledad (Capítulo IV de Octavio Paz). "La Malinche" poema de
     Rosario Castellanos. La literatura chicana sobre la mujer y el
     machismo.

8a. semana: "La mujer mexicana del Siglo XIX," Rosario Castellanos.
     Los convidades de agosto de Rosario Castellanos. Reportes orales
     sobre la mujer en México (Ver artículos en reserva). Reporte oral.

9a. semana: La primera batalla de Luisa Josefina Hernández. La noche de Tlatelolo de Elena Poniatowska. Reporte oral.

10a. semana: Hasta no verte Jesús mío de Elena Poniatowska. "La abnegación: una virtud loca" de Rosario Castellanos. La gruta del sueño de Gloria Inés Arias Nieto. "La mujer en Colombia."

11a. semana: Las colombianas ante la renovación universitaria de Lucia Cohen. "La mujer: la doble opresión" de Juan Angel Silén. NACLA "Women Struggle in Latin America" (Brasil, Cuba, etc.) Conclusión.

Bibliografía: Artículos sobre la mujer en América Latina.

Acevedo, Marta y Cristina Laurell, "Sobre el sexismo mexicano: Primeras consideraciones," (I) Siempre. "La ofensiva patriarcal y el movimiento de la mujer," (II) Siempre.

Anónimo. "The Birth Place of Machismo," Ms.   Vol. I, No. 4 (October 1972), pp. 12-17.

Brito de Martí, Esperanza. "La gran batalla de la mujer por la igualdad," Siempre (No. 1). "La intelegencia es unisex," Siempre (No. 1). "El movimiento feminista en México," Siempre. "Yo acuso al gobierno y al PRI de antifeministas," Siempre.

Castellanos, Rosario. "La mujer mexicana en el siglo XIX." "La abnegación: una virtud loca," Diorama de la cultura (Suplemento dominical de Excelsior, Domingo 21 de febrero de 1971).

Cruchaga de Walker, Rosa y Lilian Caln. "¿Quién es la mujer chilena?" Mundo Nuevo, No. 46 (April 1970), pp. 33-38.

Domingo, Alberto. "Pues ahora la mujer pretende igualarse al hombre." "Carta de una madre brasileña," Siempre. "Se ofrecen en venta dos muchachas con hambre."

Fernandez, Rosa Marta. "La mujer mexicana y la conciencia de la opresión," Siempre.

Jofre Barroso, Haydee M. "La mujer Argentina," Mundo Nuevo, No. 46 (April 1970), pp. 42-50.

Paz, Octavio. El laberinto de la soledad (Labyrinth of Solitude), Capítulos II y IV.

Peraza Landero, Rocío. "Imágenes y anti-imágenes de la mujer mexicana," Siempre.

Portugal, Ana María. "¿La peruana, 'Tapada,' sin manto?" Mundo Nuevo, No. 46 (April 1970), pp. 20-27.

Rascón, Maria Antoineta. "La mujer mexicana como hecho político: la precursora, la militante," Siempre.

Several authors. "El machismo en Hispanoamérica." "La Causa: la Mujer," in Aztlán: An Anthology of Mexican American Literature. Comp. Luis Valdex. New York: Knopf, 1972.

Silén, Juan Angel. "La mujer: la doble opresión," <u>Hacia una visión positiva del puertorriqueño</u>. Rio Piedras, Editorial Edil, 1970.

Special Issue. "Women in Struggle," <u>NACLA</u> (North American Congress on Latin America), Vol. VI, No. 10 (December 1972), Cuba, Chile y Brazil.

Gabriela Mora
Romance Language Department

City College, CUNY
New York City
Spring, 1974

WOMAN IN HISPANIC LITERATURE (Spanish 311)

Consideration of the artistic value and social meaning of selected novels, short stories, essays, poems, and plays by significant Spanish and Hispanic American writers who portray the situation of women in particular times and places. Works of the twentieth century are emphasized. The course, conducted in Spanish, is for men and women concerned with literature and the problems of society.

I. Lectura mínima obligatoria para participar en clases:

Bombal, María Luisa.	La última niebla
Bulrich, Silvina.	Tres novelas
Castellanos, Rosario.	Los convidados de agosto
Castilla del Pino, Carlos.	Cuatro ensayos sobre la mujer
De la Parra, Teresa.	Ifigenia
Delibes, Miguel.	Cinco horas con Mario

Se leerá además el siguiente material mimeografiado:

Marta Brunet, "La soledad de la sangre"; Rosario Castellanos, "Modesta Gómez"; Elena Garro, "a señora en su balcon"; Carmen Laforet, "El veraneo"; Miguel de Unamuno, "Nuestras mujeres," "A una escritora"; selecciones de Sor Juana Inés de la Cruz, Delmira Agustini, Alfonsina Storni, Juana de Ibarbourou, Gabriela Mistral y Julia de Burgos.

II. Programa de trabajo:

Febrero	4	Organización del curso
	6	Explicaciones sobre bibliografía
	8	Fray Luis de León, La perfecta casada (selecciones)
	11	Miguel de Unamuno, "Nuestras mujeres"
	13	" " " , "A una escritora"
	15	Sor Juana Inés de la Cruz (selecciones)
	20	Delmira Agustini, Alfonsina Storni (selecciones)
	22	Juana de Ibarbourou, Julia de Burgos (selecciones)
	25	María Luisa Bombal, La última niebla
	27	" " " " " " (take home exam)
Marzo	1	Gabriela Mistral (selecciones)
	4	Carmen Laforet, "El veraneo"
	6	Marta Brunet, "La soledad de la sangre"
	8	Rosario Castellanos, "Modesta Gómez"
	11	Teresa de la Parra, Ifigenia
	13	" " " " "
	15	Silvina Bulrich, Bodas de cristal
	18	" " " " "
	20	" " , Un momento muy largo
	22	Rosario Castellanos, Los convidados de agosto
	25	" " , "El viudo Román" (Los convidados)
	27	" " , "Las amistades efímeras" (Los convidados)
	29	Examen

151

Abril	1	Elena Garro, <u>La señora en su balcón</u>
	3	" " " " " "
	5	Miguel Delibes, <u>Cinco horas con Mario</u>
	15	" " " " "
	17	C. Castilla del Pino, <u>Cuatro ensayos sobre la mujer</u>
	19	" " " " " " " "

Take home exam

	22	Informe lectura individual. Sara Gallardo: <u>Enero</u>
	24	Informe. Marta Lynch, <u>La señora Ordoñez</u>
	26	" Elena Garro, <u>Los recuerdos del porvenir</u>
	29	" Elena Poniatowska, <u>Hasta no verte Jesús mío</u>
Mayo	1	" Rosario Castellanoz, <u>Balún Canán</u>
	3	" Marta Brunet, <u>María Nadie</u>
	6	" Carmen Martín Gaite, <u>Entre visillos</u>
	8	" María Luisa Bombal, <u>La amortajada</u>
	10	" Luisa J. Hernández, <u>La plaza de Puerto Santo</u>
	13	" Margarita Aguirre, <u>La culpa</u>
	15	" Silvina Bulrich, <u>Mañana digo basta</u>
	17	" Beatriz Guido, <u>La casa del ángel</u>
	20	Resumen final. Entrega de trabajos escritos

III. <u>Bibliografía para informe de lectura individual</u>:

Aguirre, Margarita (Chile).	<u>La culpa</u>
Amor, Guadalupe (México).	<u>Yo soy mi casa</u>
Bombal, María Luisa (Chile).	<u>La amortajada</u>
Brunet, Marta (Chile).	<u>María Nadie</u>
Bulrich, Silvina (Argentina).	<u>Mañana digo basta</u>
Canto, Estela (Argentina).	<u>Isabel entre las plantas</u>
Castellanos, Rosario (México).	<u>Balún Canán</u>
	<u>Oficio de tinieblas</u>
	<u>Album de familia</u>
Díaz Lozano, Argentina(Honduras).	<u>Peregrinaje</u>
Dolujanoff, Emma (México).	<u>La Calle del fuego</u>
García Iglesias, Sara (México).	<u>Exilio</u>
Gallardo, Sara (Argentina).	<u>Enero</u>
	<u>Eisejuaz</u>
Garro, Elena (México).	<u>Los recuerdos del porvenir</u>
Guido, Beatriz (Argentina).	<u>La casa del ángel</u>
	<u>El incendio y las vísperas</u>
Hernández, Luisa Josefina	<u>La plaza de Puerto Santo</u>
(México)	<u>El lugar donde crece la hierba</u>
Lombardo Caso, María (México).	<u>Una luz en la otra orilla</u>
Loynaz, Dulce María (Cuba).	<u>Jardín</u>
Lynch, Marta (Argentina).	<u>La señora Ordoñez</u>
	<u>El cruce del río</u>
	<u>Cuentos de colores</u>
Oreamuno, Yolanda (Costa Rica).	<u>La ruta de su evasión</u>
Parra, Teresa de la (Venezuela).	<u>Las memorias de Mama Blanca</u>
Petit, Magdalena (Chile).	<u>La Quintrala</u>
Poniatowska, Elena (México).	<u>Hasta no verte Jesús mío</u>

Puig, Manuel (Argentina).	Boquitas pintadas
Silva, Clara (Uraguay).	El alma y los perros
Traba, Marta (Argentina/Colombia).	Las ceremonias del verano

Autoras españolas

Ballesteros, Mercedes.	La cometa y el eco
Espina, Concha.	La ñiña de Luzmela
	La esfinge maragata
Laforet, Carmen.	La isla y sus demonios
Martín Gaite, Carmen.	Entre visillos
Matute, Ana María.	Fiesta al Noroeste
Medio, Dolores.	Diario de una maestra
Pardo Bazán, Emilia.	Doña Milagros
Quiroga, Elena.	La soledad sonora
	Plácida la joyen y otras narraciones
Soriano, Elena.	Mujer y hombre

Nélida Norris
Department of Languages and Linguistics

Florida Atlantic University
Boca Raton, Florida
Spring 1974
Fall 1970 (Univ. of Miami)

TWENTIETH-CENTURY WOMEN NOVELISTS OF SPANISH AMERICA

The following novels are to be read thoroughly and discussed in class in detail:

Clorinda Matto de Turner. _Aves sin nido_.

Gertrudis Gómez de Avellaneda. _Sab_.

Teresa de la Parra. _Ifigenia_.
_____. _Memorias de Mamá Blanca_.

Marta Brunet. _María Nadie_.

María Luisa Bombal. _La última niebla_.
_____. _La amortajada_.

Rosario Castellanos. _Oficio de tinieblas_.

Elena Garro. _Los recuerdos del porvenir_.

Beatriz Guido. _El incendio y las vísperas_.

ASSIGNMENTS: Two oral reports are required of each student during the semester based on outside reading of novels written by twentieth-century women novelists and one written report (not to exceed 20 pages) with an accompanying bibliography to be handed in at the end of the course.

Anson C. Piper
Department of Romance Languages

Williams College
Williamstown, Massachusetts
Spring 1973

LA MUJER ESCRITORA EN EL MUNDO HISPÁNICO

Programa del curso

Semana I
1. Introducción al curso

Semana II
1. Santa Teresa de Jesús, Las Moradas (trozos).
2. Sor Juana Inés de la Cruz, Poemas escogidos.

Semana III
1. Fernán Caballero, La Familia de Alvareda, Parte I.
2. "   "   "   "   "   "   , Parte II.

Semana IV
1. "   "   "   "   "   "   , Parte III.
2. Rosalía de Castro, Obra poética, Introducción
                        En las orillas del Sar, pp. 135-146.

Semana V
1. "   "   "   "   "   "   "   pp. 146-156.
2. Emilia Pardo Bazán, Los pazos de Ulloa, Cap. 1-6.

Semana VI
1. "   "   "   "   "   "   "   , Cap. 7-13.
2. "   "   "   "   "   "   "   , Cap. 14-20.

Semana VII
1. "   "   "   "   "   "   "   , Cap. 21-fin.
2. Examen de una hora.

Semana VIII
1. Gabriela Mistral, Desolación.
2. "   "   "

Semana IX
1. Carmen Laforet, Nada, Cap. 1-7.
2. "   "   "   , Cap. 8-16.

Semana X
1. "   "   "   , Cap. 17-fin.
2. Ana María Matute, Historias de la Artámila, pp. 7-56.

Semana XI
1. "   "   "   "   "   "   "   , pp. 57-104.
2. "   "   "   "   "   "   "   , pp. 105-fin.

Los últimos días del curso serán dedicados a la preparación
individual del examen general.

Marcia L. Welles
Department of Spanish

Barnard College
New York City
Spring 1973

WOMAN AS CHARACTER AND AUTHOR (Spanish 11y)

S. I

Selecciones de Alfonso X, Las Siete Partidas (1256-1263) y Libro
de los engaños e los assayamientos de las mugeres (trad. al español 1253).

S. II

Selecciones de El Conde Lucanor de D. Juan Manuel (Enxemplo XXVII
"De lo que acontesció a un Emperador et a don Alvar Fáñez Minaya con
sus mugeres").

S. III

Selecciones de: Fr. Hernando de Talavera (1428-1507), De como se
ha de ordenar el tiempo para que sea bien expendido;

Alfonso Martínez de Toledo, Arcipreste de Talavera, El Corbacho, o
Reprobación del amor mundano (1438);

Pedro Torrellas, Coplas de maldezir de las mugeres y la respuesta
de Suero de Ribera, Coplas en defensión de las donas;

Juan Rodríguez de la Cámara (o del Pardón), El triunfo de las donas
(antes de 1445).

S. IV

Selecciones de La perfecta casada (1583) de Fr. Luis de León.

Santa Teresa de Jesús, Prosa escogida (Ed. Ebro).

S. V

Selecciones de Quevedo.

Lope de Vege, La vengadora de las mugeres (1621); también Agustín
Moreto, El desdén con el desdén (1654) trata el mismo tema.

Doña María de Zayas y Sotomayor, Novelas ejemplares y amorosas
(1637) (Ed. Alianza).

Sor Juana Inés de la Cruz, Antología (Ed. Anaya).

S. VI

Feijóo, "Defensa de las mugeres" en Teatro crítico universal (1726-
1739).

Mención de Leandro Fernández de Moratín, El viejo y la niña (1790)
y El sí de las niñas (1806).

S. VII

Selecciones de Rosalía de Castro, En las orillas del Sar (1884).

Selección de cuentos de Emilia Pardo Bazán:
    "Paracaídas" en Cuentos nuevos (1894).
    "La culpable" y "La novia fiel" en Cuentos de amor (1898).

"Feminista" en Otros cuentos (1909).
y artículos como
"Mujeres" en Cuarenta días en la Exposición.

Concepción Arenal, La mujer del porvenir (en O.C., IV, 1894-1902).

Mención de Clorinda Matto de Turner, Aves sin nido (1889).

S. VIII
Postmodernismo: Selecciones de la poesía de Delmira Agustini (1886-1914), Alfonsina Storni (1892-1938), Juana de Ibarbouru (1895-), y Gabriela Mistral (1889-1957).

Epoca contemporánea

Novela: María Luisa Bombal, La última niebla. Ed. Andina (1935).
           Silvina Bullrich, Bodas de cristal. Ed. Sudamericana (1953).
                            Mañana digo basta. "   "   (1968).
           Elisa Serrana, Chilena casada, sin profesión. Ed. Zig-Zag (1963).
           Luisa Josefina Hernández, Nostalgia de Troya. Ed. Siglo XXI
                (1970).

Cuento: Ana María Matute, Los niños tontos. Ed. Destino (1956).

Poesía: Selecciones de Julia de Burgos (1917-1953), Gloria Fuertes
           (1918-), Angela Figuera Aymerich (1902-), María Beneyto (1925-).

Teatro: Obras de Maruxa Vilalta y Magdalena Mondragón.

Ann E. Wiltrout   Mississippi State University
Department of Foreign Languages   Spring 1974

WOMEN IN HISPANIC LITERATURE (FL 3003)

Catalogue description:

Women in Hispanic Literature. No prerequisites. Three lectures. A thematic study of women as literary characters and as authors as presented in representative works of eight centuries of Spanish-speaking countries.

Detailed Course Outline:

I. Middle Ages.
    A. Juan Ruiz, Archpriest of Hita, Book of Good Love, selections.
    B. Don Juan Manuel, Count Lucanor, selections.
    C. Selection of ballads.

II. Renaissance, Golden Age, and Baroque.
    A. Fernando de Rojas, La Celestina, lectures.
    B. Saint Teresa of Ávila, selections.
    C. Miguel de Cervantes, Don Quixote.
    D. Pedro Calderón de la Barca, one play.
    E. Sister Juana Inés de la Cruz, selections.

III. 18th Century.
    A. Father Benito Jerónimo Feijóo, "Defense of Women," lecture.
    B. Leandro Fernández de Moratín, Maiden's Consent.

IV. 19th Century and Generation of 1898.
    A. Gustavo Adolfo Bécquer, poetry selections.
    B. Fernán Caballero, lecture.
    C. Benito Pérez Galdós, Compassion.
    D. Leopoldo Alas, La Regenta, lecture.
    E. Emilia Pardo Bazán, lecture.
    F. José Martínez Ruiz, Doña Inés, lecture.

V. Modern and Contemporary.
    A. Federico García Lorca, one play.
    B. Gabriela Mistral, Nobel Prize winner, poetry selections.
    C. Alfonsina Storni and Delmira Agustini, poetry selections.
    D. Ana María Matute, First Memory, lecture.

Texts:

Calderón de la Barca, Pedro. Four Plays. New York: Hill and Wang, 1961.
Cervantes Saavedra, Miguel de. Don Quixote de la Mancha. Trans. P. A.
    Motteux. New York: Bigelow, n.d.
Fernández de Moratín, Leandro. Maiden's Consent, trans. Harriet de Onís.
    New York: Barron, 1962.
García Lorca, Federico. Three Tragedies. New York: New Directions, 1956.

Pérez Galdós, Benito. _Compassion_. Trans. Toby Talbot. N.Y.: Ungar, 1962.
Highlights of Spanish Literature. Eds. Seymour Resnick and Jeanne Pasmantier. New York: Ungar, 1963.

Bibliography:

I. Anthologies and histories of literature.

Brenan, Gerald. _The Literature of the Spanish People_. 2nd ed. Cam-
bridge: Cambridge University Press, 1953.
Chandler, Richard and Kessel Schwartz. _A New History of Spanish Litera-
ture_. Baton Rouge: Louisiana State University Press, 1961.
Franco, Jean. _A Literary History of Spain_, Vol. 7: _Spanish American
Literature Since Independence_. London: Benn, 1973.
Green, Otis H. _Spain and the Western Tradition_. 4 vols. Madison: Uni-
versity of Wisconsin Press, 1963-1966.
Henríquez Ureña, Pedro. _Literary Currents in Spanish America_. London:
Russell, 1963.
Hispanic Society of America. _Translations from Hispanic Poets_. New York:
Hispanic Society of America, 1938.
Resnick, Seymour and Jeanne Pasmantier. _An Anthology of Spanish Litera-
ture in Translation_. 2 vols. New York: Ungar, 1958.
Torres Rioseco, Arturo. _The Epic of Latin American Literature_. Berkeley:
University of California Press, 1959.

II. Middle Ages.

Askew, Melvin W. "Courtly Love: Neurosis as Institution," _Psychoanalytic
Review_, 52 (Spring 1965), 19-29.
Deyermond, Alan D. _A Literary History of Spain: The Middle Ages_.
London: Benn, 1971.
Don Juan Manuel. _Count Lucanor_. Trans. John E. Keller. To be published
soon.
The Poem of the Cid. Ed. William S. Merwin. New York: Mentor.
Ruiz, Juan. _The Book of Good Love_. Trans. Elisha Kent Kane. 2 edns.
New York: Rudge, 1933, and Chapel Hill: University of North Caro-
lina Press, 1968.

III. Renaissance, Golden Age, and Baroque.

Auerbach, Erich. "The Enchanted Dulcinea" in his _Mimesis_. Garden City:
Doubleday Anchor Books, 1957, pp. 293-315.
Bell, A. F. G. _Cervantes_. Norman: University of Oklahoma Press, 1947.
Bernadete, Mair José and Angel Flores. _Cervantes Across the Centuries_.
New York: Gordian, 1948.
Cervantes, Miguel de. _Don Quixote_. Trans. P. A. Motteux. New York:
Bigelow, n.d.
_____. _Exemplary Novels_. Trans. Walter K. Kelly. Emmaus, Pa.: Story
Classics, 1952.
_____. _The Interludes of Cervantes_. Trans. S. Griswald Morley.
Princeton: Princeton University Press, 1948.
Flynn, Gerard. _Sor Juana Inés de la Cruz_. New York: Twayne, 1971.

Goggio, Emilio. "The Dual Rose of Dulcinea in Cervantes' Don Quixote de la
    Mancha," Modern Language Quarterly, 13 (1952),   285-291.
Hatzfeld, Helmut. Santa Teresa de Ávila. New York: Twayne, 1969.
Hesse, Everett W. Calderón de la Barca. New York: Twayne, 1967.
Honig, Edwin. Calderón and the Seizures of Honor. Cambridge: Harvard
    University Press, 1972.
Jones, R. O. A Literary History of Spain: The Golden Age Prose and Po-
    etry. London: Benn, 1971.
Leonard, Irving A. "A Baroque Poetess," in his Baroque Times in Old
    Mexico. Ann Arbor: University of Michigan Press, 1959, pp. 172-
    192.
Lida de Malkiel, María Rosa. Two Spanish Masterpieces: The Book of Good
    Love and La Celestina. Urbana: University of Illinois Press, 1961.
Mac Curdy, Raymond. "The 'Problem' of Spanish Golden Age Tragedy: A
    Review and Reconsideration," South Atlantic Bulletin, 38 (1973),
    3-15.
Nelson, Lowry. Cervantes: A Collection of Critical Essays. Englewood
    Cliffs: Prentice Hall, 1969.
Predmore, R. L. The World of Don Quixote. Cambridge: Harvard University
    Press, 1967.
Riley, Edward. Cervantes' Theory of the Novel. Oxford: Clarendon, 1964.
Rojas, Fernando de. La Celestina. Trans. Mack Hendricks Singleton.
    Madison: University of Wisconsin Press, 1958.
Sloman, Albert E. The Dramatic Craftsmanship of Calderón: His Use of
    Earlier Plays. Oxford: Dolphin, 1958.
Spitzer, Leo. "Linguistic Perspectivism in the Don Quixote," in his Lin-
    guistics and Literary History. Princeton: Princeton University
    Press, 1948.
Teresa, Saint. The Life of Saint Teresa of Ávila, by Herself. Trans.
    J. M. Cohen. Harmondsworth, Middlesex: Penguin Books, 1957.
Thurman, Judith. "Lost Women: Sister Juana: The Price of Genius," Ms,
    I, no. 10 (April 1973), pp. 14-16, 20-21.
Wardropper, Bruce W. Critical Essays on the Theatre of Calderón. New
    York: New York University Press, 1965.
_____. "The Pertinence of 'El Curioso Impertinente,'" PMLA, 72 (1957),
    587-600.
Wilson, Edward M. and Duncan Moir. A Literary History of Spain: The
    Golden Age Drama. London: Benn, 1971.
Wilson, Margaret. Spanish Drama of the Golden Age. Oxford: Pergamon, 1969.

IV. 18th Century.

Herr, Richard. The Eighteenth-Century Revolution in Spain. Princeton:
    Princeton University Press, 1958.
Glendinning, Nigel. A Literary History of Spain: The Eighteenth Century.
    London: Benn, 1972.

V. 19th Century and Generation of 1898.

Becker, George J., ed. Documents of Modern Literary Realism. Princeton:
    Princeton University Press, 1963, pp. 166-173.

Brent, Albert. _Leopoldo Alas and La Regenta: A Study in the Nineteenth-Century Spanish Prose Fiction_. Columbia: University of Missouri Press, 1951.

Eoff, Sherman E. _The Modern Spanish Novel_. New York: New York University Press, 1961.

_____. _The Novels of Pérez Galdós: The Concept of Life as Dynamic Process_. Saint Louis, 1954.

Hilton, Ronald. "Pardo Bazán and the Spanish Problem," _Modern Language Quarterly_, 13 (1952), pp. 292-298.

Lott, Robert E. _Language and Psychology in Pepita Jiménez_. Urbana: University of Illinois Press, 1970.

Pattison, Walter T. _Emilia Pardo Bazán_. New York: Twayne, 1971.

Shaw, Donald. _A Literary History of Spain_. Vol. 5: _The Nineteenth Century_. London: Benn, 1972.

Valera, Juan. _Pepita Jiménez_. Trans. Harriet de Onís. Great Neck, .Y.: Barron's Educational Series, 1964.

VI. Modern and Contemporary:

Benavente, Jacinto. _The Passion Flower_.

García Lorca, Federico. _Three Tragedies_. New York: New Directions, 1956. (_Blood Wedding, The House of Bernarda Alba, Yerma_)

Mistral, Gabriela. _Selected Poems of Gabriela Mistral_. Trans. Langston Hughes. Bloomington: Indiana University Press, 1957.

Justification of original course proposal.

Hispanic literature is neither widely known nor appreciated outside the Spanish-speaking world despite the fact that six Nobel Prizes for Literature have been awarded to three Spaniards—José Echegaray, Jacinto Benavente, Juan Ramón Jiménez—and to three Spanish Americans—Gabriela Mistral, Miguel Angel Asturias, Pablo Neruda. The Chilean poet Gabriela Mistral was the first Spanish American, and the first woman, to be granted this coveted award.

This survey course purports to disseminate a knowledge of Hispanic literature by means of a thematic study of its women through the eight centuries of its existence. Although helpful, a reading knowledge of Spanish is not required for the course: all required readings and class lectures will be conducted in English.

Mini-Courses

In the academic year 1972-1973 Rutgers College, Rutgers University, New Brunswick, N. J., began offering two mini-courses in the Spanish department related to women: THE IMAGE OF WOMEN IN HISPANIC LITERATURE, and WOMEN WRITERS OF THE HISPANIC WORLD. These courses, which last seven weeks, are taught in English with texts in English translation. The mini-courses at Rutgers were designed to make available to freshmen course samplings of the various departments so that the student might become acquainted early with the offerings and the senior staff of the various areas. In reality, they are often attended by advanced students and are frequently taught by younger members of the faculty. They do allow for flexible scheduling and experimental topics like the ones mentioned.

Because comparatively little of Hispanic literature is available in translation, the courses have been hampered by the lack of appropriate texts. This is particularly true of the Women Writers course. Despite the limitation of texts, the students have been able to learn something of the contributions of women writers to the development of Hispanic literature and have developed a keen insight into the portrayal of male and female characters by these writers.

Listed below are the two courses, given in sequence during the fall semester, 1972:

Elaine Bunn
Department of Spanish and Portuguese

Rutgers College
New Brunswick, New Jersey
Fall 1972

IMAGE OF WOMAN IN HISPANIC LITERATURE (Spanish 171-33)

I. Texts:

The Celestina: A Novel in Dialogue. Trans. Lesley B. Simpson.
    Berkeley: University of California Press, 1955.
De Vega, Lope. Five Plays. New York: Hill and Wang, 1961.
Pérez Galdós, Benito. Tristana. Peterborough, N. H.: R. R. Smith,
    1961.
Pérez Galdós, Benito. Doña Perfecta. Woodbury, N. Y.: Barrons, 1960.
García Lorca, Federico. Three Tragedies. New York: New Directions,
    1956.
Unamuno, Miguel De. Three Exemplary Novels. New York: Grove Press,
    1960.
Queiroz, Raquel de. The Three Marias. Austin: University of Texas
    Press, 1963.
Valera, Juan. Pepita Jiménez. Woodbury, N. Y.: Barrons, 1956.

II. On Reserve:

Millett, Kate. Sexual Politics. Garden City, N. Y.: Doubleday,
    1970. Ch. 2, "Theory of Sexual Politics," pp. 23-58.
Beauvoir, Simone de. The Second Sex. New York: Alfred A. Knopf,
    1971. Ch. 6, "Patriarchal Times and Classical Antiquity," pp. 82-
    96. Ch. 7, "Through the Middle Ages . . . ," pp. 97-108.

III. Suggested further reading:

1) Otis Green's review of P. W. Bomli's <u>La Femme dans l'Espagne du Siècle d'Or</u> (The Hague, 1950), in <u>Hispanic Review</u>, Vol. XX (1952). In Prof. Green's usual encyclopedic style he adds much to Bomli's study—most important are his own bibliographic references to women's studies.

2) Important for a non-literary and sociological look at contemporary women in Spain compiled by nine women is "Mujer y aceleración histórica," <u>Cuadernos para el diálogo</u>, ns. 27/28 (Madrid, 1970). Date given is 1970 although it appeared in '71 or '72. It includes: Introduction "La mujer y la cultura"

         Chapter 1   "La educación de la mujer"
         Chapter 2   "Declaraciones de Principios (civil and ecclesiastical statements)
         Chapter 3   "Actitudes sociales retardarias"
         Chapter 4   "Nuevo plantamiento de la educación de la mujer"
         Bibliography--Extensive

IV. Tentative and incomplete list of questions to guide reading:

1) Define the woman's role in the work.
2) Is her role established on the basis of her sex alone or on some other quality?
3) Consider comments made by other characters (male and female) on her 'feminine' qualities and the validity of these comments.
4) What is her effect on other characters? Is she judged on the basis of predetermined female behavior?
5) Describe her reputation as established by others. Separate male and female attitudes toward her.
6) Is she distinguishable from other female characters?
7) Does the character reveal a self-image externally through word or deed or internally through dreams, interior monologue that disagrees with the image projected to others?
8) Is there a conflict between her private and personal good or benefit and the social and public good?
9) Do the female characters have the opportunity to determine their own future? To what extent do family and social convention determine their development? Is this beneficial or detrimental to the character herself?
10) Does the character demonstrate fanaticism, obsession, or excessive behavior? Is this due to sex-determined repression?
11) Does the author show in his handling of the plot disagreement or agreement with the established attitude of society toward women?

V. Final project:

Describe the image of the Spanish woman in literature that has emerged from your readings and our discussions in class. Refer your opinions to specific characters in specific works. Please mention at least four different works.

Considering the chronological order of the works we have read, would you say that the image of woman showed any significant changes through the centuries?

Remarks:

I began the course by discussing the role of women in selected works up to the sixteenth century (early lyric and epic poetry, ballads, courtly love, etc.). I read poetry and selected passages to them to illustrate points and get their reactions.

Each student read three selections from the reading list and gave a short report in class. These were staggered so that each student was involved during the course of the seven weeks. If I were to teach the class again I would have all the students read all the selections (choosing one or two plays).

I questioned them on the background material (Millett and de Beauvoir) before they began their readings and we used those books as a guide throughout.

The selections were limited by the availability of translations although they were adequate for our purposes.

Phyllis Zatlin Boring
Department of Spanish and Portuguese

Rutgers College
New Brunswick, New Jersey
Fall 1972

WOMEN WRITERS OF THE HISPANIC WORLD (172-32)

The syllabus for the mini-course has been limited to what is in print. The students are reading The Seagull, the first of Spain's 19th-century novels of customs, published by Fernán Caballero in 1849. The other required text is the Langston Hughes translation of poetry by the Chilean Nobel Prize winner Gabriela Mistral. These books have been supplemented by background and commentary given by the professor and by readings of poetry of Sor Juana Inés de la Cruz and Rosalía de Castro, both taken from anthologies, one story by Pardo Bazán, and a story by the contemporary Spanish writer, Carmen Laforet, also available in an anthology.

BIBLIOGRAPHY

I. Works used in 1972-73

Caballero, Fernán. (Spain) The Seagull. Trans. Joan MacLean. Woodbury,
    N. Y.: Barron's Educational Series, 1965. Paper
Castro, Rosalía de. (Spain) Selected poetry. In An Anthology of Spanish
    Poetry from Garcilaso to García Lorca. Ed. Angel Flores. Anchor Books.
    Garden City, N. Y.: Doubleday, 1961. Paper.
Sor Juana Inés de la Cruz. (Mexico) Selected poetry. In An Anthology
    of Spanish Poetry . . .
Laforet, Carmen. (Spain) "The Return." In Great Spanish Stories. Modern
    Library. New York: Random House, 1956. (Story also available in
    From Spain and the Americas: Literature in Translation. Ed. Miller,

O'Neal, McDonnell. Glenview, Ill.: Scott, Foresman, 1970. Paper.)

Mistral, Gabriela. (Chile) <u>Selected Poems of Gabriela Mistral</u>. Trans. Langston Hughes. Bloomington and London: Indiana Univ. Press, 1972. Paper.

Pardo Bazán, Emilia. "The Talisman." In <u>Classic Tales from Modern Spain</u>. Ed. William E. Colford. Great Neck, N. Y.: Barron's Educational Series, 1964. Paper.

II. <u>Other available works</u>

Bombal, María Luisa. (Chile) In <u>Short Stories of Latin America</u>. New York: Las Americas, 1963.

Chacel, Rosa. (Spain) "Twilight in Extremadura." In <u>Great Spanish Stor-ies</u>.

Garro, Elena. (Mexico) <u>Recollections of Things to Come</u>. Trans. Ruth L. C. Simms. Austin: Univ. of Texas Press, 1969.

Lispector, Clarice. (Brazil) <u>The Apple in the Dark</u>. Trans. Gregory Rabassa. New York: Knopf, 1967.

_____. <u>Family Ties</u>. Trans. Giovanni Pontiero. Austin: Univ. of Texas Press, 1972.

Matute, Ana María. (Spain) <u>School of the Sun</u>. Trans. Elaine Kerrigan. New York: Pantheon Books, 1963.

Mistral, Gabriela. (Chile) Selected poems in <u>From Spain and the Americas</u> and in <u>An Anthology of Spanish Poetry</u> . . .

Pardo Bazán, Emilia. (Spain) "The First Prize." In <u>From Spain and the Americas</u>.

_____. "The Revolver." In <u>Spanish Stories/Cuentos españoles</u>. Ed. Angel Flores. New York: Bantam, 1960. Paper.

Queiros, Rachel de. (Brazil) <u>The Three Marias</u>. Trans. Fred P. Ellison. Austin: University of Texas Press, 1963.

Storni, Alfonsina. (Argentina) Selected poems in <u>From Spain and the Americas</u>.

Teresa of Avila, Saint. (Spain) <u>The Way of Perfection</u>. Trans. E. Allison Peers. Garden City: Doubleday.

SOME WOMEN WRITERS OF THE HISPANIC WORLD

I. <u>Spain</u>

*Saint Teresa de Jesús (1515-1582) Mystic and saint; reformed Carmelite Order; wrote prose and poetry.

*María de Zayas y Sotomayor (1590-1661) Most representative writer of courtly novels; ardent feminist.

*Fernán Caballero (1796-1877) (Cecilia Böhl von Faber) Novelist; started <u>costumbrista</u> movement from which realistic novel developed.

*Gertrudis Gómez de Avellaneda (1814-1873) Born in Cuba; wrote romantic poetry, novels and drama.

Carolina Coronado (1823-1911) Romantic poet.

**Rosalía de Castro (1837-1885) Poet and novelist. Wrote poetry in both Spanish and Galician; rep-

165

	resents transition between romantic and more contemporary poetry.
**Emilia Pardo Bazán (1851-1921)	Novelist, short story writer and critic. Important interpreter of naturalism in Spain.
*Concha Espina (1877-1955)	Novelist and critic. Portrayed liberated women characters.
Eulalia Calvarriato (1905-)	Writer of novels, short stories, essays.
Carmen Conde (1907-)	Poet.

(There are dozens of women poets and novelists writing in Spain in the past 20 or 30 years. The following six novelists have all won the more or less important Nadal prize for novels:)

Elena Quiroga (1919-)	Won Nadal in 1950.
Dolores Medio (1920-)	Won Nadal in 1952.
*Carmen Laforet (1921-)	Won Nadal in 1944.
Carmen Martín Gaité (1925-)	Won Nadal in 1957.
**Ana María Matute (1926-)	Won Nadal in 1959.
Luisa Forrellad (1930-)	Won Nadal in 1953.

II. <u>Spanish America</u>

**Sor Juana Inés de la Cruz (1651-1695)	Mexico; poet and dramatist; center of intellectual life in Mexico.
*Clorinda Matto de Turner (1854-1909)	Peru; romantic novelist.
Delmira Agustini (1890-1914)	Uruguay; poet.
**Gabriela Mistral (1889-1957) (Lucila Godoy Aleayaga)	Chile; poet. Won NOBEL PRIZE
Alfonsina Storni (1892-1936)	Argentina; poet.
Teresa de la Parra (1895-1936)	Venezuela; novelist and short story writer.
*Juana de Ibarbouru (1895-)	Uruguay; poet.
Marta Brunet (1901-)	Chile; <u>criollo</u> novels and stories.
María Luisa Bombal (1910-)	Chile; novelist.
*Elena Garro (1917-)	Mexico; dramatist.
Ida Gramcko (1925-)	Venezuela; poet.
Josefina Hernández (1928-)	Mexico; dramatist.

**Extremely important writer.
*Important writer.

BRIEF COURSE LISTINGS

The University of Arizona.
   The University of Arizona is studying the formulation and implementa-
   tion of a formal Women Studies minor. Within this program, the Department of Romance Languages plans to offer a seminar on Latin-American women poets.

Hood College.
   In 1974-1975 Professor Juana A. Hernandez of the Department of Modern
   and Classical Languages will teach a course on WOMAN IN THE HISPANIC
   WORLD in order to 1) present the contributions of Hispanic women to
   literature, history, science, arts, etc., 2) study their struggle in
   society, and 3) analyze the images women project and the roles they
   are forced to play.

Mount Saint Mary's College (Long Beach, California).
   Maruxa Cargill of the Department of Spanish offered a course in 1972
   on WOMEN IN LITERATURE: VICTIMS, INSPIRERS, AND CREATORS and plans to
   repeat this course.

University of Pittsburgh.
   Constance H. Rose, assistant professor of Spanish and Comparative Lit-
   erature, taught a course on COMPARATIVE EUROPEAN TRAGEDY OF THE 17TH
   CENTURY during Winter Term 1972. English, Spanish, and French trag-
   edies of the period which focussed on women were read, such as The
   Dutchess of Malfi, Women Beware Women, Phèdre, El castigo sin venganza.
   The course was cross-referenced to the Women's Study Program. Two
   guest speakers were from the French and the English Department.

Purdue University.
   Dolores Martí de Cid of the Department of Modern Languages taught
   a course on WOMEN IN SPANISH AMERICAN LITERATURE in Spring 1974.

San Francisco State University.
   Alfred F. Alberico, Department of Foreign Languages, offered a course
   in Spring 1972 on FEMALE CHARACTERS IN SPANISH LITERATURE (Peninsular)
   and plans to repeat it.

University of Tulsa.
   Judy Salinas of the Department of Foreign Languages and Literatures
   offered a seminar in Spring 1974 on THE IMAGE OF WOMAN IN SPANISH
   AMERICAN LITERATURE (in Spanish). The course includes novels, short
   stories, and poetry both about women as the major topic and stereo-
   typed roles as well as authored by women of Spanish American letters.
   The course begins with the poetry and prose of Mexico's "Tenth Muse,"
   Sor Juana Inés de la Cruz, who battled social stigma attached to being
   a woman and a writer during sixteenth-century·colonial days in Mexico.
   It also investigates the Romantic presentation of the woman in Latin
   America as a saint or practically so or as a prostitute or whore.

The roles of woman and her presentation in the literature will be thoroughly analyzed from a stylistic and linguistic method and the women authors' works will be compared and contrasted with those written by men, wherever comparable. This course will include also the four post-modernist women of the nineteenth and twentieth centuries, one of whom, Gabriela Mistral, won the Nobel Prize for literature for her poetry about women and motherhood. It will also include women novelists' viewpoints about contemporary society as exemplified in their works.

GERMAN STUDIES

Women In Germany

by

Theresia Sauter-Bailliet

The German women's movement can be traced to Luise Otto-Peters (1819-1895)[1] whose political struggle for the emancipation of women was spurred by a deep concern for the plight of the working class. She did pioneering work during and after the German revolution of 1848. Later in the century, Clara Zetkin (1857-1933)[2] and Rosa Luxemburg (1870-1919)[3] carried on the political struggle in a more radical way. These women established the tradition in Germany of linking the women's movement with the workers' movement and of associating themselves with a political party, a fact which is confirmed by the contemporary scene: The Social-Democrats (SPD), the party in government since 1969, have a permanent women's chapter in Bonn, the "Referat Frauen,"[4] with branches on the state and local levels. The women's organization of the conservative opposition party, the Christian Democratic Union/Christian Socialist Union (CDU/CSU)[5] is structured similarly.

There are radical groups throughout Germany for which the fight for women's rights is an intrinsic part of the class struggle. Those radical groups have a similar ideology but no common party structure. The "Frauengruppe im Revolutionären Kampf" (RK) with its seat in Frankfurt is trying to constitute a political party that differs from the Communist party in that its foremost aim is the emancipation of women. They address themselves mainly to the female proletariat and intellectuals.[6]

Although the SPD has its origins in the workers' movement[7] which espoused the cause of the underprivileged, it represented the men's rather than the women's rights. A discussion of the situation of women was on the agenda for the first time at the party convention in 1867. Instead of demanding better working conditions for the thousands of exploited female workers, they asked for the abolition of female labor as such, arguing that it depreciated the value of male labor and that it endangered the family, arguments that can be heard still today. This negative stand of the SPD prevented the "Allgemeine Deutsche Frauenverein," founded by Luise Otto-Peters in 1865,[8] from merging with the party.

Not all of the men in the party upheld this anti-feminist view. Of the two factions of the party, the Eisenacher (named after the 1869 convention in Eisenach) supported women's rights. Instead of banning women from the labor market they urged that they join the labor unions on an equal footing with men. This petition was presented by August Bebel (1840-1913),[9] one of the prominent leaders of the SPD. In 1871, it was adopted by the party. But hardly had a considerable number of women joined ranks with their co-workers in the unions than a law was passed that forced them out again. This law was reversed in 1908. Since then, the number of female unionists has climbed to more than a million and that of dues-paying women of the SPD to 190,000.

August Bebel and Wilhelm Liebknecht (1826-1900) demanded women's suffrage as far back as 1875. Liebknecht declared: "A party that stands for equality contradicts itself if it denies the political rights to one

half of mankind."[10] Bebel and Liebknecht belonged to the leftist wing of
the party. They were in touch with Karl Marx (1818-1883) and Friedrich
Engels (1820-1895),[11] both of whom lived in England at the time. Marx
contributed with his writings to the emancipatory movement.[12] His ideas
were taken up by Engels, Bebel, and Zetkin. Bebel dealt with all aspects
of the status of women, and Zetkin brought Bebel's ideas into focus in her
struggle for the emancipation of women. Zetkin and Luxemburg fought within the SPD against reactionary tendencies in the male camp. When the
Marxist group split from the SPD during World War I, Luxemburg founded with
Liebknecht the communist party "Spartakusbund." Luxemburg was assassin-
ated as a revolutionary agitator in 1919.

Both the SPD and the leftists claim the legacy of their forerunners
Engels, Bebel, Otto-Peters, Zetkin, and Luxemburg. Much of the research
on the condition of women is being done by the leftists in the field of
sociology, e.g., on women and the labor force, women and the capitalist
society, women and education, abortion, etc.[13] While the leftists study
the problem within the context of a Marxist ideology, the SPD (referring to
the party, not the SPD women) has hardly ventured outside the cliché of the
traditional role of woman. In 1962, the SPD petitioned in a parliamentary
session a nationwide examination of the status of women. This big project,
called Frauenenquête, was commissioned by the then CDU government and presented to the parliament in 1966.[14] It was followed in the SPD era by the
Bericht,[15] a report of the government specifying measures to be taken to
improve the condition of women.

That the party should take the initiative and the government act
upon the recommendation is remarkable in itself. But the SPD women have
little reason to be satisfied. Gisela Helwig criticizes the outmoded concept of the family presented in the Enquête, which idealizes the housewife and mother.[16] She suspects that this patriarchal view of the family
reflects the thinking of the Department of Family Affairs, more specifically that of its then secretary Bruno Heck (CDU) and his predecessor
Franz-Josef Wuermeling (CDU). Heck's successors, Anni Brauksiepe (CDU),
Käte Strobel (SPD), and now Katharina Focke (SPD)--three of the few German women with portfolio -- have been trying to present the family without
its romantic trappings. The Bericht is an improvement over the Enquête.
It rests upon a more rational basis and is well supported by statistical
material. This inquiry will be continued and will serve as a basis--
ideally--for redressing inequities still existent in theory and practice.

Constitutionally, "equality of the sexes" has been guaranteed since
the new Federal Republic of Germany was formed. By 1958, several
different articles had been revised to reflect the principle of equality
(Gleichberechtigungsgesetz). Many laws fail to reflect this principle or
are plainly biased against women. Striking examples are the abortion
and divorce laws, which have come under fire recently. The CDU women proposed that women members of parliament representing the three parties be
commissioned to participate in the inquiry on the status of women especially in regard to the abortion and divorce laws. Since the CDU women are
traditionally conservative in their view of woman's role, the SPD women
are reluctant to cooperate. However, in April 1974 the West German parliament approved a controversial law permitting abortion during the first
three months of pregnancy. The constitutionality of the new law is now
(Fall 1974) being tested before the Supreme Court of the Federal Republic.

Formerly investigations into discrimination were conducted mainly by men. The SPD women are trying to influence their colleagues and the government by exposing existing inequities in the treatment of women.[17] One of their endeavors has been to compare the condition of women in the Federal Republic of Germany (BRD) and the German Democratic Republic (DDR). For this purpose, a workshop was conducted in Berlin in October 1973.[18] It reveals that the DDR has done much more to help their women achieve equality. Here are two of the more striking discrepancies:

1) The "Bürgerliche Gesetzbuch" (BGB) par. 1356 and 1360 of the BRD gives the husband with a good income the right to prevent his wife from seeking an outside job, arguing that the family and children would suffer, but forces the woman into the labor market if her husband is unable to work and if he has reasons not to draw from financial reserves they may have. In other words, a wife may not work if she is well-to-do, but she must work if she is poor.[19] The "DDR Verfassung" (the constitution of the DDR), especially par. 10 and 12 of the "Familiengesetzbuch," specifies the right of every woman to work. It asks husband and children to share in the household and child-rearing duties.[20]

2) In the DDR, women have equal access to technical and scientific training. In the BRD, women are geared into "female" professions. In the DDR, 25 percent of the machinists are women, in the BRD, there are none. Female electricians represent 12 percent in the DDR, none in the BRD. In 1969-1970 the percentage of women in higher education was 29.3 percent in the BRD, 43.3 percent in the DDR. In technical schools, 5.33 percent female students in the BRD compare poorly with the 47.2 percent in the DDR.

If the DDR stresses the woman's right to work and to obtain a good education, it is not out of altruistic reasons but rather to benefit from her productive labor. But it does avoid the discrimination still practiced in the BRD. The situation in the DDR is far from being ideal. The double burden of work and family rests heavily upon the woman in spite of the law. Shorter working hours for both could ease the burden, but that would go against the interests of the state. The "right to work" stated in the "Familiengesetzbuch" can also be interpreted as the state's forcing every citizen into the labor market. The SPD women try to draw from the experience of their sisters on the other side of the iron curtain and at the same time to avoid the pitfalls of their system. One of their aims is to activate women politically and have them join the party in order to strengthen their ranks and their bargaining power. A campaign has been launched to obtain more seats for women in the government on the local, state, and federal levels.[21]

Women of all political affiliations are underrepresented in political positions, especially in the parliament, where they hold only 31 out of 518 seats.[22] Their number has been decreasing from an all-time high of 48 in the 1957-1961 legislature, a warning signal for the women to be vigilant. One of the reasons for the decline could be the abolition of the quota system in the 1969-1972 legislature. German men are not liberated enough to cede to women positions of prestige hitherto reserved for men without some coercion. That a woman, Bundestagspräsidentin Annemarie Renger, was elevated to the second most important post in the government, the presidency of the parliament, is regarded by some as mere tokenism.[23]

This pattern of low representation is repeated in industry,[24] in the universities, and in the administration, where few women acceded to top positions. Jutta Menschik reports that in institutions of higher learning, only 1.4 percent of the full professors in 1960 were women.[25] The scene has hardly changed since then. It is little better in the administration. Of 2,711 federal judges and high officials in 1963, only 64 were women.[26]

Besides the prejudices that prevent women from seeking top positions, the lack of an adequate education is another important factor.[27] Since the establishment of the first girls' high school in Berlin by Helene Lange in 1889, many girls are still educated in separate schools. But even in the coeducational system which is spreading rapidly, girls often receive separate instruction in "female subjects," i.e., sewing, knitting, cooking, etc. On the other hand, in subjects like physics, chemistry, etc., boys often accumulate more hours. Fewer girls than boys attend the Gymnasium which is college preparatory. Since only high school graduates (i.e., those who passed the final examination of the Gymnasium, the "Abitur") are admitted to the universities, girls who completed only elementary school (Grund- and Hauptschule) are barred from higher education. Thirty-nine and four tenths per cent of the high school graduates were girls in 1969-1970. About two thirds of German youth--and more girls than boys--leave school with a ten-year elementary education. More than half of the student body of the Realschulen--middle schools that stand between the Hauptschulen and the Gymnasium--are girls. These middle schools mainly prepare for clerical, technical, and social--i.e., predominantly "female"--professions. At the university level, women are underrepresented, as was mentioned above. "Education" is the one single field where female students out-number the men. These prospective elementary and middle school teachers represented 64.3 percent of the student body in 1969-1970. Few women make it to the doctorate. In 1968, of the 4,676 Ph.D. candidates, 759 were women.

Not only are highly educated women in Germany in the minority, but also their education is not always put to use in a profession outside the home. It is the less educated that make up the bulk of the working women. Seventy-five percent of a total of 9.3 million are found in clerical and blue-collar jobs. Women represent 35.8 percent of the total labor force and are mainly at the bottom scale.

The picture drawn looks rather bleak, but there are signs on the horizon that promise change. The whole educational system is being re-vised, and it is most likely that women will receive more equal treatment in the emerging new system. The political groups of women are putting pressure on the government to remedy inequities and to fill more govern-ment positions with women. Slowly if reluctantly, the government will follow through.

The radical women have been vociferous in some areas like abortion, and they have been active on campuses. Their allegiance to the Marxist ideology and especially their dogmatism, however, are deterrents for many women who would otherwise gladly cooperate with them.

What is still needed is more communication with the female popula-tion in general. There are very few women's groups of students, housewives, or working women, coming together for consciouness-raising or rap sessions. Women's studies courses are conspicuously absent from the course offerings in high schools and universities. The one taught by myself in the English Department of the University of Aachen seems to stand alone.

Germans will have to unlearn in an educational process the clichés according to which they have been behaving for centuries, so that the laws and recommendations that are being made in their interest may have real bearing on the everyday life of the citizens. German feminists are learning from the progress made in the DDR, in the Scandinavian countries, and especially in the U.S.A. Since the women's movement easily crosses national boundaries, it can be said that it is truly international in scope.

University of Aachen

[1] Luise Otto-Peters was not only a political activist but also a writer and journalist. In 1848, she founded the first feminist newspaper Frauenzeitung für höhere weibliche Interessen (outlined in 1852) to which she rallied German women with the motto "Dem Reich der Freiheit werb ich Bürgerinnen" (For the land of freedom I recruit women citizens).

[2] Zetkin was the editor of the feminist journal Gleichheit. Her book, her speeches, and publications have been reprinted in Zur Geschichte der proletarischen Frauenbewegung Deutschlands (Berlin, 1958) and Ausgewählte Reden und Schriften, Bd. I, 1889-1917 (Berlin, 1957), Bd. III, 1924-1933 (Berlin, 1960).

[3] Several books by Rosa Luxemburg and her correspondance have been published. The more important ones are Sozialreform oder Revolution (1899), Massenstreik, Partei und Gewerkschaft (1906), Die Krise der Sozialdemokratie (1916), Briefe aus dem Gefängnis (Berlin, 1919-22), Briefe an Karl und Luise Kautsky, 1896-1918 (Berlin, 1923).

[4] Address: Referat Frauen beim SPD-Parteivorstand, 53 Bonn 1, Ollenhauerstr. 1. Referentin: Frau Anni Jansen.

[5] Address: CDU-Frauenvereinigung Deutschland, 53 Bonn, Friedrich-Ebert-Allee 73-75. Bundesvorsitzende: Frau Dr. Helga Wex. The "Frauenvereinigung" also represents the "CSU-Frauenunion" of Bavaria.

[6] The groups "Brot und Rosen" (Berlin), "Aktion" (Bremen, Frankfurt, Heidelberg, München), "Sozialistische Frauen Frankfurt," "Frauengruppe Aachen," "Frauenzentrum Berlin," etc., have been working together in an abortion campaign for the repeal of the abortion law par. 218. They seem to have a fairly good network of communication. More and more socialist women realize that the male socialists neglect the women, a fact that has its precedent in the history of the SPD.

[7] The history of the SPD dates back to 1863 when the "Allgemeine Deutsche Arbeiterverein" was chartered in Leipzig by Ferdinand Lasalle. The CDU is of recent date (1945), and also the small middle-of-the-road Free Democratic Party, FDP (1948).

[8] Luise Otto-Peters presided over the "Deutsche Frauenkonferenz" in Leipzig in 1865, at which the first German women's organization was chartered. In 1894, it fused with other women's groups to form the "Bund Deutscher Frauenvereine." In 1897, it joined the "Internationale Frauenbund." During the Hitler period, all women's organizations were dissolved and replaced by the "Frauenwerk" and the "NS-Frauenschaft." (The Nazi Regime degraded women to reproductive machines. Out of sheer necessity to keep the war industry going, women were drawn into the factories, from which they returned again to the hearth after the war when the war veterans returned, at least in the Western part of Germany.)

[9]His influential book Die Frau und der Sozialismus was published in 1879.

[10]The German text reads: "Eine Partei, die die Gleichheit auf ihr Banner schreibt, schlägt sich selbst ins Gesicht, wenn sie der Hälfte des Menschengeschlechts die politischen Rechte versagt." Cited after Anni Jansen's paper "Geschichtliche Entwicklung der Frauenbewegung."

[11]The two works of Engels important in this context are: Umrisse zu einer Kritik der Nationalökonomie (1844), and Die Lage der arbeitenden Klasse in England (1845).

[12]Clara Zetkin writes in Ausgewählte Reden, p. 219, that although Marx never mentioned women's emancipation as such, he provided the method by which it could be advanced.

[13]The following publications are selected as examples from the bibliography of Jutta Menschik's book Gleichberechtigung oder Emanzipation? Die Frau im Erwerbsleben der Bundesrepublik (Fischer Verlag, 1972), 2.

> Herrmann, Hedwig, Die ausserhäusliche Erwerbstätigkeit verheirateter Frauen, eine sozialpolitische Studie (Stuttgart, 1957).
>
> "Die Familie im Dienste des Kapitals; Situation und Bewusstsein der Arbeiterin im Betrieb und in der Familie," Bericht der Arbeitsgruppe "Frauenarbeit," in den Übugen am Otto-Suhr-Institut der Freien Universität (Berlin, 1970).
>
> Kinderläden, Revolution der Erziehung oder Erziehung zur Revolution by Hilde Jan Breiteneier, Rolf Mauff, et. al. (Reinbek, 1971).

A book on abortion, the Frauenhandbuch Nr. 1: Abtreibung und Verhütungsmittel, published by "Brot und Rosen" (Berlin, 1972), is not mentioned by Menschik.

[14]Frauenenquête--Bericht der Bundesregierung über die Situation der Frauen in Beruf, Familie und Gesellschaft, published by Bundesministerium für Arbeit und Sozialordnung, Bundestagsdrucksache V/909, Sept. 14, 1966.

[15]Bericht der Bundesregierung über die Massnahmen zur Verbesserung der Situation der Frau, published by Bundesminister für besondere Aufgaben Ehmke, Bundestagsdrucksache VI/3689, Aug. 1, 1972.

[16]Gisela Helwig works for the Deutschland-Archiv Köln, for which she wrote the article "Zum Ehe--und Familienverständnis in beiden Teilen Deutschlands."

[17]e.g., the SPD women's action against the discriminatory taxing system, publicized in a press conference.

[18]Auswertung des Berlin-Seminars der Arbeitsgemeinschaft Sozialdemokratischer Frauen (ASF), "Vergleich der Gesellschaftssysteme der BRD und der DDR unter besonderer Berücksichtigung der soziopolitischen Situation

der Frau," published by Referat Frauen beim SPD-Parteivorstand, 1973.

Helwig in her criticism of the Frauenenquête also draws comparisons to the DDR. Another article follows this pattern: Joachim Lieser, "Gleichberechtigung im geteilten Deutschland, Betrachtungen zur rechtlichen Entwicklung," written for the Deutschland-Archiv Köln.

[19] The text referred to reads, "Die Frau erfüllt ihre Verpflichtung, durch Arbeit zum Unterhalt der Familie beizutragen, in der Regel durch die Führung des Haushaltes; zu einer Erwerbstätigkeit ist sie verpflichtet, soweit die Arbeitskraft des Mannes und die Einkünfte der Ehegatten zum Unterhalt der Familie nicht ausreichen und es den Verhältnissen der Ehegatten, also auch ihres Mannes, nicht entspricht, dass der Stamm des Vermögens verwertet wird."

[20] Excerpts from the "Familiengesetzbuch" of the DDR, "Jeder hat ein Grundrech auf Arbeit. . . . /Die Beziehungen der Ehegatten sind so/ zu gestalten, dass die Frau ihre berufliche und gesellschaftliche Tätigkeit mit der Mutterschaft vereinbaren kann. . . . Ältere Kinder sind zum Beitrag zu den Familienaufgaben ausdrücklich verpflichtet."

[21] To this effect, the SPD women are circulating material such as "Kandidatenaufstellung--Kandidatenbefragung," edited by Anke Brunn, and their "Aktionsmodell: Mehr Frauen in den Gemeinderat."

[22] In the DDR, 159 out of 500 members of parliament are women. They constitute approximately 33 percent of the public officers in the counties and districts. The number of female mayors is especially high: there were 1172 in 1969. However, in the highest office, the "Politbüro der SED," where the decisions are made, all 15 members are male.

[23] Her vice-president, Liselotte Funcke, is also a woman.

[24] No figures could be secured. That the number is low is attested by Horst Laube, Frauen als Vorgesetzte. Published under the auspices of Rationalisierungskuratorium der deutschen Wirtschaft (RKW), Förderung der Frauenarbeit (Bad Harzburg und Frankfurt, 1964).

[25] Her source is Erika-Ruth Brunotte, "Vorurteile gegenüber Frauen," in Das Vorurteil als Bildungsbarriere, Elf Beiträge. Ed. Willy Strzelewicz (Göttingen, 1965).

[26] Her source is Statistisches Bundesamt--Statistik des Personalstandes von Bund, Ländern und Gemeinden, VII/5-40/4-336, Feb. 2, 1964.

[27] An investigation into the education of women in Germany was funded by the Rationalisierungskuratorium der Deutschen Wirtschaft in 1970. The result was published in book form by Maria Borris, Die Benachteiligung der Mädchen in Schulen der Bundesrepublik und Westberlin (Frankfurt, 1972). Another good source on the topic is: Helge Pross, Über die Bildungschancen von Mädchen in der Bundesrepublik Deutschland (Frankfurt, 1969).

In Germany, women were admitted officially to universities in 1908. There were some female students at the universities before. Alice Salomon, later founder of the social workers' organization in Germany, received her doctorate at the University of Leipzig in 1906. Her dissertation: "Die Ursachen der ungleichen Entlohnung von Männer- und Frauenarbeit."

Virgins and Other Victims:
Aspects of German Middle-Class Theatre

by

Helga Tilton

Towards the end of the eighteenth century German theatre displayed distinct functional changes. It no longer provided entertainment exclusively for the courts; the rising German middle class gradually adapted the existing theatre to its particular requirements. The German theatre became the mouthpiece of middle-class opinion. The popularity of theatre at that time was, to a large extent, based on this function. Theatre became the platform where the politically powerless citizen could express criticism of the nobility. Due to the absence of a highly differentiated class consciousness, insistence upon superior moral values became the element which provided the necessary social cohesion.

Bourgeois superior morality became one of the recurring theme of the time and was voiced again and again by the writers for middle-class theatre. Interestingly enough, moral purity, when translated into dramatic terms, appeared as a celebration of feminine purity only. The plays seem obsessed with female virginity.

This peculiar concern has led critics to interpret the melodramatic tales about innocently seduced daughters and their outraged fathers as sublimation of a struggle between the bourgeoisie and the politically dominant aristocracy. According to this view, the bourgeoisie used the theme of seduction to voice their demand for independence. The tales about seduction have been referred to as "means to create revolutionary pathways for democracy."[1]

In a sense, such interpretations are valid. The method of translating social tensions into erotic conflicts had already been introduced in France with Manon Lescaut (1731) and especially with the English Pamela (1740), which was very successful throughout Europe.

But first the idea of seduction itself had to undergo significant transformation before it could be used as a medium for the expression of conflict between bourgeois and aristocrat. The theme of seduction is age-old and has been the stock ingredient of comedies since antiquity.[2] Bourgeois theatre had first to remove the theme from its original comic environment and transfer it to the realm of the tragic. In addition, the act of seduction which originally could be initiated by either male or female --as the story of Potiphar shows--had to appear strictly as a male prerogative. For this purpose a new stock character emerged: the female virgin.

Here, George Lillo's popular--and for Germany influential--The London Merchant had prepared the way. This play celebrated the swan song of a dramatic female character who could still influence the lives of her male opponents. A pure, ineffectual but beautiful female figure was offered as substitute and was accepted by the middle-class audiences as a new feminine ideal. From Lillo's delicate Maria it was only a small step to Lessing's and Emilia. W. H. Bruford has said about the function of Lessing's plays, "Both form and content of the drama ran parallel in their development to the values and intellectual assumptions of the groups for

whom the author was primarily writing."[3] The feminine ideal, as it
emerged at that time and as it began to invade the consciousness of the
middle class, showed woman as a grotesquely reduced and passive recipient of male sexual aggression. In the plays this ideal was realized by a
virgin whose sole dramatic function lay in the fact that she could be
seduced at some point within the play. The act of seduction served to
set the tragic development in motion.

Members of the bourgeoisie were forbidden to hold explicit political
gatherings.[4] The theatre and other social institutions, such as coffee
houses,[5] became the forum for political expression.[6] This explains the
popularity of theatre at that time. As a social unit, the middle class
was economically heterogeneous; insistence upon moral superiority and
virtuous conduct provided the necessary group unity in the struggle against
the powerful aristocracy.[7] The stage became the place where the citizens
could verbalize their new system of morals and where new model characters
could be tested.

For the first time bourgeois existence was considered worthy of dramatic treatment in serious terms. The plays were so designed that the common man should recognize himself on stage. But specific occupations or
professions were rarely used as a means of characterization. Thus, exactly those elements which could have set the members of the middle class effectively apart from the non-professionally oriented aristocracy were not
realized. Instead, the issue of self-realization was totally shifted to
the realm of the private sphere: the label "father of the house" was considered adequate means for identification.

Of course, the problem does not lie in the fact that bourgeois
theatre developed dramatic stereotypes to aid the communication of its
particular ideology. Highly stereotyped communication systems are extremely important in evolutionary systems because of their new role in the
origin of the emerging class. Concern must not be with the type itself
but with the specific function of such types within a given system. And
from this point of view the dramatic content offered by the middle-class
theatre was hardly "a safety valve for unpractical dreams"[8] as it has been
called. The new theatre did in fact provide the bourgeoisie with the long
desired experience of autonomy, did indeed achieve emancipation from the
aristocratic value system. But it must not be overlooked that this feeling of liberation could become reality for the bourgeoisie only at the expense of the female members of that class. This fact also answers Bruford's
question as to why the courts, still patrons of the theatre, considered
only very few plays as potentially dangerous. With the aid of the female
virgin and the concept of her endangered honor, a politically explosive
confrontation between bourgeoisie and aristocracy was blunted, since it
was only the female who served as the recipient of aggression.

This point does not mean to imply that suppression of females was
essentially an invention of the middle class. But it was the distinction
of this class at that time to have elaborated and codified already existing elements of masculine dominance. The new system of morals, realized
as the purity of the middle-class woman, invaded the public consciousness
so completely that eventually perception of woman began to be distorted
to the extent that passivity could be interpreted as part of woman's bio-

logical make-up.

If entertainment is indeed the celebration of publicly accepted moral values, then the success of G. E. Lessing's Miss Sara Sampson and Emilia Galotti are proof of major changes within public consciousness. The problems of Sara and Emilia presupposed a major shift in public values. No writer for the court would have considered loss of female virginity as suitable material for tragic treatment. No court audience would have understood. And indeed, a production of Emilia Galotti in Vienna had the emperor laughing throughout the performance.[9]

Sara and Emilia were possible only in a very special environment. The issue at its core derived from the peculiar interpretation of woman's position in a middle-class society. As Paul Kluckhohn has shown, the development which tended to define woman as auxiliary to the male, began in the second half of the eighteenth century.[10] A social conflict which was presented on a male-oriented level could nevertheless be expressed as a conflict between lusty aristocrat and innocent bourgeois female. The woman only triggered the situation, and it was usually up to the father figure to display the full colors of middle-class virtuousness in his defense of his daughter against the lecherous aristocrat. Neither Sara nor Emilia were treated as individuals. They were used to symbolize a highly abstract set of virtues. In the case of Emilia this use became clear in the encounter between Odoardo and the prince; Odoardo especially showed no regard for Emilia's feelings and emotions. When the prince suggested that Emilia should stay with him, Odoardo's reaction showed no concern for Emilia; he was mainly annoyed that the prince dares to tell him how to dispose of his daughter. And it was for this reason that Odoardo suggested the convent.

The figure of Emilia and the other virtuous daughters which were so popular with audiences at that time were the creation of a society which had elected to see its women solely as passive victims. In order to sublimate the social tensions of one particular class, the female of that class was made the recipient of its aggressive energies. A corollary to this method of obscuring the real social conflict can be found in the excessive value which was placed on the love motif. The case of Luise Millerin was typical for this development.

Two main concerns shaped the consciousness of the middle class at that time, and they also shaped German middle-class drama: autonomy for the individual and the reinterpretation of private life as a matter of public concern. The family served as the perfect background. The family play raised the private sphere to the public level; at the same time, with the aid of the virgin type, experience of power could be created for the father figure. Only as the powerful father of the house could the politically impotent bourgeois male experience autonomy.

During this period of self-realization and emerging identity, criticism about the life style of the middle class was rejected by the public. The reception of Jacob Lenz's plays, for instance, made this very clear.[11] The fact that Lenz already used the dramatic conventions of popular works in order to criticize the still-emerging system was—predictably—met with negative audience reaction.

If one agrees with Georg Lukacs and accepts that the representation of individuality was the main concern of German middle-class drama,[12] then

182

the view of woman as archetypal victim was of vital importance for the dramatic realization of such concerns. Individuality can find dramatic expression only through the categories of dominance and submission. The interpretation of woman as destined to be submissive guarantees the experience of dominance without serious challenge. As father figure the male bourgeois can claim his right to autonomy.

From another view point, however, the bourgeois had not truly liberated himself from the feudalistic life style. Max Scheler has pointed to resentment as one of the root causes for the tensions between aristocracy and bourgeoisie.[13] The superior moral system, the backbone of the middle-class demand for individual freedom, suddenly appeared as sham. The male bourgeois did not want to eliminate the feudalistic system; he wanted the right to claim submission and obedience for himself. Middle-class marriage was redefined to that end. In the name of duty, marriage was degraded to a system which demanded physical obedience and slavish submission, the same system which the bourgeois promised to destroy for all human beings but in fact did only for men.[14]

The omniscient, almighty father became a common figure on the German stage. In this way a potentially political conflict against the powerful aristocracy was diverted to the private sphere of the family. Here the father figure ruled with authoritarian splendor. Feudalistic concepts such as passivity and physical obedience were not eliminated but were perpetuated through the new feminine ideal which developed parallel to that of the father figure. In the name of virtue and purity woman submitted to the position of permanent servant. More significantly, and as proof of the effect at that time of theatre as image-maker, woman began to accept the role of guardian of superior morality. She accepted the role of the virgin and thereby submitted to a highly detrimental form of idealization.

The popular plays of the time mainly celebrated two themes. Following Diderot, the strong father populated the stages in many variations, ranging from that of Emilia Galotti to that of Friedrich Schröder's Das Blatt hat sich gewendet. Following the Emilia formula, the theme of the seduced virgin usually appeared parallel to the father theme. The obsession which manifested itself in repetitions of the theme of femal purity revealed the bourgeois as a hypocrite. Lessing was the first of the middle-class writers to reflect the growing influence of masculine dominance within the consciousness of his class. The plays of the earlier Christian Gellert showed serious efforts to reflect female psychology in meaningful terms. By the time Sara and Emilia appeared, women functioned as a dramatic stereotype to serve a male-oriented purpose. It is revealing to recall Lessing's reaction when asked whether by giving the play her name he wanted to give the character of Emilia more weight. He denied this, saying that women and slaves are incapable of moral sense.[15]

Passivity and obedience were presented as God's special gift to woman. The resulting human cripple was liberally compensated with beauty and hailed as the feminine ideal. The popular Pamela, which showed how sexual innocence could sell if correctly marketed, for title and castle, had set the tone which allowed the interpretation of woman as an object. With such a background Lessing could construct effortlessly an entire plot on little else than the difficulties arising from the loss of the maidenhead.

Once successful, variations of virginity and the resulting complications became a stock situation in German middle-class theatre. It must be kept in mind, however, that these seemingly tragic complications could only be registered as such within a male-dominated social structure. To illustrate this point, it is only necessary to reverse the roles in Emilia Galotti and imagine a male Emilia who chooses death instead of pleasure.

After the successes of Miss Sara Sampson and Emilia Galotti, dramatic representation of woman began to display a problematic reduction in scope. The emergence of such types as the female virgin and their uncritical acceptance by the audiences, the absence of effective alternatives, and the resulting penetration of the public consciousness by these types are to a large extent a major source of present difficulties which thwart meaningful change in the perception of woman. Deeply ingrained habits of perceiving females as passive objects, the absence of an alternative symbolic environment—in this sense, neither Minna von Barnhelm nor Nathan der Weise became models for successive writers—makes constructive reinterpretation of woman a difficult task.

The type of the virgin remained an important figure on the German stage. The exuberant period of Storm and Stress brought a further variation on that theme. The peculiar vision of the female virgin as the passive object of male aggression was for that generation of writers a well-integrated part of their literary tradition. Given their desire to depict a world without the stilted abstractions of their literary ancestors, these writers set out to discover what they consider to be reality. Given their desire to alter social problems, they brought the plight of the unwed mother to the stage and constructed rather eloquent pleas for her demise. In this connection, it must not be overlooked that these plays which deal with the unwed mother were, despite a rather progressive surface, essentially uncritical towards the assumptions of their literary ancestors.

Heinrich Wagner's Die Kindermörderin (1776) and the more famous Gretchentragödie of Urfaust were typical. Such plays were problematic in so far as they appeared to demand social change while in reality they tended to reinforce the existing social conditions. Just as the responsibility for the virgin's purity rested with the father figure, so the responsibility for the pregnancy lay with the seducer. Quite often he was catapulted into a situation where his decision to restore the girl's honor by marriage literally meant that he decided whether she should live or die. The request for pity was a superficial one and had a reactionary core. These plays still upheld traditional middle-class moral values. The woman had engaged in what was considered to be illicit pleasure and had to be severely punished. From a psychological view, the fact that these plays inevitably ended with the girl's death points to barely suppressed hostility towards female sexuality. This approach which punished woman while presenting her to the audiences as an object of pity can hardly be surpassed in its blatant disregard for sincerity.

As the middle class began to gain political power, the resulting self-confidence precipitated the need to elaborate the superior system of values. Discovery of the Greeks led to reinterpretation of Greek mythology and eventually the bourgeois borrowed the myth for himself. This provided a perfect opportunity to decorate biological differences between the sexes with an aura of the universal, the absolute, and the inevitable. The myth enabled writers to hide the artificially created concept of female passivity behind a respectable façade.

Examples can be found in Friedrich Hebbel's works. The entire spectrum of carefully developed feminine attributes--audience-tested since Lessing--was now presented as a manifestation of universal powers. Throughout his works Hebbel invoked visions of a precarious balance between hostile masculine and feminine forces. The possibility for the creation of a more reasonable and constructive image of woman diminishes abruptly, if sociological reality is interpreted as reflection of universal forces.

The myth of universal sexual polarity provided Hebbel with what he considered a necessary tragic core for his plays.[16] His works were, in a sense, the highpoint and endpoint of that tradition which used the figure of the virgin for the realization of male middle-class dreams of independence. Hebbel employed the concept of virginity to suggest the invincibility of the female principle; he translated its loss into victory of the male principle. This idea was particularly blatant in Judith, where God himself in his wisdom made use of the heroine's virginity. However, in Hebbel's universe no female could represent a real threat to the male principle. The author used the traditional method for dealing with female sexuality. Motherhood was seen as woman's eternal curse. This idea was only implied in Judith but was cynically admitted in Maria Magdalena.

Due to the rather unique function of the theatre as image-maker for the middle classes at that time, permanent distortions of the perception of women could develop and penetrate the public consciousness freely. The dramatic tradition which served the middle class ended with Hebbel. New interests precipitated different dramatic types and concerns. Modern interests no longer revolve around the depiction of sexual conflicts. Modern interests lie beyond the point where reflection of the individual's private life is thought to capture reality in adequate terms.

Now the writer finds that he must defend his activity and justify the very existence of his work. In the face of middle-class ideals, which are now widely interpreted as questionable and susceptible to distortions, the playwright feels compelled to take a radical stance. The concept of counter-art expresses one possible reaction. Recycling of tradition becomes literary method.[17] Tradition is deliberately used as formula so that the past can be scrutinized indirectly.

Constructive reinterpretation of woman as dramatic character seems to create problems. Traditional male-oriented stereotypes impede efforts to depict woman as an autonomous being. This impediment can be seen in the works of writers who expressively denounce the values of the bourgeoisie but, at the same time, seem unable to conceive female dramatic characters without use of the traditional images and concepts put forth by this class.

The impact of concepts such as universal sexual polarity, concepts which interpreted human biology in terms of human destiny, can be seen in the struggles of a writer like Peter Hacks. Like many of his contempories, Hacks shares the modern obsession and no longer presents the traditional myths as predetermined manifestations of higher forces. He demonstrates the working out of the myth as the result of human actions. Specifically, Hacks attacks the content of the bourgeois consciousness. This attack also leads to a partial reevaluation of woman's situation within this particular social structure. Hacks does not shrink from this question and his Alkmene in Amphitryon indeed transcends the limits imposed by the bourgeois dramatic tradition. Hacks ridicules the problematic concept of female virtuousness by exposing it as a manifestation of masculine inadequacy.

On the other hand, plays such as Omphale and his version of Die Kindermörderin show Hacks losing the battle against the impact of tradition. Omphale especially addresses itself to the problem of sexual roles within a given social organization and concludes that motherhood is the unalterable destiny of woman. The play asserts that Omphale is unable to act as a hero since her function is to give birth to heroes.

In Die Kindermörderin Hacks points out what is readily acceptable to modern audiences: he insists that the play must concentrate on class differences.[18] He shows the seduction of the middle-class girl by an officer as the confrontation of two entirely different systems of human virtue. Following closely the traditional treatment of the theme, the play makes the girl the carrier of bourgeois honor which is assaulted by the aristocrat. And since Hack's version of the seduction theme is no longer concerned with peddling a superior moral system to a susceptible audience, the author can be honest and admit that there is no reason for the officer and aristocrat to subscribe to the bourgeois system.

Hacks does not vent any suppressed feelings of hostility towards female sexuality: neither the girl nor the child die. The fact that both survive and set out to try to make a new life for themselves is indeed an improvement in the status of the dramatic figure of the seduced virgin. But the play does not go quite far enough. It does not point to the concept of illegitimacy itself as the primary means to suppress woman and force her into a state of permanent dependency. Hacks unmasks the melodramatic tradition of the seduced virgin as an outgrowth of a specific class consciousness. Yet he still succumbs to the incredible power of that very tradition.

Attempts to create autonomous female characters seem as yet unable to transcend a highly problematic tradition. Deeply ingrained habits of perceiving females as victims of their own peculiar biology rather than as victims of specific social forces appear almost impossible to overcome.

New York

Notes

[1]W. H. Bruford, Theatre, Drama, and Audience in Goethe's Germany (London, 1950), p. 242. Similarly Georg Lukacs, Faust und Faustus, Ausgewählte Werke, Vol. II (Rowohlts deutsche Enzyklopädie, München, 1968), p. 179.

[2]Hellmut Petriconi, Die verführte Unschuld (Hamburg, 1953), p. 7.

[3]Bruford, p. 356.

[4]Ernest K. Bramsted, Aristocracy and the Middle Classes in Germany (Chicago and London, 1964), p. 23.

[5]Jürgen Habermas, Strukturwandel der Öffentlichkeit (Neuwied, 1962), p. 85.

[6]Bruford, p. 106.

[7]Arnold Hauser, Sozialgeschichte der Kunst und Literatur (München, 1963), p. 577.

[8]Bruford, p. 355.

[9]Ibid., p. 190.

[10]Paul Kluckhohn, Die Auffassung der Liebe in der Literatur des 18. Jahrhunderts und in der deutschen Romantik (Tübingen, 1966), p. 307.

[11]Rudolf Genee, Hundert Jahre des königlichen Schauspiels in Berlin (Berlin, 1888), p. 10.

[12]Georg Lukacs, "Zur Soziologie des Modernen Dramas," Schriften zur Literatursoziologie, Soziologische Texte, Band 9 (Neuwied und Spandau, 1968), p. 294.

[13]Quoted in Bramsted, p. 185.

[14]Ralf Dahrendorf, Gesellschaft und Demokratie in Deutschland (München, 1968), p. 72.

[15]Lessings Werke, ed. Kurt Wölfel (Frankfurt, 1967), p. 668. In a letter to Karl Lessing: "Die jungfräulichen Heroinen und Philosophinnen sind garnicht nach meinem Geschmacke. Wenn Aristoteles von der Güte der Sitten handelt, so schliesst er die Weiber und Sklaven ausdrücklich davon aus. Ich kenne an einem unverheirateten Mädchen keine höhere Tugenden, als Frömmigkeit und Gehorsam."

[16]Friedrich Hebbel, "Vorwort zur Maria Magdalena," Werke, Vol. I, ed. Gerhard Frick, Werner Keller, Karl Pörnbacher (München, 1963), p. 327.

[17]Hugh Kenner, The Counterfeiters (Bloomington and London, 1968) develops this aspect of modern literature in greater detail.

[18]Peter Hacks, "Vorrede zur Kindermörderin," Stücke nach Stücken (Berlin und Weimar, 1965).

Selected Bibliography:

Bramsted, Ernest K. _Aristocracy and the Middle Classes in Germany._ Chicago and London: 1964.

Brombacher, Kuno. _Der deutsche Bürger im Literaturspiegel von Lessing bis Sternheim._ München: 1920.

Bruford, W. H. _Theatre, Drama, and Audience in Goethe's Germany._ London: 1950.

Dahrendord, Ralf. _Gesellschaft und Demokratie in Deutschland._ München: 1969.

Glaser, Hermann. _Eros in der Politik._ Köln: 1967.

Haberman, Jürgen. _Strukturwandel der Öffentlichkeit._ Neuwied: 1962.

Hauser, Arnold. _Sozialgeschichte der Kunst und Literatur._ München: Becksche Sonderausgabe., 1963.

Kluckhohn, Paul. _Die Auffassung der Liebe in der Literatur des 18. Jahrhunderts und in der Romantik._ Tübingen: 1966.

Kosellek, Reinhart. _Kritik und Krise: Ein Beitrag zur Pathogenese der bürgerlichen Welt._ Freiburg und München: 1959.

Lukacs, Georg. _Faust und Faustus: Vom Drama der Menschengattung zur Tragödie der Modernen Kunst._ München: Rowohlts deutsche Enzyklopädie, 1968.

_____. _Schriften zur Literatursoziologie._ Neuwied und Spandau: 1969.

Marcuse, Herbert. "Studie über Autorität und Familie," _Ideen zu einer kritischen Theorie der Gesellschaft._ (edition suhrkamp, 300) Frankfurt: 1963.

Petriconi, Hellmut. _Die verführte Unschuld._ Hamburg: 1953.

Schaer, Wolfgang. _Die Gesellschaft im deutschen bürgerlichen Drama des 18. Jahrhundertz._ Bonn: 1963.

Selver, Henrik. _Die Auffassung des Bürgers im deutschen bürgerlichen Drama des 18. Jahrhunderts._ Diss. Universität Leipzig. Leipzig: 1931.

Inculcating a Slave Mentality: Women in German Popular

Fiction of the Early Twentieth Century

by

Ruth K. Angress

Germany in the twentieth century has not been especially innovative
in its popular literature.* Westerns, science fiction, and murder myster-
ies are largely Anglo-Saxon in origin and development. They are avidly
consumed in Germany but only inferior imitations are produced there. Even
the middle-brow romance is lacking in skilled practitioners who write in
the relatively sophisticated and original style and with the mastery of
human psychology that distinguishes that genre in England and America.

One of the problems seems to be a tendency to endow family sagas--
a favorite with Germans--and the so-called "women's novels" (Frauenromane)
with an ideology or a pseudo-depth that will redeem these books from being mere entertainment. The resultant mixture is peculiarly German, not
capable of export and, I submit, quite pernicious. I should like to examine some of the pre-Nazi best sellers of this type.

From the standpoint of a woman, we are dealing here with a kind of
slave literature. That is to say, only those female characters are permitted to lead meaningful lives who are willing not only to put up with
the status quo but to serve it heart and soul. This is quite different
from a legitimate treatment of a slave mentality, i.e., from an analysis
of the neuroses and conflicts that result when one group of people is
forced to accept the superiority of another. The books I have in mind are
not a literature about a slave mentality, but rather they feed these very
neuroses and tensions instead of illuminating them. They repress the very
possibility that conflict may follow the unquestioned acceptance of a
status quo. They advocate selflessness, but demonstrate it not in the
rulers but only in the ruled. Thus, attitudes that should be exposed as
either sick or counter-productive are glorified as the Beautiful, the
Good, and the Eternally Feminine.

In Germany as elsewhere there is a book market geared specifically
to a female public. The unprejudiced observer might expect that novels
billed as "Frauenromane" would deal with the achievements of exceptional
women or, alternately, with the everyday life of ordinary women, treating
that life with appreciation and in detail. Such is not the case. Exceptional women are suspect, and professional, artistic, or administrative
excellence is non-existent for them. Nor are ordinary women often seen
performing or worrying about the household chores that make up their lives,
and not much room is given to kitchen and nursery where they spend their
time. Pregnancies are omitted, children are born in two sentences, one
and a half dealing with the father's excitement and one half with the pal-
lor of the mother. Once born, they seem to manage without diapers, i.e.,
the actual trouble, skill, and hard work of child care is not treated.
Analogous passages dealing with a man's work do, however, emphasize the
harshness and dignity of his work.

If, then, everything is omitted that makes up the lives of women,

189

and traditional feminine tasks are not given their due as socially useful, what are these books about? The answer is that they constitute variants in prose of the patriarchal hierarchy. They are "women's novels" only in the sense that they contribute to women's willingness to accept their status as second-class citizens. Nearly always do girls and women in them not only act but think and feel in the shadow of a man, led by a man. If a man disappoints a woman, another man will comfort her. In those rare scenes where women are among themselves, they exchange giggly imbecilities or they enact jealous scenes or they discuss available bachelors. Never do they talk to each other of God and man (in the generic sense), their experience of solitude, the meaning of friendship, a sense of discovery or doubt in the justice of the world. On the contrary: with one exception, independence of mind is treated as a fault of character and is punished accordingly, usually through the withdrawal of male approbation.

The exception is the case of the mother, preferably widowed, who has to take care of a son who is still a minor. This figure recurs with great frequency, presumably because it permits an expansion of the narrow scope imposed on the author by the rules governing the other female characters. It should be noted, however, that the relative independence of the mother figure is permissible only because it is of benefit to a male. It is axiomatic that the child must be a son. Only minor characters are parents of daughters. The heroine proves her higher worth through male progeny, and already during pregnancy both parents refer with X-ray certainty to the embryo as "he."

Now the superiority of sons over daughters is of course an ancient and primitive cultural prejudice, worth singling out only because it is warmed over and served up in twentieth-century novels destined for women. But the context in which this is done is significant, for that context is property. Men are heirs. Notice how respect for ownership and readiness for motherhoood merge into one in the following passage from Nataly von Eschstruth's The Bears of Hohen-Esp (Die Bären von Hohen-Esp) (1902): "Here in the castle of your forefathers, I am seized by a passionate, awesome longing, by jubilant enthusiasm when I think that I may be called on to give an heir to this old, doughty house of bears, to continue it in a son who will be as noble, as chivalrous and magnificent as all those heroic men." The heroic qualities of the family are apparent only in the existence of the impressive piece of real estate that has inspired this outburst, since the owner himself, the husband of the speaker, turns out to be a gambler who loses everything, except the family estate, and then kills himself.

Nataly von Eschstruth was an aristocrat at the Prussian court who wrote a large number of very successful novels, some of which she dedicated to Emperor Wilhelm II himself. She took care to endow them with all the right sentiments, including a solid, upper-class pre-war patriotism that may have seemed harmless enough at the time, though with hindsight it appears ominous. A very different, non-political and deliberately inner-directed writer was Agnes Günther, who wrote only one novel, 750 pages of it, entitled The Saint and her Fool (Die Heilige und ihr Narr). It was her life's work. She labored over it with an energy and perseverance, in sickness and close to death, that stand in odd contrast to the quality of the product. When she died in 1911, the formidable manuscript was still un-

published. The book was published in 1913 and after World War I it became one of the most sensational of German best sellers, with more than a
million copies sold.

In Günther's novel the heroine, Princess Rosmarie, is an only child,
and from the outset her father makes her aware that she is only a poor substitute for the son who could inherit the principality of Brauneck. Rosmarie suffers from her "inferiority"; yet instead of analyzing the debil-
itating effect of such a treatment on the psyche of a child or censuring
the father, the author herself moves with the current of the prejudice.
She arranges her plot so that Rosmarie later gives birth to a son (what
else?), and this son inherits Brauneck, together with the name and rank of
his maternal grandfather. A complicated judicial procedure is required to
bring all this about and to raise Rosmarie to the level of a son, since
the family line with all its possessions is continued through her. Günther
tells of these machinations as the fulfilment of Rosmarie's life. Not a
shadow of doubt or criticism enters, no hint of the futility of such patriarchal attitudes in a woman.

With the fusion woman/property/home, we have come to the core of
the problem. The relationship of woman and property is crucial. It is
most easily understood where woman herself is a piece of property. She can
become a proprietor in her own right only after she has been married, once
she has been property, after she has been (the pun is intentional) had.
Again a quote from Eschstruth, from the novel Gänseliesl, where a man ex-
claims in connection with an engagement: "Is it true, has Reimar dared to
desire you for his property?" ("Sie zum Eigentum zu begehren?") And in
the same book: "Is that woman a widow that she can traipse around the
world on her own and dispose so independently over such sums?" Of course
the substance of these outraged exclamations only reflects the economic
facts of life of the period. Yet there is a sharp, almost comical contrast
between the background of courtliness which is the premise of Eschstruth's
novels and the blatant resentment which greets the threat of feminine economic independence. The author, however, does not draw the obvious conclusions nor imply that the reader should.

Yet woman is not always a possession, she also functions as the pre-
server or, alternately, the squanderer of property. And what is property?
The answer to this question may be found in succinct form in a passage
from The Barrings (Die Barrings) by William von Simpson, a family saga
which appeared in 1937 (yet is not a Nazi book!). On a solemn occasion,
the head of the family speaks of the family estate Wiesenburg: "Your
great-grandfather Barring gave us Barrings with our dear Wiesenburg the
greatest thing that can be given to men, gave us a home which no one can
take from us. And together with a secure home he left us as our foremost
task the duty to guard our own hearth, our inherited earth as the greatest
good in life." There is a trick of language here that cannot be translated. Old Barring does not say "ein Heim," he says "die Heimat," thus
making the homeland out of a home. This sleight-of-hand permits the
author to confuse a private estate with the fatherland, and thus we find
that to increase one's holdings is a patriotic deed. To accumulate wealth,
particularly in the form of real estate, becomes the highest duty. Once
this train of thought is established, women are smoothly fitted into
their niche: "That we were able to do this is largely due to the devoted

and selfless help of our womenfolk." And finally: "Wiesenburg is grateful. It won't let you down, if you'll keep faith."

In the last passage the estate itself has been raised to the level of a living being, and efficiency has become faithfulness. In terms of women, this means that there is only one step from neglecting their husbands' estate to marital infidelity. This outlook gradually leads the reader to dividing women into two groups: first the good ones, who conserve and enlarge their husbands' or sons' property and are consequently faithful, and then the wicked ones, who waste money and, through an illogical chain of association, are also bad mothers and unfaithful, or at least dangerously sensual, wives. The point is, money comes first, everything else is a natural development of a deficient sense of respect for wealth. The plot of the book deals with the gradual loss of the estate because of a wasteful woman. The process is given a historical and symbolic significance through a personal relationship between old Barring and Bismarck. Long excerpts from Barring's diary deal with events in the capital and the politics of the day. Wiesenburg is in every respect a part and a microcosm of Germany. The basic fault of Gerda, the wicked woman, is that she does not realize this. But the reader may well be inclined to sympathize with her and question the sanctity of real estate. At the end of the book she is going to sell Wiesenburg, and she therefore has to be seen committing a variety of spiteful actions which will put her proclivity to make debts into the right light, i.e., show it up as a dangerous vice. So she is made to neglect her children and treat them with a lack of sensitivity that is not altogether plausible. By a process of escalation she becomes cruel to both children and animals. The ideology of the book demands that Gerda become more and more contemptible in human terms at the expense of verisimilitude.

Agnes Günther also writes of a bad woman whose basic qualities are a tendency to waste money and a lack of reverence towards the old castle in which she lives as well as toward the others that her husband is busily restoring. Rosmarie/s stepmother betrays tradition by demanding new (and modern) furniture, longing for central heating, buying an automobile, and not being automatically horrified at the sight of rich Americans. Although her husband spends large sums on his restoration projects, his expenditures are ideologically justified, while hers open the road to all further wickedness: she is an inadequate wife, she cannot bear children (the reasons are a mystery-laden mixture of biology and morals), she tortures her stepdaughter and in the end even tries to kill her. Like Gerda Barring, she uses money for her own ends, and this lies at the root of all her evil-doing.

Significantly, in all such cases we are dealing with women who refuse to submit and to serve. They are women who follow their own tastes and needs, who want to assert themselves, in short, to be independent. The novels of Rudolf Herzog show a virtual obsession with authority and dependence in masculine and feminine roles. Herzog wrote a History of Prussia (Preussens Geschichte, 1913) in which he spells out the fundamental importance of a healthy patriarchal family system to the functioning of a state. His very poor and very popular novels must have been conceived as an educational enterprise of national scope. In these books it is no longer German soil but German factories that constitute the fatherland. We have come a step further in the equation of private property and holy Germany. Herzog's heroes are determined by a work ethic, and essentially they don't do much else than increase their holdings. But of course this pursuit is sublimated into patriotism of the highest order.

Let us consider The Stoltenkamps and their Women (Die Stoltenkamps und ihre Frauen, 1917), a novel that deals with the development of German steel in the nineteenth and early twentieth centuries. (In other words, this is basically a Krupp novel.) It closes with a glimpse of the steel factories working full blast at the height of World War I, that is, with a nationalistic justification of a private industry. The hero is both the owner and the administrator of the fatherland, and anyone who refuses to cooperate with him is guilty of high treason. Accordingly he is surrounded by faithful women, faithful friends, and faithful workers. This means that he is not only central to the novel, but he is also central to these other lives which have no independent value that is not derived from their contribution to his activities. In the women characters this devaluation of individuals is carried furthest, but it can be seen best if one compares the plight of women to the analogous situation of the workers in the book.

Although Herzog claimed to have written in praise of labor and although he produces sentiments like, "A new aristocracy is arising, an aristocracy of labor" ("Ein neuer Adel kommt herauf, ein Adel der Arbeit"), yet he actually writes in praise of the existing power structure in factory and family. Not by accident does he call the employers the "masters" ("die Herren"). The employee should resemble a well-trained horse, a comparison that is put into the mouth of an elderly worker who speaks words of wisdom to young Stoltenkamp, instructing him on the submissiveness which he must exact from his crew: "There's got to be pressure ("Schenkeldruck"), or you won't gain respect." Anyone who doesn't relish the pressure and joins a union is shown to be selfish without redeeming qualities.

There is the question of what the employer, the master, owes to his workers. The answer is: "The whole power of the employee belonged to the firm to which he bound himself. But the firm had to pay each employee so that his wages were a perfect expression of the worth of his labor." A perfect expression? Elsewhere Herzog explains that man should work for the sake of a cause, or for the sake of "sacred labor" herself and he explicitly introduces as antagonist a man who works for the sake of a higher living standard and stands condemned by his materialistic ambition. Hence: the worker proves his good character by accepting his wages, which he has not helped determine, as the fair equivalent of his labor.

So much for the worker, and now the women. Old Stoltenkamp dies with the pace-setting words: "I had the right wife, one who did not ask questions and always had faith. That made me feel so good." The widow is 32 years old, her oldest son Fritz is 16. From hereon she has no other need or ambition than to live for him and his firm. As with the workers, Herzog again employs the trick of having the less privileged speak in defense of their own submission, thus lending it a spurious validity. The mother says to her teenage son: "I am and shall remain your mother, but as of today you are the head of the family." The author stresses her voluntary choice of a life which to the unbiased reader must appear depressing, by implying, but not spelling out, that the mother could have married again

during the first years of her widowhood. We never see her with another
man. She is shown only in her total dedication to her son and his work.
Not that she acquires a genuine or independent interest in that work. The
bookkeeping which she does for him gives her a purely vicarious pleasure,
and she generalizes the satisfaction which the author has her feel when
she says: "You can't give a woman a better or more cheerful life than
what you are doing for your mother. To take part in the troubles and cares
of the person one loves, to help him carry them and overcome them and then
be permitted to see the rewards in the success of the beloved person."
The beloved person is, of course, always the man, while the woman is inevitably cast for the auxiliary action.

Thus, Mrs. Stoltenkamp does her son's secretarial work, "for we
Stoltenkamp women must keep active for our men, in order to achieve the
right kind of cheerfulness." Yet only she, the mother, has the right to
be a priestess in the inner sanctum, to keep vigil over German steel. For
the rest, Herzog is at pains to exclude women from the masculine realm.
When a sister shows an interest in the factory, she is told in unequivocal
words that "a Stoltenkamp girl has no business meddling with the work of
her brothers." When the sister is obstinate, her brother buys her shares
and then walks through his factory as "its only lord and master."

Even more infantile are the intentions behind the title figure of
Herzog's later novel, The Boys of Mrs. Opterberg (Die Buben der Frau Opterberg, 1921). Here the heroine is first met at the source of the Rhine in
the mountains where she has wandered on an excursion with her son and her
adopted son. The father is at home, not dead as in The Stoltenkamps, but
Herzog gets him out of the way by making an insignificant, artistically
inclined weakling of him, so that the stress falls once again on the
mother-son relation. With symbolic emphasis this mother is often referred
to as a source and is identified with the Rhine as a German river. She
overflows with patriotic doctrines and maxims and lacks any quality that
does not pertain to her real and symbolic motherhood. She stands forever
ready to help her children and their friends and waits in some unspeci-
fied limbo of latency when she is not needed.

The boys are her only comrades, she pronounces. (The implied
slight to the father is not meant to reflect on her, hence must be uncon-
scious on Herzog's part.) But when her son later marries, his wife is to
concern herself exclusively with her husband. For the true wife, says
Christiane Opterberg, is a comrade who marches in step with her man. Although she has done very little for her husband in the course of the novel,
having to attend to the unconsciously infantile ego needs of her son, she
now paints the ideal wife as one who "has her heart in the right place,
especially at the moment when her husband needs it" ("besonders wenn's der
Mann gerad beansprucht"). "And she must have brains in the right place,
too, so that she can take part in everything that makes up the husband's
intellectual life, only she mustn't come on as a know-all and school mistress, for that would take away the man's pleasure in being the stronger."

This obsession with defining the role of women and circumscribing it
ever anew is anchored, I believe, in a profound mistrust towards women.
When dealing with "bad" women, this mistrust turns into the fear that they
could take something away from men, that they might harm or diminish
that very property which plays so large a part in these novels, as we have

said, and which is so closely linked to male identity. This is why a straight line leads from the wasteful woman to the adulteress. If a man wastes money, for example a playboy of a brother, the reader is asked to sympathize up to a point. We have already mentioned the example of a rather attractive gambler in an Eschstruth novel, the father of the hero of The Bears of Hohen-Esp. Such men can be forgiven, because it is not important whether they are submissive or not. But the sensuous woman constitutes a threat to the hero, for she has her own emotional life, and if she regards their joint property as just that, namely as belonging to her, too, then the rider-horse relationship is seriously jeopardized. Sabine, the younger Mrs. Opterberg, is such a woman who refuses to serve.

Sabine reaches the height of her supposed malice and low point of feminity when she is something less than enthusiastic at the prospect of maternity. She suggests that one might wait a while before getting her pregnant and has the effrontery to imply that she herself has a right to make such a decision. She clearly rejects the role of a slave by saying: "I wouldn't dream of giving up my freedom." Herzog has a lot to say about freedom, about German freedom, about the freedom of men. But a woman who uses this expression in a meaningful context, as a claim to physical self-determination, thereby loses the sympathies of the author and his obedient readers. Sabine's fate in the novel is sealed after this pronouncement. A few pages later her husband catches her with another man and gets divorced.

True love comes to Martin Opterberg with his second engagement to a girl who celebrates the occasion by singing, "Let us stand fast / In the tempest's blast" ("Haltet aus im Sturmgebraus"). The rejection of adult sexuality has received a pointedly nationalistic twist: the messy sensuous marriage is equated with the lost war, the new chaste love with the resurrection of Germany. Still referring to the engagement part, Herzog writes: "Thus Martin Opterberg celebrated the peace treaty of Versailles." A double defeat, on the personal and the national level, is countered by a double defiance through a second marriage and through a sense of "the blood of his Germanic ancestors coursing through his veins." The new Mrs. Opterberg (her symbolic first name is Linde, the national tree) is selfless, devoted, pure, clear-eyed, very young, and she worships her mother-in-law.

The feminine counterpart to this infantile projection of the maternal mistress and the submissive, erotically undemanding wife as ideal women can be found in Agnes Günther's The Saint and her Fool. Essentially the novel is a glorification of sexual repression. The novel deals with a princess whom we first meet as a misunderstood, introverted child, whom the adults consider retarded, although she suffers only from a gift for ESP and from the insensitivity of her surroundings. Her admirer and later husband, Count Harro von Thorstein, calls her "Seelchen" (little psyche, with an obvious allusion to Goethe's "schöne Seele"), and nearly half a novel passes before she is called by her real name, Rosmarie. Throughout she is shown in a suffering posture, which is no mean trick, considering that she is noble, beautiful, wealthy, with an eminently eligible bachelor and later a loving husband at her feet. Yet Agnes Günther manages to present her as a victim: suffering is a talent which women can display without fear of male competition.

Repressed sexuality becomes a pervasive theme once Rosmarie marries

Harro, after she has spent a soulful and pathetic childhood. Now Harro
has promised his father-in-law that the marriage will not be consummated
for a time, because his bride is too young. Neither the reader nor Rosmarie are informed of this arrangement. The wedding takes place, and is
couple of old aunts appear to spend the wedding night, providing what is
meant to pass as a comic interlude: there is some discreet jesting about
naked aunts, while the new husband, who is a painter among his other ac-
complishments, retires to his studio. Although Rosmarie is a grownup
woman, she doesn't notice that anything is amiss. And now Günther invents
a situation that is of the essence of the book, perhaps also of the essence
of soft-core pornography. Harro is working on a painting which he cannot
finish for lack of inspiration and the right model. His virginal wife
brings him the ultimate sacrifice by posing for him in the nude, so that
he can paint her as a fairy next to a legendary fountain. The scene permits Rosmarie to be simultaneously shameless and pure. A young female
middle-class reader might have a bad conscience when she dreams herself
into the role of a fallen woman, but she can with a good conscience identify with this princess who is exposing all her maidenly charms in what is
essentially a symbolic consummation of her marriage. Symbolism has the
further advantage that it skirts and evades the realities of the sexual
act, thus meeting and feeding the neurotic fears of repressed and imaginative virgins. To top it all, the husband is of course fully satisfied,
since his wife has inspired him to paint his best work.

The counterpart to Herzog's bad woman who doesn't want children is
Günther's good woman who isn't supposed to have children yet and who is
spared by good men. Here we should remember our grandmothers' all too
well-founded fear of childbirth. The possibility of dying was very real
to pregnant women, but, significantly, it isn't treated as an independent
issue, worthy to be investigated. Günther turns it into a mystery, but at
least the danger is recognized, although it becomes inextricably mixed with
fear of the sexual act. Herzog ignores it altogether or turns it into a
reproach against the woman.

Strangely enough, the only conflict in Günther's novel and therefore
the propelling mechanism of the plot, such as it is, takes place between
women and consists of an older woman harming the younger one in an erotically symbolic way: e.g., she scalds her stepdaughter's arm on her wedding day. Only the wicked woman is aggressive; there are no aggressive
men in the book. I am inclined to see here another representation of virginal repressions. The father as well as the husband are on the one hand
masculine stereotypes, but on the other hand they are incomplete, static,
inhibited, and not quite adult. Yet they are also strong and energetic--
Harro is not only an artist, he is also a military officer, an architect,
and physically of athletic build, while his father-in-law looks and acts
like the great lord he is ("Grand Seigneur, sehr sogar"). These desirable specimens of manhood are never seen fighting among themselves or
forcing their attention on women, as the story of the wedding amply demonstrates. It is significant that throughout the long first part of the
novel, the relationship of the couple is that between an adult and a child,
free of erotic tension, while from the reader's point of view they are
already a pair.

In contrast to Agnes Günther, Rudolf Herzog shows masculine activity as being indeed closely related to aggressiveness. The triumph of German steel at the end of the Stoltenkamps is adumbrated in the first sentence of the book: "The fist of the fourteen-year-old boy hit the scolding man right between the eyes." This action earns unqualified admiration: "You are a reliable fellow, Fritz." ("Auf dich ist Verlass, Fritz.")

There seems to be a distinct difference in the treatment of male aggressiveness as presented by male and female authors in this type of book. Günther is not alone. The other women also have a tendency to draw masculine characters who are energetic and active on the one hand, but are lacking in passion or involvement with other human beings, and hence cannot really be seen as feminine love or sex objects. Their attraction lies elsewhere, I believe. They may have been conceived as complementary figures to the pathetically limited lives of the female characters. In their freedom of action they open an added dimension, needed to hold the reader's interest and fulfill her capacity for empathy. In other words, they are extensions of the women, somewhat as in Hesse's work, where the female characters are often used as projections of the male psyche rather than as separate and autonomous characters. The more passive the woman is (not sexually, but in her daily life), the more active the man has to appear to achieve a balance and to offer the reader what she is looking for as a person, particularly a young person, but what she must not wish to find in the female figures, namely ambition, freedom, courage and mobility.

Let us, in this connection, consider the function of horseback riding, an aristocratic sport for both sexes which plays a prominent part in Eschstruth's novels. Now the sticky question arises: how well may a girl ride? In this, as always, she must not lose in femininity what she might gain in other respects. Hence not too well. For whoever rides well gives the impression of being strong, even dominant, certainly in control. And women are to be weak, unless they have to take care of young men. At the beginning of The Bears of Hohen-Esp, a girl has to appear as both weak and strong, because later in the novel she is going to be one of those motherly administrators. In the meantime she must not lose any obligatory passivity. She is introduced with her horse, and the description reads: "That vigorously beautiful girl who's mastering the frightened horse is at bottom only a weak suffering (!) humble and infinitely gentle woman." The hand that describes the woman takes away the very virtues which the other hand has just bestowed on the human being. The sad fact is that excellence of any kind is incompatible with the ideal of womanhood these books present.

Thus, the girl on horseback has to be without any athletic ambitions. She is permitted to ride well, just as she is permitted and supposed to be sexually attractive, but only up to a point. And in any case, she is not allowed to strive for either effect or even to know about it. The reader, however, does know, for the admiration of this kind of innocence or ignorance is not possible without consciousness, and thus its imitation can only be a matter of hypocrisy. Indeed, hypocrisy is a quality that is implicitly advocated in women's literature, and it has no analogy in the corresponding boys' literature or the war novels primarily aimed at men.

In the case under discussion these "rules" are all the more deplorable as Nataly von Eschstruth had a rather sharp eye for eccentric women and would have been a far more interesting novelist if she had been more

daring. There is a mannish princess in Gänseliesl who dresses comfort-
ably and is serious about riding and hunting. As soon as she becomes too
autonomous, however, her author makes up by turning conventional and either
censures and punishes poor Sylvie or shows her in an altogether different
light, doing things that don't really suit her, such as singing folk songs
with her heart trembling in her voice. When Sylvie competes or perspires
while riding, the men scorn and resent her, and the author is on the side
of the men. The slave mentality propagated in all these books stipulates
that competition is for masters only, not for the auxiliary forces, not
for servants, not for women. In order to complete and round off the subject of competitive sports and skillful horseback riding which was begun
with women, the novel turns to men. The novelist shows male competitiveness
and adventurousness pushed to the point of foolhardiness, as when a young officer rides across a railroad track, leaping the barriers after they have
come down and while the train is approaching at a distance of a hundred
yards.

The case is similar with women who know how to do sums. The woman
who can figure is the calculating female. Precisely because money and
property play such a decisive role in their world, girls and young women
are supposed to be ignorant and unworried about the two factors that will
determine their lives. Witness Rosmarie who is so sweet and innocent when
she talks about interest rates that Harro says with patronizing affection:
"This is hilarious; do you even know what interest rates are?" Yet Rosmarie is a rich heiress.

It is, incidentally, quite a mystery how and when the efficient
widowed mothers acquire their economic know-how. Again, the reader is
asked to do what the heroine mustn't, namely calculate and wish her a good
match. But when a character in the novel realizes what her interests are,
she loses her appeal. For example, in The Bears of Hohen-Esp there is a
girl without means, called Thea, who makes a deliberate effort to catch a
man. The attempt is hopeless, and the author shows no sympathy for a girl
who is conscious of her situation, that is, of belonging to the upper
classes without the requisite dowry. Mere poverty is excusable in a novel but a conscious attempt to do something about it is not, at least not
in a girl. And yet, exasperatingly, Eschstruth understands very well that
this is a political-social problem, for at the end of the book one of the
other characters has this to say about Thea: "Season after season she
danced in vain. Now she has joined the women's movement and writes very
angry and venomous articles against men. If she has her way, the strong
sex will be destroyed within a year." Now Thea is in a situation which
might very well point the way to the feminists, for she must notice that
the ideal of chivalry is a sham. Yet instead of exposing the conditions
of which Thea is a victim, Eschstruth makes her responsible by ridiculing
her.

Woman, then, is treated as property, and property in turn (whether real
estate or factory or just plain money) is equated with fatherland (in some
contexts it would be better to say motherland); that land with all its ad-
juncts is idealized by being burdened with its past and its literature, especially in frequent references to and quotations from Goethe. The cycle
closes with woman not as a citizen but as ideal possession and embodied
inwardness. If she rebels against her role, she betrays her men and in so

doing she betrays her homeland and hence humanity at large. It is easy
to see the dishonesty which makes out of a powerful man of property a
guardian of the fatherland, and labels the striking worker unpatriotic.
There is a close analogy in these young women who are required to be soulful, inner-directed, and unselfish, and thereby to uphold values that are
not in their best interests, and to pretend, moreover, that these values
are universal, no to say Eternally Feminine, when in fact they stand in
patent contradiction to what is really required of these girls, namely
money and sex. These books make square pegs fit into round holes. The
reader learns from them and from these creatures who always please and
never try to please that one one must not desire the only things that are
desirable. She is given a set of useless models and is left with the ir-
reconcilability of being a fully developed human and an attractive woman
at the same time.

In today's Germany The Barrings is a book club selection (Bertels-
mann Lesering) and The Heirs of the Barrings is a best seller. Agnes
Günther is still so popular that as late as 1957 a book of photos was
worth publishing, entitled Aus Agnes Günthers Wunderland, with text by her
son. Even more importantly, however, today the subjects and values of
these books have sunk to a lower level yet and have become part and par-
cel of the cheap paperback market, the so-called "Heftromane," which are
pure formula writing, and unfortunately have a very wide distribution. In
the "Frauenromanserien" sex is even now taboo! Side by side with these
sub-literary productions, we find more pretentious "modern" family novels,
like Will Heinrich's Geometry of a Marriage. Here eroticism is treated
openly, but the contrasting types of the devoted and the calculating wom-
en are still pitted against one another, though the quality of their characters is now shown in their sexual behavior. And the calculating woman
is still the one with a head for business, an eye on money, though now
she is a political reactionary which is meant to make her as unappealing
as her predecessors' cosmopolitanism used to be. Now, as then, the evidence of her inferiority is her refusal to bear children.

In conclusion it is instructive to glance back at the beginnings of
the German popular novel. Handbooks on German literature usually tell
that the first German "Unterhaltungsroman" was written by a woman, Sophie
LaRoche's Fräulein von Sternheim. Now the heroine of this work happens to
have many more facets to her life and character and is far more of a three-
dimensional person than the heroines of the books we have discussed. To
be sure, the complexities of her love life dominate much of the novel, but
she is also concerned with self-fulfilment and her immediate usefulness to
society. In pursuit of these goals she becomes an educator and demonstrates her ability to lead both an active and a contemplative life, quite
apart from sex and marriage. The novel appeared in 1771 and was a great
success. The moral is that in the eighteenth century it was possible to
present, even on a relatively low literary level, a heroine who was not
only a female but a human being as well. It took the sophistications of a
later period to reduce the women of popular fiction to fragments of their
real selves and to present the mutilated pieces to a female audience for
consumption and enjoyment.

                                              University of Virginia

*Lecture given at the Third National Popular Culture Association
Meeting, Indianapolis, April 1973.

Women in the Third Reich

by

Ann Leek

This short paper was written as part of the requirements of an undergraduate course in German Civilization at the University of Massachusetts.
It is a brief description of life for women in Germany from 1933 to 1945.

In Hitler's Germany a little girl started to perform her duty to the
Reich when she was ten years old. She became a member of the Young Girls
and took part in social evenings, competed in sports, heard lectures in
Nazi history, and learned the Horst Wessel song and the Deutschland song.
From fourteen to eighteen, she was kept busy with the League of German
Girls, where she continued with sports and also went to youth camps. Since
she could not join the National Socialist Women's League until she was
twenty-one, there remained three unsupervised years. In 1938, however,
this loophole was closed by the advent of a new Party organization for
eighteen to twenty-one year olds. This division was known as Faith and
Beauty and was considered voluntary although it, too, would probably have
become mandatory had not World War II intervened.

This was only a part of the control of the Nazi government. Because
so many agricultural workers had moved into the cities, there was an urgent
need to replace them. From this need was born the Agricultural Year for
Girls. Every young girl had to serve the Reich for one year. In the cities, there were few vacant jobs, and this gave yet another possibility for
the State to make use of teenage girls, the mandatory Household Year.
After 1938, those who left school were able to receive their certificates
only after showing proof of completion of a year's work for the State.
The daughters of wealthy families could avoid this task by pretending to
work in the homes of family friends. Girls from poor homes had no choice
other than taking an unpaid year of work on a farm or being a mother's
helper for a large family in the city.

During this time, educating women was not government policy. Study
at a university was made very difficult by the setting up of a numerus
clausus, by which only one student in ten could be female. Already in
1933, married women in the professions were dismissed and, in the working
classes, young women were encouraged to leave their jobs as soon as they
married. A loan of one thousand marks was offered to the young couple if
the woman agreed to give up her job. One quarter of the loan would be
cancelled with the birth of each child. In this way, the government
hoped to free many jobs for unemployed men and to encourage large families
of future Nazi workers.

Producing many children was the noblest work a woman could do for
the State and was compared with that of a soldier fighting for his country.
A childless marriage was highly suspect, especially among civil servants,
who were considered disloyal if they had no children. Every year on the
twelfth of August (the birthday of Hitler's mother), mothers were presented with the Honor Cross of the German Mother, which came in three
classes: bronze for more than four children, silver for more than six

children, and gold for more than eight children. To give Germany (or the Führer) as many children as possible was the only means by which a woman could gain respect. At most, an ambitious woman would go no higher than being a leader in the National Socialist Women's League, or in the women's branch of the German Work Front.

In spite of the feeling against working women, the poor kept on working as before. It was mostly the middle classes who were affected by the Regime. Young middle-class girls in the high schools were encouraged to take Home Economics courses instead of studying in academic fields. As a result of this, they were referred to as having passed the "Pudding Matriculation."

Even the appearance of women came under attempted control. Newspapers like the Völkische Beobachter and Schwarzes Korps raged against the use of cosmetics, the popular "boy-look" hairstyle and the latest styles in clothing. In some cities, women were forbidden to smoke in restaurants. To be a good Nazi, a woman was supposed to be not too intelligent, to have stereotyped "Gretchen" looks, and to be the mother of many children.

That was ideal. The reality was often different, and as the war drew closer, women were pressured to go to work in the factories. In May, 1941, Hitler announced the increased entry of women into the armaments industry.

Thus from the beginning to the end of the Third Reich, the German woman was used. She had free choice to elect Hitler to power, but this was the last free choice she was to have in the twelve years of his government.

Of great help in preparing this paper were two books:

Bleuel, Hans Peter. Das Saubere Reich. Scherz Verlag, 1972.

Grunberger, Richard. The Twelve Year Reich. New York: Holt, Rinehart, and Winston, 1971.

Women and German Literature: A Bibliography

by

Ritta Jo Horsley

General works and survey treatments.

Adolf, H. "Literary characters and their subterranean sources. The
Amazon type in literature," Comp. Lit. Proceedings (1959), 256-62.

Angermann, A. "Pfarrerstöchter in der deutschen Dichtung." Deutsche
Pfarrerstöchter. 1955, pp. 39-59.

Batts, Michael S. "Tristan and Isolde in modern literature. L'éternel
retour," Seminar 5 (1969), 79-91.

de Beauvoir, Simone. The Second Sex. New York, 1953. (Not specifically German)

Braun, F. "Die Idee der Liebe in der Dichtung Österreichs," in F. B.,
Das musische Land. 1962, pp. 29-53.

Cornillon, Susan K, ed. Images of Women in Fiction: Feminist Perspective. Bowling Green, Ohio, 1972.

Demetz, Peter. "The Elm and the Vine. Notes toward the history of a
marriage topos," PMLA 73 (1958), 521-32.

Ellmann, Mary. Thinking About Women. New York, 1968. (Not specifically German)

Figes, Eva. Patriarchal Attitudes: Woman in Society. London., 1970.

Foster, Jeanette H. Sex Variant Women in Literature: A Historical
and Quantitative Survey. New York, 1956.

Furness, Raymond. "The Androgynous Ideal: Its Significance in German Literature," Modern Language Review LX, No. 1 (1965), 58-64.

Gornick Vivian and Moran, Barbara K., eds. Woman in Sexist Society:
Studies in Power and Powerlessness. Basic Books, 1971. (Not
specifically German)

Greer, Germaine. The Female Eunuch. New York, 1970. (Not specifically German)

Guthke, Karl S. "Die Herkunft der weltliterarischen Typus der 'Femme
Fatale' aus der deutschen Volkssage," Germanisch-Romanische
Monatsschrift = NF 6 (1965), 294-96.

Hatterer, Lawrence J. The Artist in Society: Problems and Treatment
of the Creative Personality. New York: Grove Press, 1966.
(Chapter on the Woman Artist)

Hays, H. R. The Dangerous Sex: The Myth of Feminine Evil. New York:
Pocket Books, 1965.

Klein, Viola. The Feminine Character: History of an Ideology. 1948.
(Chapters on Freud, Weininger, Havelock Ellis, and others)

Klüber, H. Das Bild der Frau in der Dichtung der Epochen. Münster,
Regensburg. 1. Von Dantes Göttle. Komödie zu Becketts End-
spiel. 64 p. 2. Antigone von Sophokles zu Anouilh. 1965,
39 p. 3. Elektra von Aischylos zu O'Neill. 1965, 39 p.

Loderhose, K.-E. Das Antlitz der Mutter im Spiegel der Literatur.
Bad Homburg, Berlin, Zürich: Gehlen, 1959, 103 p.

Majut, R. Deutsche Philologie im Aufriss. II. 1960. "Der Roman
des tragischen Frauenschicksals," pp. 1427-35; "Der Roman der
deutschen Familie," pp. 1668-75; "Der Eheroman," pp. 1692-96.

Masters, R. E. L., and Lea, Edward. The Anti-Sex: The Belief in the Natural Inferiority of Women. New York: Julian Press, 1964.

Millett, Kate. Sexual Politics. New York, 1970.

Mitchell, Juliet. Psychoanalysis and Feminism, Freud, Reich, Laing, and Women. New York: Pantheon, 1974.

Norton, David. "Toward an Epistemology of Romantic Love," Centennial Review, 14 (1970), 421-43.

Rogers, Katharine. The Troublesome Helpmate: A History of Misogyny in Literature. Seattle: University of Washington Press, 1966.

de Rougement, Denis. Love in the Western World. New York: Pantheon, 1956.

Stern, Karl. The Flight from Woman. New York: Farrar, Straus and Giroux, 1965. (Chapters on Schopenhauer, Kierkegaard, Goethe, and others).

Weber, Marta. Das Frauenbild der Dichter. Bern, Munich, 1959. 272 p.

About erotic and pornographic literature.

Arnold, Heinz Ludwig, ed. Dein Leib ist mein Gedicht. Deutsche erotische Lyrik aus fünf Jahrhunderten. Bern, Wien, 1970. 318 p.

Alexander, Rolf B. Das ist Porno: Eine vergleichende Untersuchung. Munich, 1970. 264 p.

Durbach, Errol. "Form and Vision in Erotic Tragedy: From Aphrodite to Freud," Mosaic 1 (1967/68). No. 4, 35-52.

Emrich, Wilhelm. "Kunst und Pornographie: Kriterien zu ihrer Unterscheidung," in W. E., Polemik, 1968, pp. 220-34.

Eros in der Literatur des 20. Jahrhunderts. Munich: Desch, 1969, 350 p.

Herchenröder, Jan. "Belletristik und Pornographie," Welt und Wort 23 (1968), 111.

Lenning, W. "Sexus und literarische Intelligenz," Eckart Jahrbuch (1964/65), 191-202.

Mertner, Edgar and Mainusch, Herb. Pornotopia. Das Obszöne und die Pornographie in der literarischen Landschaft. 1970.

Purdy, Strother B. "On the Psychology of Erotic Literature," Literature and Psychology 20 (1970), 23-29.

Schlaffer, Heinz. Musa iocosa. Gattungspoetik und Gattunsgeschichte der erotischen Dichtung in Deutschland. Stuttgart: Metzler, 1971. 244 p.

Schreiber, Hermann. Erotische Texte. Sexualpathologische Erscheinungen in der Literatur. Munich: Lichtenberg, 1969. 206 p.

Streblow, Lothar. Erotik, Sex, Pornographie. Munich: Lichtenberg, 1968. 202 p.

Walser, Martin. "Die Unschuld des Obszönen," Der Literat 9 (1967), 151-2.

Zwerenz, Gerhard. Bürgertum und Pornographie. 106 Fussnoten. Frankfurt, 1971. 116 p.

Middle Ages and folk literature.

Bernard, M. Speculum Virginum. Geistigkeit und Seelenleben der Frau im Hochmittelalter. Köln-Graz, 1955.

Bindschedler, Maria. "Weiblich Leitbilder in der alten Literatur," Reformatio 18 (1969), 102-113.

Brietzmann, Franz. Die böse Frau in der deutschen Literatur des
     Mittelalters. Berlin, 1912.
Capellanus, Andreas. The Art of Courtly Love. J. J. Parry, trans.
     Frederick Lock, ed. and abridg. New York: Ungar, 1957.
Chitwood, Garrett Clayton. "Love and Guilt: A study of suffering in
     selected medieval works." Diss. Case Western Reserve University
     1970. DA 31 (1970/71) 3497-98A.
D'Arcy, M. C. The Mind and Heart of Love. Lion and Unicorn: A
     Study in Eros and Agape. London, 1945.
Gerhards, Gisela. Das Bild der Witwe in der deutschen Literatur des
     Mittlealters. 1962.
Gibbs, Marion. "The Role of Woman in Wolfram's Parzival," German
     Life and Letters 21 (1968), 296 ff.
     _____. Wîplîchez wîbes reht: A Study of the Women Characters in
     the Works of Wolfram von Eschenbach. Pittsburgh: Duquesne Uni-
     versity Press, 1972. 246 p.
Greif, I. "Die Frau in der deutschen Volkssage." Diss. Göttingen
     1937.
Heer, Friedrich. The Medieval World. New York: Mentor Books, 1961.
     Ch. 7, "Courtly Love and Courtly Literature," and Ch. 13, "Jews
     and Women."
Kaiser, Elsbet. Frauendienst im mittelhochdeutschen Volksepos. 1921.
Kirchberger, E.-L. "The Role of Woman as Mother in the German Epic
     of the 12th and early 13th Centuries." Diss. University of
     Wisconsin 1949.
Koch, Gottfried. Frauenfrage und Ketzertum im Mittelalter. Berlin:
     Akademie, 1962.
Koebner, Richard. "Die Eheauffassung des ausgehenden Mittelalters."
     Diss. Berlin 1912.
Lehmann, A. Le Rôle de la femme dans l'histoire de France au Moyen
     age. Paris, 1952.
Lewis, C. S. The Allegory of Love. Oxford, 1936.
McDonnell, E. W. The Beguines and Beghards in Medieval Culture. New
     Jersey, 1954.
Meinert, M. C. "Die Stufen der Idolisierung des Frauenbildes im
     frühen deutschen Minnesang." Diss. Cape Town 1961. (typewritten)
Mertes, Renate. "Die Liebe in der antikisierenden Dichtungen des 12.
     Jahrhunderts. Versuch einer Bestandsaufnahme mit besonderer
     Berücksichtigung des Theben-, Eneas- und Trojaromanes." Diss.
     Wien 1971. (typewritten)
Mohr, Wolfgang. "Die 'Vrouwe' Walthers von der Vogelweide," Zeit-
     schrift für deutsche Philologie 86 (1967), 1-10.
Mowatt, D. G. "Tristan's Mothers and Iwein's Daughters," German Life
     and Letters 23 (1969-70), 18 ff.
Newman, F. X., ed. The Meaning of Courtly Love. Albany: SUNY Press,
     1968.
Pearce, Lynette. "Relationships in Hartmann's Iwein." Seminar 6
     (1970), 15-30.
Phillips, Dayton. Beguines in Medieval Strasbourg. Stanford, 1941.
Power, Eileen. "The Position of Women." Legacy of the Middle Ages,

Eds. C. G. Crump and E. F. Jacobs. Oxford, 1926. pp. 401-433.

Schneider, Annerose. "Zum Bild von der Frau in der Chronistik des frühen Mittelalters," Forschungen und Fortschritte 35 (1961), 112-114.

Sprenger, Jacob. Malleus Maleficarum. Die Hexenhammer. 1484.

Stammler, Wolfgang. Frau Welt. Eine mittelalterliche Allegorie. Fribourg, 1959. 112 p.

Tax, Petrus W. Wort, Sinnbild, Zahl im Tristanroman, Studien zum Denken und Werten Gottfrieds von Strassburg. 1961. (Symbolik des Liebestodes)

Thiel, Gisela. Das Frau-Welt Motiv in der Literatur des Mittelalters. 1956.

Völker, Barbara. "Die Gestalt der vrouwe und die Auffassung der Minne in den Dichtungen Frauenlobs." Diss. Tübingen 1966.

Weigand, H. J. Three Chapters on Courtly Love in Arthurian France and Germany: Lancelot--Andreas Capellanus--Wolfram von Eschenbach's Parzival. Chapel Hill, 1956.

Weinhold. Die deutschen Frauen in dem Mittelalter. 1897.

Wiegand, Herbert E. Studien zur Minne und Ehe in Wolframs Parzival und Hartmanns Artusepik. Berlin, 1972.

Ziegler, M. Die Frau im Märchen. Leipzig, 1937.

16th and 17th Centuries.

Berent, Eberhart. "Frauenverehrung und Frauenverachtung in der Dichtung des frühen Barock." Studies in Germanic Languages and Literature. Robert A. Fowkes and Volkmar Sander, eds. New York, 1967, pp. 21-34.

Coupe, W. A. "Ungleiche Liebe, A 16th-Century Topos," Modern Language Review (1967), 661-71.

Schmidt, Rudolf. "Die Frau in der deutschen Literatur des 16. Jahrhunderts." Diss. Strassburg 1917.

Stern, Gerhard Wilhelm. Die Liebe im deutschen Roman des 17. Jahrhunderts. Reprint of the Berlin 1932 edition. Nendeln/Liechtenstein: Kraus, 1967. 251 p.

18th Century.

Brosy, Joseph. "Das Bild der Frau im Werk Lessings." Diss. Zürich 1951.

Bruford, W. H. Germany in the 18th Century. Cambridge (England), 1965 (1935).

Blaze de Bury. Les Salons de Vienne et de Berlin. Paris, 1861.

Goette, Rose. Die Tochter im Familiendrama des 18. Jahrhunderts. Bonn, 1964.

de Goncourt, Edmond and Jules. The Women of the 18th Century. Balch, 1927.

Grossmann, M. "Die Bildgestalt der Mutter in deutschen Selbstzeugnissen bis zur Romantik." Diss. Jena 1945. (typewritten).

Hanstein, Adalbert von. Die Frauen in der Geschichte des deutschen Geisteslebens des 18. und 19. Jahrhunderts. Bd. I. Leipzig, 1899.

Hargrave, Mary. Some German Women and their Salons. London, 1912.

Hoffmann, Therese. Das klassisch-frühromantische Frauenideal.
Leipzig, 1932.

Jäckel, Günter, ed. Das Volk braucht Licht. Frauen der Goethezeit
in ihren Briefen. Berlin: Verlag der Nation, 1966.

Kipka, Karl. Maria Stuart im Drama der Weltliteratur, vornehmlich
des 17. und 18. Jahrhunderts. 1907.

Kluckhohn, Paul. Die Auffassung der Liebe im 18. Jahrhundert und in
der deutschen Romantik. Tübingen, 1966 (1922).

Köberle, Sophie. "Von der Bildung des Frauenzimmers: Nach Mädchen-
büchern des 18. Jahrhunderts," Zs für Jugendliteratur (1968),
145-52.

Labroisse, G. M. "Emilia Galotti's Wollen und Sollen," Neophilo-
logus 56 (1972), 311-23.

Mittner, L. "Freundschaft und Liebe in der deutschen Literatur des
18. Jahrhunderts." Stoffe, Formen, Strukturen. Albert Fuchs,
Helmut Motekat, eds. Munich, 1962, pp. 77-138.

Pascal, Roy. The German Sturm und Drang. Manchester, 1953. (Especially Ch. III, "The Sturm und Drang and the Social Classes")

Petriconi, Helmut. Die verführte Unschuld: Bemerkungen über ein
literarisches Thema. 1953.

Schreiber, S. Etta. The German Woman in the Age of Enlightenment.
New York, 1948.

Staiger, Emil. "Rasende Weiber in der deutschen Tragödie des 18.
Jahrhunderts," Zeitschrift für deutsche Philologie 80 (1961),
364-404. Also in E. S. Stilwandel, Zürich, 1963, pp. 25-75.

Touaillon, Christine. Der deutsche Frauenroman des 18. Jahrhunderts.
1919.

Trunz, Erich. "Eine Betrachtung über Freundschaft, Liebe und Familien-
gefühl im Schrifttum der Goethezeit," Deutsche Vierteljahrs-
schrift 24 (1950), 214-42.

Goethe.

Borchardt, Frank L. "Goethe, Schiller, Sphinx, Centaur, and Sex,"
Monatshefte 64 (1972), 247-55.

Eissler, K. R. Goethe: A Psychoanalytical Study 1775-1786.
Detroit, 1963. 2 vols.

Jantz, Harold. The Mothers in Faust: The Myth of Time and Creativity. Baltimore, 1969.

_____. "The Place of the 'Eternal Womanly' in Goethe's Faust
Drama," PMLA 68 (1953), 791-805.

Krogmann, Willy. "Untersuchungen zum Ursprung der Gretchentragödie."
Diss. Rostock 1928.

_____. Das Friederikenmotiv in den Dichtungen Goethes. 1932.

_____. Goethes Ringen mit Wetzlar. 1932.

Kühn, Paul Goethe und die Frauen: Die Frauen um Goethe. II Bde.
Leipzig, o J.

Larrett, William. "Wilhelm Meister and the Amazona: The Quest for
Wholeness," PEGS 39 (1969), 31-56.

Loeb, Ernst. "Liebe und Ehe in Goethes Wahlverwandschaften," Weimarer
Beiträge 16, Heft 8 (1970), 163-180.

Lukacs, Georg. "Faust-Studien 4: Die Gretchen-Tragödie," in Faust und Faustus. Rowohlt, 1967. (=rde 285), pp. 179-193.
Politzer, Heinz. "Gretchen im Urfaust," in his Das Schweigen der Sirenen. Stuttgart, 1968.

Romanticism.

Bailliet, Theresia S. "Die dichterischen Gestaltungen der heidnischen und christlichen Frau im Werk Eichendorffs." Diss. University of Washington 1969. DA 30 (69/70), 2518A.
_____. Frauen im Werk Eichendorffs. Verkörperungen heidnischen und christlichen Geistes. Bonn: Bouvier, 1972. 240 p.
Berndt, Albrecht. Die Bedeutung der Frau in der Dichtung deutscher-Romantiker. 1937.
Floeck, Oswald. Die Elementargeister bei Fouqué und anderen Dichtern der romantischen und nachromantischen Zeit. 1909.
Hoffmann, Ernst Fedor. "Die Anekdote 'Mutterliebe' als Modell Kleistchen Deukens," Monatschefte 64 (1972), 229-36.
Kern, Hans. Vom Genius der Liebe: Frauenschicksale der Romantik. Leipzig, 1942.
Klin, Eugeniusz. "Das Problem der Emanzipation in Friedrich Schlegels Lucinde," Weimarer Beiträge (1963), 76-99.
Kuoni, Clara. Wirklichkeit und Idee in Heinrich von Kleists Frauenerleben. Frauenfeld: Leipzing, 1937.
Nägele, Rolf. "Die Muttersymbolik bei Clemens Brentano." Diss. Zürich 1959.
Praz, Mario. The Romantic Agony. Oxford, 1933.
Schier, Alfred. Die Liebe in der Frühromantik mit besonderer Berücksichtigung des Romans. Marburg, 1913.
Schmidt, A.-M. "Féminité du romantisme allemand," Nouvelle Revue Française 5 (1957), 702-708.
Tanneberger, I. Die Frauen der Romantik und das soziale Problem. 1928.
Thorslev, P. L. "Incest as a Romantic Symbol," Comp Lit 2 (1965), 41-58.
Wilde, Jean T. The Romantic Realist: Caroline de la Motte Fouqué. New York, 1955.

19th and early 20th Centuries.

Adler, Alfred. Möblierte Erziehung: Studien zur pädagogischen Trivialliteratur des 19. Jahrhunderts. Munich: Fink, 1970.
Anthony, Katherine. Feminism in Germany and Scandinavia. New York, 1915.
Bandet, J. L. "Blanka von Kastilien ou les ambiguités de la vertu," Etudes germaniques 27 (1972), 193-206.
Basil, Otto. Ein wilder Garten ist dein Leib. Die Frau um die Jahrhundertwende. Auswahl und Nachwort von Otto Basil. Wien: Forum, 1968.
Beckmann, Emmy. Quellen zür Geschichte der Frauenbewegung. 1955.
Bennett, Veldon J. "The Role of the Female in the Works of Hermann Hesse." Diss. Utah 1972. DA 33 (1972/73), 2314-15A.

Bergemann, Paul, *Die werdende Frau in der neuen Dichtung*. Leipzig, 1898.

Binion, Rudolph. *Frau Lou. Nietzsche's Wayward Disciple*. Princeton, 1968.

Bramsted, Ernest K. *Aristocracy and the Middle Classes in Germany. Social Types in German Literature 1830-1900*. Chicago: Phoenix Books, 1964. (Sections on family journals and women popular writers)

Brink, Louise. *Women Characters in Richard Wagner: A Study on the Ring of the Niebelung*. New York: Nervous and Mental Disease Pub., 1924.

Danzenroth, E., ed. *Frauenbewegung und Frauenbildung*.

Décaudin, Michel. "Un mythe 'fin du siècle': Salomé," *Comp Lit Studies* 4 (1967).

Dosheimer, Elise. *Das zentrale Problem in den Tragödien Hebbels*. 1925. (The conflict of the sexes).

Dunhofen, I. "Die Familie im Drama vom Beginn des Naturalismus bis zum Expressionismus um die Zeit des 1. Weltkriegs," Diss. Wien 1958 (typewritten).

Engels, Friedrich. *The Origin of the Family, Private Property, and the State*. 1884.

Frey, D. "La Mère. De Gorki à B. Brecht à travers 30 ans d'histoire," *Etudes de Lettres*. Ser. 2, 6 (1963), 125-51.

Gizycki, Lily. *Die neue Frau in der Dichtung*. 1896.

Glass, Frieda and Kische, D. *Die wirtschaftlichen und sozialen Verhältnisse der berufstätigen Frauen*. Berlin, 1930.

Gnanck-Kühne, Elisabeth. *Die soziale Lage der Frau*. Berlin, 1895.

Gruenberg, Elsa. *Daemon and Eros in Some Plays of Gerhart Hauptmann*. 1959.

Guntrum, Heidi. "Die Emanzipierte in der Dichtung des Naturalismus," Diss. 1928.

Gwiggner, G. "Die Probleme der Frauenbewegung im weiblichen Schrifttum der Zeit von 1800-1930," Diss. Wien 1948 (typewritten).

Hahn, Walther. "Zu Stifters Konzept der Schönheit in 'Brigitta,'" *Adalbert Stifter Institut des Landes Oberösterreich: Vierteljahresschrift* 18 (1969), 121-32.

Hamann, Richard and Hermand, Jost. *Deutsche Kunst und Kultur von der Gründerzeit bis zum Expressionismus*. Berlin: Akademie Verlag. I. *Gründerzeit*, 1965, II. *Naturalismus*, III. *Impressionismus*, 1966.

Hansson, Laura. *Wir Frauen und unsere Dichter*. 1896.

Hermand, Jost. "Undinen-Zauber. Zum Frauenbild des Jugendstils." *Wissenschaft als Dialog . . . Festschrift Wolfdietrich Rasch*. Renate von Heydebrand and K. G. Just, eds., Stuttgart, 1969, pp. 9-29.

Hoppe, Else. *Der Typus des Mannes in der Dichtung der Frau: eine internationale Revue*. Hamburg, 1960. (originally 1934.)

Hori, Isao. "Die weiblichen Gestalten als verführerische Wesen in Grillparzers Dramen," *Doitsu Bungaku* 44 (1970), 59-68. In Japanese with German summary.

Horn, Fritz. Das Liebesproblem in Richard Dehmels Werken. Nendeln/
Liechtenstein: Kraus, 1967. (Reprint of 1932 edition.)

Howitt, W. The Rural and Domestic Life of Germany. 1842.

Juergensen, H. "Die Mutter in Adalbert Stifters Werken," Modern Language Notes 64 (1949), 483-86.

Junge, M.-E. "Die Auffassung der Familie im Roman des 19. Jahrhunderts," Diss. Hamburg 1948 (typewritten).

Kleinschmidt, Gert. Illusion und Untergang. Die Liebe im Drama
Franz Grillparzers. Lahr/Schwarzwald: Schauenburg, 1967. 117 p.

Knodel, John. "Malthus Amiss: Marriage Restrictions in 19th-Century
Germany," Social Sciences, 47 (Winter, 1972), 40-45.

Kössler, B. "Das Eheproblem im deutschen Roman des 19. Jahrhunderts."
Diss. Wien 1952 (typewritten).

Lange, Helene and Bäumer, Gertrud, eds. Handbuch der Frauenbewegung.
Berlin, 1901.

Lehnert, Herbert. "Jugendstil-Erotik und ihre soziale Ambivalenz,"
in Wahrheit und Sprache, 1972, pp. 189-99.

Leuchter, Johanna. "Sex Roles in Three of Hesse's Novels," Images of
Women in Fiction, ed. M. S. Cornillon, 1972, pp. 175-180.

Lewald, Fanny. Gefühltes und Gedachtes (1838-1888). L. Geiger, ed.
Dresden, 1900.

Ludwig, Renate. "Frauengestalten im Werk Tehodor Fontanes," Jahrbuch
für Brandenburgische Landesgeschichte 21 (1970), 41-45.

Morgenstern, Lina. Frauenarbeit in Deutschland. Berlin, 1893.

Mörsdorf, J. Gestaltwandel des Frauenbildes. 1958.

Neikirk, Joan Cantwell. "The Role of Woman in the Works of Ödön von
Horvath," Diss. Wisconsin 1971. DA 31 (1970/71), 6622-23A.

Pataky, Sophie. Lexikon deutscher Frauen der Feder. Eine Zusammen-
stellung der seit dem Jahr 1840 erschienenen Werke weiblicher
Autoren, nebst Biographien. Berlin, 1898. 2 Vols.

Puppe, Heinz Werner. "Die soziologische und psychologische Symbolik
im Prosawerk Hermann Hesses." Diss. Innsbruck 1959. (Urmutter-
archetypos)

Rasch, Wolfdietrich. "Sozialkritische Aspekte in Wedekinds Dichtung:
Sexualität, Kunst und Gesellschaft." Festschrift Fritz Martine.
Helmut Dreuzer and Käte Hamburger, eds. Stuttgart, 1969, pp.
409-426.

Rass, Waltrand. "Die Frauengestalten in der Dichtung von Franz Krane
witter," Diss. Insbruck 1972 (typewritten).

Remmers, Käthe. Die Frau im Frühnaturalismus. 1931.

Rieff, Philip. "Sexuality and Domination," Chs. IV and V in his
Freud: The Mind of the Moralist. New York: Anchor Books, 1961.

Roszak, Theodore. "The Hard and the Soft: The Force of Feminism in
Modern Times." Masculine/Feminine. Betty Roszak and Theodore
Roszak, eds. New York: Harper Colophon Books, 1969, pp. 87-104.

Sagarra, Eda. Tradition and Revolution: German Literature and Society 1830-1890. London, 1971.

Sammons, Jeffrey. "Theodor Mundt and Women's Heroism in Early Nineteenth-Century Germany," Yale University Gazette 47 (1972),
109-11.

Schmid-Jürgens, E. I. Ida Gräfin Hahn-Hahn. Berlin, 1933. (Reprinted
    1967: Nendeln/Liechtenstein: Kraus.)

Schönfeld, Margarete. Gutzkows Frauengestalten. Ein Kapitel aus der
    literarhistorischen Anthropologie des 19. Jahrhunderts. (Re-
    print of the Berlin, 1933 edition.) Nendeln/Liechtenstein:
    Kraus, 1967. 120 p.

Schütze, Johannes. "Dickens Frauenideal und das Biedermeier." Diss.
    Erlangen 1947.

Sengle, Friedrich. Biedermeierzeit. Deutsche Literatur im Spannungs-
    feld zwischen Restauration und Revolution. 1815-1848. Bd I.
    Stuttgart, 1971.

Sichelschmidt, Gustav. Hedwig Courths-Mahler. Deutschlands erfol-
    greichste Autorin. Eine literatursoziologische Studie. Bonn:
    Bouvier, 1967. 87 p.

Strecker, Gabriele. Frauenträume, Frauentränen. Über den deutschen
    Frauenroman. Weilheim/Obb: Barth, 1969. 181 p.

Sveistrup, Hans and Zahn-Harnack, Agnes v. Die Frauenfrage in Deutsch-
    land: Strömungen und Gegenströmungen. Berg: August Hopfer,
    1934 ff. (An 800-page bibliography.)

Thomalla, A. Die "femme fragile." Ein literarischer Frauentypus der
    Jahrhundertwende. Düsseldorf: Bertelsmann, 1972. (Literatur
    in der Gesellschaft, 15)

Titche, Jr., Leon. "The Concept of the Harmaphrodite: Agathe and
    Ulrich in Musil's Novel Der Mann ohne Eigenschaften." German
    Life and Letters 23 (1969/70), 160 ff.

Turner, David. "Fontane's Frau Jenny Treibel: A Study in Ironic
    Discrepancy," Forum for Modern Language Studies 8 (72), 132-47.

Wachtler, Gundi. "Der Archetypus der grossen Mutter in Hermann
    Brochs Roman Der Versucher." Hermann Broch: Perspektiven der
    Forschung. Manfred Durzak, ed. Munich: Fink, 1972, pp. 231-50.

Webb, Karl. "Themes in Transition: Girls and Love in Rilke's Buch
    der Bilder," German Quarterly 43 (1970), 406-17.

Weirauch, Anna Elisabet. The Scorpion. (Germany, 1930) New York:
    Greenberg, 1932.

    _____. The Outsider. (Sequel to the above.)

Wyss, Hugo. Die Frau in der Dichtung Hofmannsthals. Zürich, 1954.

Recent Literature.

Alldridge, J. C. Ilse Aichinger. Oswald Wolff, 1969. 128 p.

Alexander, Mary. "Virgo-Virago? Werner Bergengruens Novelle Jung-
    fräulichkeit," German Life and Letters 23 (1969/70), 206-16.

Alker, E. "Das Problem der Liebe in der modernen Literatur," Anima
    (Olten) 12 (1958), 219-26.

Becher, H. Liebe und Ehe in der modernen Literatur. Frankfurt:
    Knecht, 1959. 64 p.

Beckmann, Heinz. "Die Frau in der modernen Literatur," Zweitwende 42
    (1971), 194-201.

Bender, Wolfgang. "Ingeborg Bachmann." Deutsche Literatur seit 1945 in Einzeldarstellungen. Dietrich Weber, ed. Stuttgart: Kröner, 1968, pp. 505-23.

Blöcker, Günter. "Auf der Suche nach dem Vater," Merkur 25 (1971), 395-98. (On Ingeborg Bachmann.)

Freese, Wolfgang. Mystischer Moment und reflektierte Dauer. Zur epischen Funktion der Liebe im modernen deutschen Roman. 1969.

Gerstenslauer, Wolfgang. "Undines Wiederkehr: Fouqué--Giraudoux-- Bachmann," Die Neueren Sprachen 19 (1970), 514-527.

Glenn, Jerry. "Hofmannsthal, Hacks, Hildesheimer: Helen in the 20th Century," Seminar, V, 1 (1969), 1-20. (On heroism and love.)

Kirkpatrick, Clifford. Nazi Germany, Its Women and Family Life. Indianapolis, 1938.

Kunze, I. "Zum Frauenbild in der Literatur des 'Bitterfelder Weges,'" Wissenschaftliche Zeitschrift . . . Gesellschafts-u. sprach- wissenschaftliche Reihe. Leipzig, 15 (1966), 687-697.

Langer-Elsayed, Ingrid. Frau und Illustrierte im Kapitalismus. Köln: Pahl-Rugenstein Verlag, 1971.

Le Fort, Gertrud von. The Eternal Woman: The Woman in Time, Time- less Woman. Milwaukee: Bruce, 1954.

Menschik, Jutta. Gleichberechtigung oder Emanzipation. Die Frau im Erwerbsieben der Bundesrepublik. Fischer Taschenbuch, 1971. (Texte zur politischen Theorie und Praxis.)

Merrifield, Doris F. Das Bild der Frau bei Max Frisch. Freiburg: Becksman, 1971. 150 p.

Mohr, Heinrich. "Produktive Sehnsucht: Struktur, Thematik, und politische Relevanz von Christa Wolfs Nachdenken über Christa T.,"

Patai, Raphael. Woman in the Modern World. New York: Free Press, 1967.

Pross, Helge. Über die Bildungschancen von Mädchen in der Bundes- republik, edition suhrkamp 319, 1969.

Runge, Erika. Frauen. Versuche zur Emanzipation. edition suhrkamp 359.

Seim, Jürgen. Das Thema Liebe in der Lyrik unserer Zeit. Wuppertal- Barmen: Jugenddienst-Verlan, 1969. 35 p.

Strecker, Gabriele. Frausein heute. 1965

Weinmayer, Barbara. "Frauenromane in der BRD," Kürbiskern (1971), 80-92.

Wolf, Christa. "Die zumutbare Wahrheit: Prosa der Ingeborg Bach- mann," Frankfurter Hefte 27 (1972), 744-51.

Runge, Erika. _Frauen._ _Versuche zur Emanzipation._ Suhrkamp (es 359).
Schwarzer, Alice. _Frauenarbeit-Frauenbefreiung._ _Praxis-Beispiele und_
    Analysen. Suhrkamp (es 637).
Thönnessen, Werner. _Frauenemanzipation._ _Politik und Literatur der_
    deutschen Sozialdemokratie zur Frauenbewegung 1863-1933. Euro-
    päische Verlagsanstalt, 1969.

   *This is a composite reading list of two versions of the course.
The second time the course was given in Spring 1974 as a special senior
seminar at the University of Massachusetts, Amherst. The course was co-
taught with Sigrid Bauschinger, Associate Professor at the University,
and I am indebted to her for additions and revisions. We dealt with the
works as literary expressions but within the special focus of the course.
The bibliography listed here supplemented but did not replace background
readings normally expected in a course in contemporary German literature
of East and West Germany.

Sidonie Cassirer   Mount Holyoke College
Department of German   Spring 1973*

CONTEMPORARY WOMEN WRITERS IN EAST AND WEST GERMANY

Texts:

Bertolt Brecht. Die Mutter, rororo 917.
Anna Seghers. "Aufstellen eines Maschinengewehrs im Wohnzimmer der Frau
    Kamptschik" in Aufstellen eines Maschinengewehrs im Wohnzimmer der
    Frau Kamptschik. Luchterhand (SL 14).
_____. "Crisanta"; zur Wahl: "Der Ausflug der toten Mädchen" in
    Ausgewählte Erzählungen, rororo 1119.
_____. Aufstand der Fischer von St. Barbara. Bibliothek Suhrkamp.
Christa Wolf. Nachdenken über Christa T. Luchterhand (SL 31). "Blick-
    wechsel" in Lesen und Schreiben. Luchterhand (SL 90).
Erika Runge. Eine Reise nach Rostock, DDR, besonders: "Eine Diskussion
    mit Frauen." Suhrkamp (es 479).
Ingeborg Bachmann. Auswahl aus den Gedichten (hektographiert).
_____. "Alles"; "Undine geht" in Das dreissigste Jahr DTV 344.
_____. "Ihr glücklichen Augen"; "Probleme, Probleme" u.a. in Simultan.
    Piper, 1972.
Gabriele Wohmann. Erzählungen. Langewiesche-Brandt, 1966 (Auswahl).
_____. Sonntag bei den Kreisands. Eremiten-Presse B10/11.
_____. Die Bütows. Eremiten-Presse.
Helga Novak. In einem irren Haus. Luchterhand (SL 46). Auswahl.
_____. Auswahl aus den Gedichten in Ballade von der reisenden Anna.
Marieluise Fleisser. Pioniere in Ingolstadt in Gesammelte Werke I.
    Suhrkamp, 1972.
_____. "Das Pferd und die Jungfer" in Gesammelte Werke III. Suhrkamp,
    1972.

Sekundärliteratur zur Frauenfrage (Auswahl):

Das Argument 22, 3, ('62), 6. Aufl. Sept. 1970.
    "   "   23, 4, ('63), 6. Aufl. Mai 1970.
Bebel, August. Die Frau und der Sozialismus. Übers: Woman under So-
    cialism, Schocken (SB 323).
Ellmann, Mary. Thinking about Women. Harcourt Brace and World, 1968.
Kursbuch 17, ('69) "Frau, Familie, Gesellschaft."
"Engels and Revolutionary Theory" in K. Millett, Sexual Politics. Double-
    day, 1970. 108-111 (Auch nützliche allgemeine Bibliographie).
Mitchell, Juliet. "The Longest Revolution," in B. and Th. Roszak, Mascu-
    line/Feminine: Readings in Sexual Mythology and the Liberation of
    Women. Harper and Row, 1969. pp. 160-173.
Rowbotham, Sheila. Women, Resistance and Revolution, Kap. 33 und passim.
    Vintage 954 (Das Buch enthält nützliche bibliographische Hinweise).
Pross, Helge. Über die Bildungschancen von Mädchen in der Bundes-
    republik. Suhrkamp (es 319).

Christiane E. Keck
Department of Modern Languages

Purdue University
Lafayette, Indiana
Spring 1972, Spring 1974

FRAUENGESTALTEN DER DEUTSCHEN LITERATUR (German 640)

(This course was taught on an undergraduate level and also as a graduate seminar.)

We shall look at a great variety of women as they are found in major literary works by German male and female authors, in order to provide a deeper insight into the feminine psyche through literature and to see woman's place in the particular society as reflected by these works.

There will be brief oral reports and a term paper.

Required Readings:

Goethe	Iphigenie
Goethe	Die Wahlverwandtschaften
Schiller	Maria Stuart
Kleist	Penthesilea
Grillparzer	Sappho
Hebbel	Judith
Hauptmann	Rose Bernd
Meyer	Die Richterin
Storm	Immensee
Fontane	Effi Briest
Droste-Hülshoff	Die Judenbuche
Schnitzler	Reigen
Mann	Lotte in Weimar
Strindberg	Miss Julie
Ibsen	Hedda Gabler

Ritta Jo Horsley
Department of German

University of Massachusetts
Boston
Spring 1971, Fall 1973
Spring 1974

IMAGES OF WOMEN IN GERMAN LITERATURE
Course and Variations

Introduction

Since spring 1971 I have taught three versions of a course on images of women in German literature. The first (German 396) was an honors seminar for majors in German (conducted in German), which examined the dominant images and roles of women in German, Swiss, and Austrian literature from the eighteenth century to the present. It followed a basically chronological approach and viewed the portrayal of women in the larger context of the general social and cultural ideals of a given time.

The second and third versions (German 275) were offered in English translation to students with no knowledge of the language or (in many cases) the culture. This course (the first time with over fifty, the second with twenty students) was an introduction both to German culture and to its attitudes toward women. We studied characteristic images of men as well as of women in these two classes to provide the necessary complementary background to the view of women. The first time around I attempted to interpret the images chronologically, as representing certain movements or periods within German literary and cultural history (this time going back to the medieval period). It proved almost too much of a challenge, given the students' unfamiliarity with the subject.

In the most recent version of the 275 course I tried to refine somewhat the way we used the literature: the first part of the course dealt with works which we interpreted as representing the actual social condition of women's (and men's) lives; in the second part we read works more clearly expressing the myths and fantasies of male-dominated culture. This approach enabled us to focus our discussions more clearly and fruitfully.

General Aims of the Courses

My own interests and my understanding of what needs to be done in such courses have moved, perhaps along with the development of the general consciousness, from a reaction of excitement at "discovering" the existence and effects of sexism and patriarchal society in my own life and relationships, to the desire to analyze and more clearly understand the ways in which patriarchy has functioned historically and continues to function in the oppression of women and the dehumanization of both sexes. Thus, the objectives of my teaching have broadened from an initial attempt to discern and criticize the characteristic ideals, myths, and stereotypes of woman in German literature to an increasingly political approach aimed at setting these images into, and explaining them from, their specific social-historical context, to gain a better understanding of the patterns and laws by which patriarchy maintains itself. Unchanged since the beginning has been the goal of liberation from stereotyped thinking and uncritical reception of sexist attitudes.

I have summarized below the kinds of questions we attempted to deal with.

1. In studying the images of women and men, we first attempted to discern, usually in a chronological survey, how the literature of a given period viewed the sexes. We looked for the stereotypes, images, and roles which were characteristic of different eras in literary and cultural development, such as the strong, witty, intelligent heroine of the Enlightenment who was followed by the sensitive, emotional ideal of Empfindsamkeit and the simple, naive, motherly, and non-intellectual woman of Storm-und-Stress writings. We tried to examine these roles and images from a feminist perspective. What are the implications for a woman's life of the roles or ideals projected? Are women shown as individuals, with a life and concerns of their own rather than as secondary characters existing in relation to men? If a woman is a strong, independent character, is she successful or punished, admired or mocked? When a woman is portrayed as admirable by the author, do the qualities that are valued reinforce traditional positions of dependence and subordination? Are the relations between men and women seen as constructive and healing or destructive and threatening? What of the relationships between women?

2. We attempted to go beyond an awareness of what the characteristic images and roles were to discern why we found particular images at a given time and place. We asked what factors--social, economic, political, religious, literary, psychological--seemed to influence or determine a particular vision of male and female, and what relationship the literary images had to real life. Through such questions we hoped to deepen our understanding of how the institutions of patriarchy have operated within the culture, particularly in literary production.

    For example, some works attempt to mirror accurately, critically, and/or satirically actual conditions (Lenz, Büchner, Hebbel's Maria Magdalena, Hauptmann's Einsame Menschen, Fontane's Effi Briest), although even here the portrayal of women is colored by the bias inherent in male-dominated culture. Other works and eras show a more obvious and inadvertent expression of values: the family and mother cults of the Biedermeier era reflect the general withdrawal to conservatism and domesticity, the quietism of the political atmosphere, as well as perhaps free love. The virulent misogyny of the later nineteenth century is at least in part a reaction against the growing women's movement.

    It is important to be aware of the limitations of the general validity of a given image, such as the classical idealization of woman in some writings of Goethe, Schiller, Humboldt, Schlegel, and the early Romantics, which represented a very small elite segment of the population. Elisa oder das Weib wie es sein soll, 1795, and other similar tracts popular at the time are a more accurate indication of the views of the broad middle class in their prescription of woman as an obedient servant, existing for the benefit of her parents and husband.

3. We tried to raise our consciousness concerning the effect that such categorizing and attitudes about the sexes have had on the life and culture of the times and of today. For example, the literature of Empfindsamkeit both reflected and influenced the life of its time; people read much and modelled themselves on literary characters as can be seen in the Werther cult. Many women of the late eighteenth century accepted the developing literary ideal of woman as a sensitive and gifted lover and tried to live

their lives on this model. We need to study more primary documents--letters, diaries, memoirs--and popular literature, to be able to see the interrelation of literary images and ideals and real life.

An important aspect (of the Wirkung) is the continuity of the literary tradition itself, the way in which images and stereotypes are inherited and passed on. The sharp duality of the sexes and of woman's domestic, supportive role appears throughout the nineteenth century, though with differing valuations, in Schiller, Schopenhauer, Nietzsche, Weininger, Freud. We can begin to see our own attitudes as a product of such continuous traditions, as, for example, in the enormous importance of Freud's ideas for contemporary conceptions of male and female.

4. We tried to discern what is characteristically German in the attitudes or explanations investigated. We need collaboration with students of other literatures to do the comparative work necessary here. My own knowledge is inadequate to do more than suggest possibilities to be explored:

a. The Hausfrau syndrome to an extreme, developing in the nineteenth century and glorified by the National Socialists.

b. An unusually sharp dualism of the sexes, with extreme emphasis on "masculine" virtues, especially in the late nineteenth century: honor, reason (versus feeling), struggle, hardness, military and business achievement; officer cult, duelling, Männerbund groups, veneration of Greek culture, Nietzsche's critique of Christianity and its "weak" "feminine" virtues.

c. Idealizations of woman as redeemer of man, often from some excess in his nature or in his interpretation of society's expectations. Woman is often seen as more humane, more complete. This seems a part of the classical-humanistic tradition of the eighteenth century and its revivals: Minna von Barnhelm, Musarion, Iphigenia, Brigitta, Helene Altenwyl; and in a more mythicized way Novalis' Sophie, Hesse's archetypal mother images, Jensen's Gradiva (cf. Freud's interpretation).

d. Connected to the above is a strong emphasis on the maternal image of woman, sometimes with a correspondingly infantile, regressive image or aspect of the male. The Romantics (especially Novalis, Brentano) and Hesse are obvious examples, and Siegfried Kracauer, **From Caligari to Hitler**, suggests this is the case for many German films of the 20's. Sometimes the mother is perceived as evil and threatening (Barlach, Der tote Tag); but also associated romantically with death and love (Rilke's Cornet), with the return to the womb and a longing for undifferentiated mystical being. A similar longing for unity is perhaps expressed in the various manifestations of an androgyne ideal (Böhme, Schlegel, Trakl, Musil).

e. Mythicizing the female in a demonic, supernatural direction. Especially in the later Romantics we see the opposition of demonic, super- or sub-human, unknown, transcendent, powerful, dangerous, anti-social, non-Christian female to the innocent, sweet, Christian, bourgeois, conventional, "safe" girl (Tieck, Eichendorff, Hoffmann).

Course Descriptions

I. German 396, Honors Seminar on Images of Women. Spring 1971.

Open to qualified seniors in German. The seminar members read in German works

217

from the eighteenth century to the present with the intent of discerning changing roles of, attitudes toward, and myths about women as reflected in German literature. Readings, reports, and a paper.

Syllabus

1. Introduction. The power of a stereotype: Betty Friedan, "The Happy Housewife Heroine," The Feminine Mystique, Ch. 2. Recurrent myths and images: Simone de Beauvoir, The Second Sex, Ch. 9, "Dreams, Fears, Ideals."

2. Enlightenment. Lessing, Minna von Barnheim.

3. Empfindsamkeit. Goethe, "Die Bekenntnisse einer schönen Seele," from Wilhelm Meisters Lehrjahre.

4. Storm and Stress. Goethe, poems (e.g., "Der Wandrer"); Schiller, "Die berühmte Frau," Kabale und Liebe.

5. Classical ideals of femininity. Schiller, selected poems and excerpts (e.g.,"Würde der Frauen," "Die Geschlechter," excerpt from Über Anmut und Würde); Goethe, Iphigenie, selection from Hermann und Dorothea.

6. Romanticism (1) A. W. Schlegel, parody of Schiller's "Würde der Frauen" Friedrich Schlegel, Lucinde; Novalis, Hymnen an die Nacht, Geistliche Lieder (selections).

7. Romanticism (2) Ludwig Tieck, Der Runenberg; Brentano, Heine, selected poems; Eichendorff, Das Marmorbild.

8. Eros, morality, and the family in the mid-nineteenth century. Büchner, Woyzeck; Stifter, Brigitta, Der Kondor; Hebbel, Maria Magdalena.

9. Advance and reaction in the later nineteenth century. The New Woman and her contemporaries. Hauptmann, Einsame Menschen; Fontane, Effi Briest.

10. Philosophical, economic, and psychological views of woman. Schopenhauer, "On Women"; Nietzsche, selections; Otto Weininger, excerpts from Geschlecht und Charakter; Friedrich Engels, from Origin of the Family, Private Property, and the State; and Freud, "On Femininity."

11. Woman as a sexual creature. Schnitzler, Liebelei; Wedekind, Erdgeist.

12. Twentieth-century images of the mother. Ernst Barlach, Der tote Tag; Brecht, Der gute Mensch von Sezuan; Hesse, Demian.

13. Two women poets. Selections from the poetry of Annette von Droste-Hülshoff and Else Lasker-Schüler.

14. Feminine consciousness in fiction. Ingeborg Bachmann, selections from Das dreissigste Jahr (especially "Ein Schritt nach Gomorrah," "Undine geht").

Format

We met weekly to discuss reading and have reports on background or outside material (we used Katherine Rogers, The Troublesome Helpmate and Kluckhohn,

Liebesauffassung). For reasons of time we omitted item 8 and some other individual works from the syllabus. The students prepared papers on the role
of women in <u>Wilhelm Meisters Lehrjahre,</u> on Kleist's <u>Penthesilea,</u> on love
in the life and poems of Else Lasker-Schüler, on Wedekind's <u>Lulu,</u> on Brecht's
<u>Der gute Mensch von Sezuan,</u> and on Dürrenmatt's female characters.

Works relating to the syllabus

Friedrich Heer. <u>The Medieval World</u>. New York: Mentor Book, 1961. Esp.
    Ch. 7, "Courtly Love and Courtly Literature; Ch. 13, "Jews and
    Women."

Eileen Power. "The Position of Women," in <u>Legacy of the Middle Ages</u>.
    C. G. Crump and E. F. Jacob, eds. Oxford, 1926, pp. 401-433.

F. X. Newman, ed. <u>The Meaning of Courtly Love</u>. Albany: SUNY Press, 1968.

W. H. Bruford. <u>Germany in the 18th Century</u>. Cambridge (England), 1965
    (1935).

Paul Kluckhohn. <u>Die Auffassung der Liebe im 18. Jahrhundert und in der</u>
    <u>deutschen Romantik</u>. Tübingen, 1966 (1922).

S. Etta Schreiber. <u>The German Woman in the Age of Enlightenment</u>. New
    York, 1948.

Mario Praz. <u>The Romantic Agony</u>. Oxford, 1933.

Lieselotte Dieckmann. <u>Goethe's Faust. A Critical Reading</u>. Engelwood
    Cliffs, N. J., 1972.

Henry Hatfield. <u>Goethe. A Critical Introduction</u>. New Directions Paper-
    book, 1963.

Harold Jantz. <u>The Mothers in Faust. The Myth of Time and Creativity</u>.

———. "The Place of the 'Eternal-Womanly' in Goethe's Faust Drama,"
    <u>PMLA</u>, 68 (1953), 791-805.

Ernest K. Bramsted. <u>Aristocracy and the Middle Classes in Germany. So-</u>
    <u>cial Types in German Literature 1830-1900</u>. Chicago: Phoenix Books,
    1964.

Eda Sagarra. <u>Tradition and Revolution: German Literature and Society</u>
    <u>1830-1890</u>. London, 1971.

Philip Rieff. "Sexuality and Domination," Chs. 4 and 5 in his <u>Freud: The</u>
    <u>Mind of the Moralist</u>. New York: Anchor Books, 1961.

Theodore Roszak. "The Hard and the Soft: The Force of Feminism in Modern
    Times," in <u>Masculine/Feminine</u>, Betty Roszak and Theodore Roszak, eds.
    New York: Harper Colophon Books, 1969, pp. 87-104.

Eleanor Burcke Leacock. "The Emergence of Monogamy and the Subjugation of
    Women," in her introduction to Engels, <u>The Origin of the Family,</u>
    <u>Private Property and the State</u>. New World Paperback, 1972, pp.
    29-43.

Raymond Furness. "The Androgynous Ideal: Its Significance in German Literature," Modern Language Review, 60 (January 1965), 58-64.

Clifford Kirkpatrick. Nazi Germany, Its Women and Family Life. Indianapolis, 1938.

Kate Millett. Sexual Politics. Garden City, N. Y., 1970, pp. 159-168.
Cf. her bibliography also.

Works relating to the woman question

Simone de Beauvoir. The Second Sex. New York, 1953
Mary Ellmann, Thinking About Women. New York, 1968.
Germaine Greer. The Female Eunuch. New York, 1970, 1971.
Kate Millett. Sexual Politics. Garden City, N. Y., 1970.
Katherine Rogers. The Troublesome Helpmate, A History of Misogyny in Literature. Seattle: University of Washington Press, 1966.
Diana Trilling. "The Image of Woman in Contemporary Literature," in Robert Jay Lifton, ed., The Woman in America. Boston, 1964.
Virginia Woolf. A Room of One's Own. New York, 1929.

II. German 275. Women and Men in German Literature. Fall, 1973.
A study of images of women and men in German literature from the eighteenth century to the present, with the aim of understanding the social forces and historical contexts that produced them, and the cultural attitudes which they both mirror and shape. Given in English; no knowledge of German required.

Syllabus

I. Introduction
       Grimms' Fairy Tales (selection).
       Simone de Beauvoir. The Second Sex, "Introduction."
       Betty Friedan. The Feminine Mystique, "The Happy Housewife Heroine."
II. Women and Men in Social Context: What does literature reveal about social reality?
       Schiller. Intrigue and Love (Ungar).
       Hebbel. Maria Magdalena (handout).
       Büchner. Woyzeck (handout).
       Fontane, Effi Briest (Ungar).
       Hauptmann, Lonely Lives (handout).
III. Ideals, Myths, Fantasies, and Theories. How does literature reflect and shape private and social attitudes, cultural myths, and traditions about feminine and masculine "nature"?
       de Beauvoir. The Second Sex, Ch. IX, "Dreams, Fears, Idols."
       Goethe. Iphigenia in Tauris (Ungar).
       Schiller. "Honor to Woman," "The Sexes," "Virtues of Woman" (handout).
       Novalis. Selections from Hymns to Night and Sacred Songs (handout).
       Heine. "The Lorelei," "King Harald Harfagar."
       E. T. A. Hoffmann. "The Mines of Falun" (handout).
       Wedekind. Earth Spirit (handout).
       Hesse. Narcissus and Goldmund (Bantam).
       Thomas Mann. "Tristan" (handout).

Schopenhauer. "On Women."
Nietzsche. Selections from Zarathustra, Beyond Good and Evil.
Otto Weininger. Selections from Sex and Character.
Günter Grass. Cat and Mouse (Signet).
Friedrich Engels. Selections from Origin of the Family, Private
    Property, and the State.
Ingeborg Bachmann. "A Step toward Gomorrah," and "Undine Goes,"
    from The Thirtieth Year (handout).

In addition to completing the readings and participating in class and group discussions, students are expected to hand in the following written assignments:

1. Formulate a list of questions and concerns which you think should be considered in our approach to the material to gain from literature a greater understanding of ourselves as women and men and of the forces which have shaped and continue to shape us. May be in outline form (will not receive a letter grade).

2. Discuss a character (male or female) from one of the works in section 2. Show how his/her character, behavior, and fate are influenced by social forces and institutions (e.g., family, religion, social and economic class, moral code, education, political system). To what extent is the character's sex a limiting or determining factor in the way these forces affect him/her? (This should be a well-written essay, 5-7 pages, which will be graded.)

3. Write a statement exploring what it means to you to be a woman or man today. How do you feel your personality, expectations, options, relationships have been shaped or affected by your gender? Indicate what insights into your own experience or into present social reality you may have gained from our reading and discussions. This may be in note or journal form and will not be graded.

4. Discuss the concept(s) of femininity or masculinity, or the ideas ("myths") associated with female or male "nature," as portrayed in one of the following: Iphigenia, Mines of Falun, Earth Spirit, Narcissus, Cat and Mouse. What attributes are ascribed to the sex and how are they valued (positively, negatively, ambivalently)? If possible, give your own critical evaluation of how the sex is portrayed. A 5-7 page essay to be graded.

5. Either a final examination or (if approved by instructor) a 7-10 page essay on a chosen or suggested theme.

Observations

About 20 students, 3/4 women, ranging widely in background and interest. Most were new to both German and Women's Studies. The course met three hours per week; the first two were spent in discussion of the material, the third session was devoted to small group meetings in which issues raised in class could be pursued further and related more concretely to our own lives and concerns. I tried to sharpen the feminist focus of the course to encourage more direct and critical response to the material, and this, combined with the smaller size and more frequent contact, made it more effective than the previous year's course, in terms of both the thoroughness with which the material was covered and the degree of personal involvement, mutual sharing, and growth of awareness of the effects and workings of patriarchal society.

III. <u>German 478</u>. Independent Study: Readings on the Women's Movement and in German Women Writers. Spring, 1974.

Bi-weekly meetings to discuss readings and have reports. Conducted in English and German. The students (four women from the previous semester's course) and I read some things in common; others were reported on by various members.

Paper topics on the image of the mother in Brecht, on the portrayal of women in works of Brecht and Christa Wolf, and on Ingeborg Bachmann's <u>Simultan</u>. Materials used included:

Katherine Anthony. <u>Feminism in Germany and Scandinavia</u>.
Ingeborg Bachmann. <u>Das dreissigste Jahr</u>.
      . <u>Simultan</u>.

Vicki Baum. <u>Stud. chem. Helene Willfuer</u>.
Shulamith Firestone. <u>Dialectics of Sex</u>.
Jost Hermand and Richard Hamann. <u>Deutsche Kunst und Kultur</u> . . . II. <u>Naturalismus</u>.
Helene Lange and Gertrud Bäumer, eds., <u>Handbuch der Frauenbewegung</u>.
Kate Millett. <u>Sexual Politics</u>.
Juliet Mitchell. <u>Woman's Estate</u>.
Sheila Rowbotham. <u>Women, Resistance and Revolution</u>.
Anna Seghers. <u>Der Aufstand der Fischer von St. Barbara</u>.
Martha Vicinus, ed., <u>Suffer and Be Still</u>. Women in the Victorian Age.
Christa Wolf. <u>Der geteilte Himmel</u>.
      . <u>Nachdenken über Christa T</u>.

Krishna Winston
Department of German

Wesleyan University
Middletown, Connecticut
Spring 1973

WOMEN AND GERMAN LITERATURE (German 170)
(In translation)

Weekly Schedule	Class Readings and Reports	Suggested Collateral Reading
1.	Tacitus Merseburg Incantations Hrosvitha v. Gandersheim	Power, Medieval People
2.	The Nibelungenlied Medieval Poetry (Penguin)	Oldenbourg, The World is not Enough
3.	Gottfried, Tristan and Isolde	de Rougement, Love in the Western World
4.	Grimmelshausen, Courage Baroque poetry (Penguin)	
5.	Poetry of the Enlightenment (Penguin), Lessing, Emilia Galotti	Goethe, Iphigenia
6.	Wieland, "Love and Friendship Tested" (in Ten German Novellas) Goethe, The Elective Affinities	Bruford, Culture and Society in 18th-Century Germany
7.	" " " " " Poetry (Penguin) Schiller, Maria Stuart	Eissler, Goethe
8.	Kleist, "The Marquise of O--" La Motte Fouqué, "Undine"	B. v. Arnim, Goethe's Correspondence with a Child
9.	Romantic Poetry (Penguin) Grillparzer, Medea	
10.	Gotthelf, "The Black Spider" Droste-Hülshoff, Stories	
11.	Hebbel, Maria Magdalena Fontane, Effie Briest	Huch, Ursleu the Younger Ebner-Eschenbach (in German Classics, Vol. XIII)
12.	Hauptmann, The Beaver Coat " The Heretic of Soana (in Ten German Novellas)	A. Mahler Werfel, The Bridge is Love
13.	Schnitzler, "Fräulein Else" (in Ten German Novellas) Kafka, The Castle	Adler, Understanding Human Nature
14.	Brecht, The Good Woman of Setzuan	Aichinger, Herod's Children

Böll, Acquainted with the
Night

Additional topics for reports: Courtly love; Brant, Ship of Fools; Brecht,
Mother Courage; Lessing, Nathan the Wise; Goethe, Faust, The Sorrows of
Young Werther, Hermann and Dorothea; figure of St. Joan in Schiller, The
Maid of Orleans, Shaw, St. Joan, Brecht, St. Joan of the Stockyards; Women
of the Romantic Period; Kleist, Penthesilea; Heine and Women; Young Ger-
many and Women's Rights; Schopenhauer on Women; Marx and Engels on Women;
Helene Böhlau; Lou Andreas-Salomé; Freud and Adler on Women; Hitler and
Women; Women in the Group 47; Women in East Germany.

Required Reading:

The Nibelungenlied
Gottfried v. Strassburg, Tristan
    and Isolde
The Penguin Book of German Verse
Grimmelshausen, Courage the Adven-
    turess
Lessing, Emilia Galotti
Goethe, The Elective Affinities
Schiller, Mary Stuart
Kleist, The Marquise of O-- and
    Other Stories
Gotthelf, "The Black Spider"

Hauptmann, The Beaver Coat
Kafka, The Castle
Brecht, The Good Woman of
    Setzuan
Steinhauer, ed. Ten German
    Novellas
The German Classics, ed. Kuno
    Francke
    Vol. V: La Motte Fouqué,
        "Undine"
    "   VI: Grillparzer, Medea
    "   VII: Droste-Hülshoff,
        Stories
    "   IX: Hebbel, Maria
        Magdalena
    "   XII: Fontane, Effie
        Briest

Suggested additional reading:

Ailer, Understanding Human Nature
Aichinger, The Bound Man and Other Stories
    "   Herod's Children
Arnim, Bettina. Goethe's Correspondence
    with a Child, Vols. 1 and 2
de Beauvoir, The Second Sex
Böll, Acquainted with the Night
Bruford, Culture and Society in Eight-
    eenth-Century Germany
Eissler, Goethe: A Psychoanalytic
    Study
Ellmann, M. Thinking About Women

Francke, Kuno, ed. The German
    Classics
Vol. I: Goethe, Iphigenia
    "   XIII: Ebner-Eschenbach
    "   XV: Schopenhauer, On Women
    "   XVIII: Ricarda Huch, Ursleu
        the Younger
    "   XIX: works by Böhlau and
        Viebig
Millett, Sexual Politics
Oldenbourg, Z. The World is Not
    Enough
Peters, My Sister, My Spouse
Power, Eileen. Medieval People
de Rougemont. Love in the West-
    ern World
Werfel, Alma Mahler, The Bridge
    is Love

Kalamazoo College:
     Joe K. Fugate, chairman of the Department of German, offered a
senior seminar DIE GESTALT DER FRAU IN DER DEUTSCHEN LITERATUR DES 19.
UND 20. JAHRHUNDERTS in Spring 1973.

University of Connecticut:
     George Reinhardt of the College of Liberal Arts and Sciences con-
ducted a graduate seminar in German: DICHTERINNEN UND FRAUENGESTALTEN IN
DER DEUTSCHEN LITERATUR DES NEUNZEHNTEN JAHRHUNDERTS in Spring 1973.

University of Texas at Austin:
     Janet King, Department of Germanic Languages, taught a senior course
PERCEPTIONS OF MALE AND FEMALE IDENTITY IN GERMAN LITERATURE AFTER LESSING
during the second summer session, 1973.

University of Washington (Seattle, Washington):
     Diana Behler, Department of Germanic Languages and Literature, and
member of the Department of Comparative Literature, introduced a Junior
Level course THE IMAGE OF WOMAN IN GERMAN LITERATURE (in English) in the
Winter Quarter 1972. The course was structured historically with the intent to discern any possible "development" in the relationship between
women and society throughout the ages. Readings were from the Middle Ages
to modern times. In Spring 1973 the focus of the course was expanded to
include American and English literature and was offered within the Comparative Literature program.

Wilson College (Chambersburg, Pennsylvania):
     Josef M. Kellinger, chairman of the Department of German, taught a
course OUTSTANDING WOMEN WRITERS IN GERMAN LITERATURE OF THE 20TH CENTURY
in Fall 1973. The focus was on work after 1945. Authors and works dis-
cussed: 1) Ilse Aichinger, Die grössere Hoffnung; Wo ich wohne. 2)
Ingeborg Bachmann, Das dreissigste Jahr; Gedichte, Erzählungen, Hörspiele,
Essays; Simultan. 3) Marie Luise Kaschnitz, Wohin denn ich; Ferngespräche;
Nicht nur von hier und heute. 4) Elisabeth Langgässer, Gedichte; Das
Labyrinth; Märkische Argonautenfahrt; Das unauslöschliche Siegel. 5)
Luise Rinser, Gefängnistagebuch; Septembertag; Ich bin Tobias. 6) Nelly
Sach, Späte Gedichte. 7) Anna Seghers, Das siebte Kreuz; Aufstand der
Fischer von St. Barbara; Die Kraft der Schwachen. 8) Christa Wolf, Der
geteilte Himmel; Nachdenken über Christa T.

RUSSIAN STUDIES

The Metamorphosis of an Icon: Woman in Russian Literature

by

Maria Banerjee

Soviet literature, in its official manifestation as socialist realism, is a curious phenomenon. Whether praised as the ultimate chapter
in art's long history of struggle to conquer reality, or derided as a ser-
vile and hybrid style which parodies its own intent, it is always assumed
to be something more and less than pure literature. The uninitiated may
well wonder at the high stakes and risks of the Soviet literary game.
But it should be remembered that in Russia, realism was the norm long before it became socialist. The novel especially has always served as a
battleground for the intelligentsia. Indeed, it was the Russian literature of the golden age with its array of archetypal characters and paradigmatic plots that helped shape the historical consciousness which cul-
minated in the Russian Revolution. Even today, in the bourgeois USSR, the
visitor can hardly fail to notice Lenin, the Revolution's essential hero,
presiding over every public place in his fin-de-siècle costume as the intelligence of the last hour.

The heroic stylization of woman--redeemer of the Russian past, har-
binger and co-builder of the socialist future--is another inheritance from
the previous century. Eighteenth-century empresses apart, it is only with
the advent of Romanticism that female heroines became dominant in Russian
literature. Not unexpectedly, woman gained a special place for herself in
the fictional world by first stooping to the role of victim.

The unfortunate Liza of Nikolai Karamzin's sentimental romance is a
Gretchen in sarafan.[1] Seduced and later abandoned by the city-bred aristocrat Erast, she fulfills her erotic fate by drowning in the very same pond
that had witnessed her trysts. For the reader familiar with German Romantic ballads or West Slavic folklore, Liza's characteristics are as pre-
dictable as her suicide. She is a flower rooted in a particular corner of
Russian nature, her sensuality is innocent by definition, and in death she
becomes the spirit that animates and graces the landscape. For the literary historian, Liza's merit is that she attempts to formulate her feelings
in Karamzin's Russian, a new literary language submitting to the pressure
of novel emotions, styles of experience, and modes of love-making. For
all her Germanic origins and her semi-French idiom, Liza was found irre-
sistible by her reading public. The pond where she reputedly drowned became a place of pilgrimage for genteel Muscovites. More importantly, her
brief and imitative excursion in the land of Tendre opened the way for a
procession of Russian heroines, victims or would-be victims, vindicated
by the integrity of their emotional selves.

The tragic pas-de-deux of the mating dance is, of course, a favorite theme of the Romantic novel, in Russia as elsewhere. But the theme
shows its vigor by surviving into the critical phase of disillusionment
out of which the Realists drew their vision. Alexander Pushkin's Tatyana
and her Byronic partner Onegin are typical Romantics, but their choreo-
graphy is plotted by an imagination as ironic as it is generous and by a
subtly discriminating intelligence. Onegin is a "master of the tender

passion," a Napoleon of the boudoir who has understood the first law of
seduction: "The less we love a woman/the more her love for us increases."[2]
In the celebrated first chapter of Pushkin's novel in verse, which evokes
the pleasures of St. Petersburg and through the lyric complicity of the
narrator, the ephemeral enchantment of youth, Onegin reigns supreme, the
male lover as the sole subject in a world of glittering objects. The
women are elusive silhouettes, shapes or fragments of shapes in motion,
fixed in a momentary stasis by the lorgnetted eye of Onegin, whose male
desire alone confers authenticity to their presence. But the lyrical
climax of the chapter is usurped from the hero by the poet himself who, in
the famous "feet digression" unrolls in a quick succession of precise images
the breathtaking reel of his own erotic memory. Fetishism? Perhaps, but
more significantly, the erotic metonymy finally comes to rest in the metaphor of time: "Brief as your footprints on the grass, / The happiness of
youth must pass,"[3] the ironic master of Pushkin's lyric muse.

Tatyana, the fated victim of Onegin's sexual charisma, is a figure
of originality. Her rustic name and the very likeness of her were designed to break the poetic conventions of the day. With the cunning of a
budding realist, Pushkin endowed Tatyana's sister Olga with all the expected "poetic" attributes, only to show later how quickly these turn to
everyday prose as the impostor-heroine dons the cap of a banal marriage.
By contrast, Tatyana embodies the poetry of the real world. She is, in
fact, the muse of Pushkin's realism. Her close identification with Russian country life and lore and the naive spontaneity of her emotions would
seem to qualify her for the purely Romantic role of a Russian Haidée. Despite appearances, Pushkin has advanced to square two beyond Romanticism
by a simple inversion of its terms: it is Tatyana's native Russianness
that strikes the reader as so exotic. This characteristic gave an ideological edge to Tatyana's romance which was not lost on any of her important
readers, from Vissarion Belinsky to Fedor Dostoevsky.[4] If anything, they
over-reacted to it and in the process changed Tatyana from real woman to
a figure of myth.

In her mythological role, Tatyana is the national ideal of nature
incarnate. Like any mystical entity, she cannot be properly defined but
must be apprehended in terms of a set of paradoxes: she is passionate yet
innocent, original and traditional, bold and modest, all at the same time.
It is perhaps easiest to understand her dialectically, by opposition to
Onegin who, in his turn, has undergone a similar transformation from
character into symbol. When Tatyana visits the abandoned inner sanctum of
Onegin's study and discovers a statuette of Napoleon poised on a shelf of
fashionable books, she asks, "Isn't he a parody?"[5] Her first look at him
had been that of adolescent infatuation, but the second look of love un-
covers a bit of reality under the hero's mask.

With this awareness begins Tatyana's evolution from object to subject. In the eighth and last chapter of the poem she stands on the edge
of becoming the consciousness of the novel. But the lyric poet in Pushkin
partly resists the grim rigors of the ironist and gives some leeway to
Tatyana's heart. Pushkin would never have said, "Tatyana, c'est moi."
Even as she recites for Onegin's benefit the stern lessons of time, "la
morale est dans la nature des choses,"[6] she tempers irony with pity. For

on Pushkin's battlefield of love, where time commands, there can be no real winner. And if Onegin comes out as time's fool, Tatyana, his teacher, is left with the mere consolation of a Stendhalian overview of her own as well as of her emotions, exhilarating but dry.

The Russian ideological critics, in their characteristically crude but sturdy shorthand, rewrote that standoff as a triumph for the Russian woman. In the essay "The Russian at the rendez-vous," Nikolai Chernyshev-sky gave his allegorical version of the Tatyana-Onegin relationship: the issue, clearly, was not sex but action. Chernyshevsky urged, "Forget about them, those erotic questions! They are not for a reader of our time 1857, occupied with problems of administrative and judiciary improvement, of financial reforms, of the emancipation of the serfs."[7] To get instant relevance, Chernyshevsky substituted, for Onegin, the politically impotent intelligentsia, and for Tatyana, the narod, the victimized but fabulously vital Russian people.

The men of the sixties, who liked to call themselves "realists," heeded Chernyshevsky's advice and dedicated their considerable energies to a frontal attack on the most cherished ideals of their fathers. "Nature isn't a temple but a workshop," barked out Bazarov the nihilist, who also demythified woman with his astounding comment on the object of his attraction, Madame Odintsova. "Such a fine body! . . . It ought to go at once to the anatomical theater."[8] At the same time the "new woman" came forward in the sixties, no longer man's toy and torment, but an active, business-like partner in the building of a rational society. But first her mind had to be put in order--by man. She revealed herself a quick learner in the field of reductionist logic. Here is Vera Pavlovna, the heroine of Chernyshevsky's Utopian novel What is to Be Done?, analysing her happy second marriage: "This continuous, strong, healthy excitement necessarily develops the nervous system . . . consequently my intellectual and moral forces grow in proportion to your love."[9] It should be understood that this rational union was made possible by the heroic stage-management of Vera Pavlovna's first husband and teacher Lopukhov, who first took her away from her petty-bourgeois family. After Vera Pavlovna had shown a preference for his friend Kirsanov, Lopukhov escaped the irrational horrors of the love triangle into America, burying his old identity under a fake suicide, having reassured his wife that he was acting out of purest egotism. On second thought, this elaborate plot might be translated into a back-handed argument in favor of divorce, but even so, there remains a troublesome chink in Chernyshevsky's armor of reason. Vera Pavlovna's first marriage was never consummated, in deference, one suspects, to the author's own rather Victorian delicacy. But then, radicalism and prudery are the twin virtues of the priesthood of the Russian intelligentsia.

Both of the two greatest writers of the age, Dostoevsky and Count Tolstoy, rejected the rationalist solution to the "woman question," each for his own reasons. For Dostoevsky, sex was the crucial testing ground of the ego. The spirit being egalitarian, the power drive was evenly distributed between Dostoevsky's males and females, so that one might rather talk of a polarity of the proud and the humble than of the polarity of sexes. Compare the two couples--proud Raskolnikov versus meek Sonya Marmeladova, meek Prince Myshkin versus proud Nastasia Filipovna. Yet these men and women, for all their excitability, remain curiously sexless. The sexual crisis is for them an ordeal as catastrophic as murder, which often accompanies it, but still an ordeal in which the body plays the least part.   It is as if Dostoevsky had put Freud upside down, representing sexuality as a metaphoric activity, a shadow-boxing show of the spirit, without physical substance but suggestive of hidden meanings.

A Gentle Creature (1876) is the quintessential Dostoevskian tragedy of pride masquerading as a "tragedy of the bedroom" The plot revolves around the theme of the duel. At the outset the combatants, husband and wife, are unevenly matched. "I was forty-one and she was only sixteen. That fascinated me--that feeling of inequality."[10]Moreover, she is an orphan and destitute, down to her last trinket, a family ikon, which she comes to pawn. With this pathetic offering the tragic romance between the pawnbroker and the "meek one," as he calls her, begins. But the middle-aged suitor carries on him a hidden wound of festered pride from a duel he once refused to fight as a young officer, in defiance of the aristocratic conventions of his regiment. That is why he had gone underground as a pawnbroker and why he now chooses her, the gentle spirit, to be his wife and the instrument of his vindication.

But he soon discovers that the young girl has her own resources of pride to challenge him with. "Which of us began it first?" he asks, now that it is all over, addressing an imaginary jury while her dead body lies stretched out on the sitting-room table.[11] In the power struggle, which is a disguised battle for dignity, "she," the objectively weaker antagonist, possesses one great advantage: she has youth's privilege of scorn and indignation. "You see," he explains, "young people are generous. I mean, young people who are good are generous and impulsive. But they have little tolerance. If anything doesn't turn out the way they like, they immediately begin to despise you."[12] In the hands of the young woman, the middle-aged man's history can become an incriminating dossier. Yet, characteristically, he responds by a show of force to her demand for justice. And the one-time rebel now claims the authority of convention for his side:

> I wasn't going to justify myself, was I? You see, it was the pawnshop that was the chief source of trouble between us. Mind you, I knew that a woman, and particularly a girl of sixteen, simply must submit to her husband. Women have no originality. That--that is axiomatic--yes, I regard it as axiomatic even now. Even now! Never mind what's lying there in the sitting-room. Truth is truth, and John Stuart Mill himself can do nothing about it![13]

In spite of his bluster, the would-be male supremacist opts for a strategy of indirection. Feigning indifference towards the young wife, he provokes her into making a secret appointment with an officer. In her game, this is a subtle move forward, an invitation for him to fight the old duel at last, this time over her. Unaware that her husband is eavesdropping behind the door, she acts for herself and crushes the officer's amorous advances by a combination of wit and candor. The husband emerges from his hiding place with his honor intact, to claim the rightful possession of his wife and lead her back home.

But the battle is not over and that same night, she tests him for courage by placing a gun at his temple, while he pretends to be lying asleep. Both of them understand the significance of the moment and this is how he remembers it:

> Besides, I realize with the whole force of my being
> that at that very moment a struggle was going on be-
> tween us, a life and death struggle, a duel in which
> I--the coward of the day before who had been expelled
> by his fellow-officers for cowardice--was engaged. I
> knew it, and she knew it too, if she had guessed the
> truth and knew that I was not asleep.[14]

But by a willful caprice of resentment--Dostoevsky emphasizes the deliberateness of the decision--he chooses to interpret the outcome as a victory for himself. "I had conquered and she was conquered forever. . . . She was conquered but not forgiven."[15] He exiles her from the marriage bed to a "little iron bedstead with a screen." The fatal revolver had separated the lovers like the modern version, or perversion, of the sword of chastity which the knight of the medieval romances used to put between himself and his love.

A long, dream-like winter follows and life is postponed by the obdurate lover. When "the scales suddenly fall off his eyes," as he puts it, in the epiphany of a spring evening--"my world came crushing about my ears and I just collapsed at her feet"--she turns away in terror from the violent return of his love.[16] His new-found idolatry, like an onrush of spiritual lust, is as humiliating to her as his former indifference. She escapes him into death, crashing to the pavement with the family ikon of Virgin and Child in her hand, as gentle in her flight as a Russian Ophelia, herself an image of nature violated by the sickness of the spirit.

Tolstoy's epic entanglement with woman, in life and art, is too well known to need recounting. Of all the great novelists of Russia's nineteenth century it is he, the squire of Yasnaya Polyana, who most deserves the term of sexist. Orphaned in early childhood, coddled by a doting aunt, Tolstoy grew up with an inordinate need of female warmth. From his youth to his fifties he remained a champion of the human nest. In his first significant venture into the realm of feminine psychology, Family Happiness,[17] he subjected the heroine Masha to the lessons of reality, which turn out to be the lessons of Jules Michelet and his four stages of female development--from daughter to lover, wife, and finally mother (of sons, presumably). The didacticism of the novella is all the more irksome because Tolstoy employed the services of Masha herself as diarist, in order to tell the story of her romantic debacle.

"Romanticism," Tolstoy would say to Maxim Gorky, "is the fear of looking into the eyes of truth."[18] At the zenith of his powers Tolstoy saw the truth of womanhood embodied in Natasha when, in the epilogue of War and Peace, deserted by the spirit of music, she becomes the willing agent for a Schopenhauerian cunning of nature. Not only did Tolstoy dare to look at his Natasha in the nursery, but he praised what he saw as a sublime and very Russian victory--the triumph of vegetative being over consciousness, of mass and space over the arrogant splendors of individuality.

After War and Peace, Tolstoy's view of nature gradually darkened, as he found by look, touch, and feeling that even his own body was mortal. In Anna Karenina pure sexuality is tragic precisely because it is natural, and while Tolstoy tried to superimpose the epic romance of Kitty and Levin on Anna's fate, that design did not quite succeed in controlling the emotional energies of the novel. With Anna, Tolstoy bade goodbye to Dionysus and allowed the critical mind to prevail in him. Gorky would note, "Woman, in my opinion, he regards with implacable hostility and loves to punish her. . . . It is the hostility of the male who has not succeeded in getting all the pleasure he could, or it is the hostility of spirit against 'the degrading impulses of the flesh.' But it is hostility." [19]

Hatred made a radical out of Tolstoy. In The Kreutzer Sonata, sex and the family were revalued from the perspective of a moral maximalist. Curiously enough, the Tolstoyan underlying view of the Victorian marriage as a conspiracy of sexually decadent males and venal females, aided and abetted by dressmakers, the opera, and moonlight, could have been endorsed by the most ardent feminist. According to Tolstoy, the upper-class, urban society of his time was nothing but a brothel, and hospitals were full of sexually crippled, hysterical women. But if woman is a victim, she is also an accomplice of her enslavement and, by the grim dialectic of the master and slave relationship she, in turn, becomes man's tormentor. "On one hand woman is reduced to the lowest stage of humiliation, while on the other she dominates. Just like the Jews: as they pay us back for their oppression by a financial domination so it is with women!" [20]

Pozdnyshev, who finally murdered his wife out of jealousy, and who mixes these general observations with the relentless narration of his life's wreck, is also a logician. This is how he develops the question of the inequality of the sexes:

> Woman's lack of right arises not from the fact that
> she must not vote or be a judge--to be occupied with
> such affairs is no privilege--but from the fact that
> she is not man's equal in sexual intercourse and has
> not the right to use a man or abstain from him as she
> likes--is not allowed to choose a man at her pleasure
> instead of being chosen by him. [21]

Germaine Greer herself would not object to the definition of the problem but she would probably be appalled at the solution. Sexual equality based on the use of contraceptives clearly is not for Pozdnyshev nor, for that matter, for Tolstoy. Pozdnyshev's statement was merely a logical probe into the realm of absurdity, but he would rather opt for the eschatological alternative of total abstinence from sex, for everyone. To the objection, "If everyone thought this the right thing to do, the human race would cease to exist," he answers, "And why should we exist." [22] This is not only the half-crazed murderer speaking, but Tolstoy himself, an angry old man deadlocked by the antinomy of nature and spirit. From here, he has just a short way to go towards Astapovo station to die, wifeless at last and unaccommodated.

But the tragedians could not stop the new Russian woman from assuming her station as the heroic vanguard in Russian life and fiction.

Ivan Turgenev, the most temperate among the Russian realists, gave her a
place of honor in his prophetic novel On the Eve (1859). His Eliena represents a challenge to the Russian male: she rejects three suitors--the
artist Shubin who has sensuality but no values, the intelligent Bersen-
iev who has values but no vitality, and the ambitious Kurnatovsky. Shubin
philosophizes, "Our Russians are all either small fry, rodents, petty
Hamlets. . . . When will our time come? When will men be born among us?" 23
Eliena, of course, will not wait and commits her life and faith to the
Bulgarian nationalist revolutionary Insarov. Her gesture of dedication
has distinctly religious overtones. She meets her lover/comrade in an
abandoned country chapel, thus confirming the monasticism of the Russian
revolutionary tradition. With a Turgenevian touch of scepticism and mel-
ancholy, Insarov dies in Venice, in an almost Jamesian atmosphere of beauty and decay, without even setting foot on Bulgarian soil. But Eliena
survives him to join the Slavonic rebels, fulfilling her destiny as woman
and militant in a semi-mythical widowhood.

In the 1870's the type of the exalted revolutionary woman flourished
among the Narodniki. A few decades later, the same combination of asceti-
cism and activism marched under the banner of scientific Marxism. V. I.
Lenin's wife and comrade, Nadezhda Krupskaya, conformed to this type. In
the first heady years of the Bolshevik Revolution woman's liberation movement opened up on two fronts--the economic and the sexual. But Lenin himself, while endorsing enthusiastically the entrance of "working women comrades" into the labor arena on equal terms with men, stopped short of the
idea of total sexual emancipation. Indeed, he considered "free love" a
modern aberration which threatened injury to the good name of the Revolution. In an exchange of views with the feminist Clara Zetkin he warned
that excesses of sexual freedom were "purely bourgeois, an extension of
bourgeois brothels."24Instead, he advised his women comrades to "work sys-
tematically with the youth. That is a continuation, an extension and exal-
tation of motherliness from the individual to the social sphere. . . ." 25
I tend to think that Lenin was not so much a sexist as he was a prude, for
he did not exempt men, at least in theory, from the same rigid code of
sexual conduct. In Joseph Stalin, however, the Elienas met their master.
In the days of the early purges, when Nadezhda Krupskaya herself tried to
intervene on behalf of some old comrades, Stalin informed her that if she
did not stop meddling, he could easily find someone else to be Lenin's
widow.26

In spite of the psychological setbacks for woman's liberation in the
USSR, the achievements on the labor front have been remarkable. It is not
my intent to denigrate the Soviet woman's contributions to the building
of the Moscow subway, the defense of Leningrad under siege, or the exploration of space. What concerns me, beyond the debate about the Soviet women's
many roles and the tallying of contribution with economic and political
reward, is the strange impoverishment of her inner being. Xenia Gesiorowska
has put it this way:

> There is a Russian toy, a wooden doll called Matry-
> oshka. Produced for centuries by village craftsmen,
> Matryoshka represents a typical Russian beauty: dark-
> browed, shawl around her plump body. The doll can be
> taken apart; inside is found another doll, different

only in size and color of her shawl. This one, in
turn, contains still another replica, and so on, until
at least half a dozen of them stand around the original
Matryoshka. . . . The crowd of stereotyped characters
obscures the picture: the heroine, the original model
does not deserve to be noticed . . . to be sought out
. . . among the crowd.[27]

In my conversations with educated Soviet women during a visit to
Moscow, Leningrad, and Kiev in the spring of 1971, I noticed an emphasis
on the theme of privacy. Some women even hazarded the opinion that it
might be liberating not to have to work, not to have to send children to
day care centers. I do not intend to present here a back-handed defense
of bourgeois privacy, nor indulge in cold-war comparativism. Our problems
remain with us. But the Soviet experience can teach us something about
the dangers of committing women to rigid, a priori definitions of roles,
no matter how attractive they may seem at a given time. I, for one, believe that there can be no single model or mould for the free woman.
Right now, in the Soviet Union, where the inner space of the feminine
psyche still remains largely terra incognita, the woman everybody is waiting for is not another Valentina Tereshkova, but a modern Eleanor of
Aquitaine.*

Smith College

*Lecture given as part of the Forum "Women Writers, Woman Image in
the Foreign Literatures," December 1972 at the Annual Meeting of the Modern Language Association. The Forum was sponsored by the MLA Commission
on the Status of Women in the Profession.

NOTES

[1] N.M. Karamzin, _Bednaja Liza_. It was first published in 1792. For an English translation, see Harold B. Segel, _The Literature of Eighteenth Century Russia_, vol. II, 78-93.

[2] A. S. Pushkin, _Eugene Onegin_. Trans. By Vladimir Nabokov, 4 vols., Pantheon Books, (Chaps. I, VIII; Chaps. IV, I).

[3] Ibid (Chaps. I, XXXI).

[4] "Pushkin," an address delivered by Dostoevsky on June 8, 1880, at a meeting of the Society of Lovers of Russian Literature. See F. M. Dostoevsky, _The Diary of a Writer_. Trans, by Boris Brasol. New York, 1954, pp. 967-980.

[5] _Eugene Onegin_ (Chaps. VII, XXIV).

[6] Ibid., Epigraph to Chap. 4 (Necker: "La morale est dans la nature des choses").

[7] N. G. Chernyshevsky, "The Russian at the _Rendez-vous_," in _Selected Criticism_ by Belinsky, Chernyshevsky and Dobrolyubov, Dutton paperback, p. 12

[8] _Fathers and Sons_, in The Vintage Turgenev, Vol. I, p. 202 and p. 234.

[9] N. G. Chernyshevsky, _What is to Be Done?_, Vintage, p. 302.

[10] "A Gentle Creature" in _The Best Short Stories of Dostoevsky_, Modern Library, p. 255.

[11] Ibid., p. 258.

[12] Ibid., p. 256.

[13] Ibid., p. 260.

[14] Ibid., p. 271.

[15] Ibid., p. 272.

[16] Ibid., p. 282.

[17] "Family Happiness" (1859), in Leo Tolstoy, _The Death of Ivan Ilich and other Stories_, Signet.

[18] Maxim Gorky, _Reminiscences of Tolstoy, Chekhov and Andreyev_, Compass Books, p. 7.

[19] Ibid., p. 14.

[20]"The Kreutzer Sonata," in Leo Tolstoy, The Death of Ivan Ilich and Other Stories, Signet, p. 178.

[21]Ibid.

[22]Ibid., p. 183.

[23]On the Eve, in the Vintage Turgenev, Vol. II, pp. 125-126.

[24]Quoted in Ysabel de Palencia, Alexandra Kollontay. New York, 1947, p. 119.

[25]Ibid.

[26]Robert H. McNeal, Pride of the Revolution, The University of Michigan Press, Ann Arbor, 1972, p. 259. "Stalin is supposed to have said, 'I shall make someone else Lenin's widow.' In some versions of the story he even specified his choice. Elena Stasova, R.S. Zemlyachka, and even one Artiukhina have been among those nominated."

[27]Xenia Gasiorowska, Women in Soviet Fiction, 1917-1964, Madison, University of Wisconsin Press, 1968, p. 14.

The MLA Commission on the Status of Women in the Profession was first appointed in 1969. It is funded on an annual basis by the Modern Language Association of America, whose members, approximately 30,000 in number, are one-third women.

The Commission has worked both to improve employment opportunities for academic women and to publish information designed to alter ideas of women, in courses and in scholarship in the modern languages and in women's sudies.

Study I, reported in PMLA, in May, 1971, surveyed the status of women studying and teaching in the modern languages. (Fifty per cent of graduate students in the languages are women: as professors, they are clustered in the lower ranks and in the less prestigious institutions.) Study II, reported in PMLA in May, 1972, laid down guidelines for the improvement of the employment situation of academic women and surveyed progress toward affirmative action in departments granting the Ph.D. in the languages. Study III, reported in PMLA in January, 1976, resurveyed the status of women in the modern languages using data obtained by the American Council on Education: it showed the gains of women in the profession between 1968-9 and 1972-3 were at best slight. It also enabled The Commission to study factors correlated with the acquisition of rank, tenure and salary for women and for men.

Annually, The Commission has sponsored at the MLA Convention in December, a Forum and a series of Workshops on women writers, on feminist criticism, on textbooks, on teaching women's studies, on children's literature, and the like.

The current Co-chairpersons of the MLA Commission are Gloria De Sole and Jean A. Perkins. The mailing address: c/o Jean A. Perkins, Dept. of Modern Languages, Swarthmore College, Swarthmore, Pa. 19081.